BASKETBALL

BASKETBALL

Subhash K. Goyal

Crescent
CRESCENT
PUBLISHING CORPORATION

[The responsibility for the facts stated, conclusions reached and plagiarism, if any, in this book is entirely that of the Author. And the Publisher bears no responsibility for them, whatsoever.]

Basketball

First Published : 2009

ISBN 978-81-8342-155-3

Published by :

CRESCENT PUBLISHING CORPORATION
4831/24, Prahlad Street,
Ansari Road, Darya Ganj,
New Delhi - 110002
Ph. : 23272541, 23257835
Fax : 91-011-23257835
e-mail : campusbooks@hotmail.com

Printed at :
Roshan Offset Printers
Delhi

Preface

A court game played by two teams of five players each basketball is a sport which is extremely popular around the world. The basic objective of the game lies in putting a ball through a hoop, or basket, and thus score more points than the opposing team. Devised by James Naismith, an instructor in physical education, basketball was an instructor in physical education, basketball was initially intended to serve as an exiting indoor exercise for the winter months in a norther climate. Today it is a lightly popular outdoor game, appealing to many for its scope for displaying athletic powers, fast-paced action and building up of team solidarity.

This book in the series of books on various sports has been designed as a manual which provides comprehensive insight into the arena of basketball. Engaging in detailed discussion of the history of the game, the book pours forth incisive and important information on the rules and equipment of basketball, the emergence and progress of professional tournaments, the crowning glories and defining moments of the game, as well as the valuable .players of basketball. In addition, it also presents compendious but articulate material on contemporary basketball, dealing with its issues as well

It is hoped that the relevant and comprehensive information of the book finds favour with basketball enthusiasts.

Subhash K. Goyal

Contents

1

Introduction

Basketball is a team sport in which two teams of five active players each try to score points against one another by throwing a ball through a 10 foot (3 m) high hoop (the *basket*) under organized rules. Basketball is one of the most popular and widely viewed sports in the world. Points are scored by passing the ball through the basket from above; the team with more points at the end of the game wins. The ball can be advanced on the court by bouncing it (*dribbling*) or passing it between teammates. Disruptive physical contact (*fouls*) is not permitted and there are restrictions on how the ball can be handled (*violations*).

Through time, basketball has developed to involve common techniques of shooting, passing and dribbling, as well as players' positions, and offensive and defensive structures. While competitive basketball is carefully regulated, numerous variations of basketball have developed for casual play. In some countries, basketball is also a popular spectator sport. While competitive basketball is primarily an indoor sport, played on a basketball court, less regulated variations have become exceedingly popular as an outdoor sport among both inner city and rural groups.

Basketball is a team sport in which two teams of five active players each try to score points against one another by throwing a ball through a 10 foot (3 m) high hoop (the *basket*) under organized rules. Basketball is one of the most popular and widely viewed sports in the world.

Points are scored by passing the ball through the basket from above; the team with more points at the end of the game wins. The ball can be advanced on the court by bouncing it (*dribbling*) or passing it between teammates. Disruptive physical contact (*fouls*) is not permitted and there are restrictions on how the ball can be handled (*violations*).

Through time, basketball has developed to involve common techniques of shooting, passing and dribbling, as well as players' positions, and offensive and defensive structures. While competitive basketball is carefully regulated, numerous variations of basketball have developed for casual play. In some countries, basketball is also a popular spectator sport.

While competitive basketball is primarily an indoor sport, played on a basketball court, less regulated variations have become exceedingly popular as an outdoor sport among both inner city and rural groups.

History

In early December 1891, Dr. James Naismith, a Canadian physical education student and instructor at YMCA Training School (today, Springfield College) in Springfield, Massachusetts, USA, sought a vigorous indoor game to keep his students occupied and at proper levels of fitness during the long New England winters. After rejecting other ideas as either too rough or poorly suited to walled-in gymnasiums, he wrote the basic rules and nailed a peach basket onto a 10-foot (3.05 m) elevated track. In contrast with modern basketball nets, this peach basket retained its bottom, so balls scored into the basket had to be poked out with a long dowel each time. A soccer ball was used to shoot goals. Whenever a person got the ball in the basket, they would give their team a point. Whichever team got the most points won the game.

Naismith's handwritten diaries, discovered by his granddaughter in Spring 2006, indicate that he was nervous about the new game he had invented, which incorporated rules from a Canadian children's game called "Duck on a Rock", as many had failed before it. Naismith called the new game 'Basket Ball'. e first official basketball game was played in the YMCA gymnasium on January 20, 1892 with nine players, on a court just half the size of a present-day National Basketball Association (NBA) court. "Basket ball", the name suggested by one of Naismith's students, was popular from the beginning.

Women's basketball began in 1892 at Smith College when Senda Berenson, a physical education teacher, modified Naismith's rules for women. Basketball's early adherents were dispatched to YMCAs throughout the United States, and it quickly spread through the USA and Canada. By 1895, it was well established at several women's high schools. While the YMCA was responsible for initially developing and spreading the game, within a decade it discouraged the new sport, as rough play and rowdy crowds began to detract from the YMCA's primary mission. However, other amateur sports clubs, colleges, and professional clubs quickly filled the void. In the years before World War I, the Amateur Athletic Union and the Intercollegiate Athletic Association vied for control over the rules for the game.

Basketball was originally played with a association football ball. The first balls made specifically for basketball were brown, and it was only in the late 1950s that Tony Hinkle, searching for a ball that would be more visible to players and spectators alike, introduced the orange ball that is now in common use. Dribbling, the bouncing of the ball up and down while moving, was not part of the original game except for the "bounce pass" to teammates. Passing the ball was the primary means of ball movement. Dribbling was eventually introduced but limited by the asymmetric shape of early balls. Dribbling only became a major part of the game around the 1950s as manufacturing improved the ball shape.

Basketball, netball, dodgeball, volleyball, and lacrosse are the only ball games which have been identified as being invented by North Americans. Other ball games, such as baseball and Canadian football, have Commonwealth of Nations, European, Asian or African connections. Although there is no direct evidence as yet that the idea of basketball came from the ancient Mesoamerican ballgame, knowledge of that game had been available for at least 50 years prior to Naismith's creation in the writings of John Lloyd Stephens and Alexander von Humboldt. Stephen's works especially, which included drawings by Frederick Catherwood, were available at most educational institutions in the 19th century and also had wide popular circulation.

International Basketball

The International Basketball Federation was formed in 1932 by eight founding nations: Argentina, Czechoslovakia, Greece, Italy, Latvia, Portugal, Romania and Switzerland. At this time, the organization only oversaw amateur players. Basketball was first included in the Olympic Games in 1936, although a demonstration tournament was held in 1904. This competition has usually been dominated by the United States, whose team has won all but three titles, the first loss in a controversial final game in Munich in 1972 against the Soviet Union. In 1950 the first FIBA World Championship for men was held in Argentina. Three years later, the first FIBA World Championship for Women was held in Chile. Women's basketball was added to the Olympics in 1976, with teams such as Brazil and Australia rivaling the American squads.

FIBA dropped the distinction between amateur and professional players in 1989, and in 1992, professional players played for the first time in the Olympic Games. The United States' dominance continued with the introduction of their Dream Team. However, with developing programs elsewhere, other national teams started to beat the United States. A team made entirely of NBA players finished sixth in the 2002 World Championships in Indianapolis, behind Yugoslavia, Argentina, Germany, New Zealand and Spain. In the 2004 Athens Olympics, the United States suffered its first Olympic loss while using professional players, falling to Puerto Rico (in a 19-point loss) and Lithuania in group games, and being eliminated in the semifinals by Argentina. It eventually won the bronze medal defeating Lithuania, finishing behind Argentina and Italy.

Worldwide, basketball tournaments are held for boys and girls of all age levels. The global popularity of the sport is reflected in the nationalities represented in the NBA. Players from all over the globe can be found in NBA teams. Steve Nash, who won the 2005 and 2006 NBA MVP award, is Canadian; Kobe Bryant is an American who spent much of his childhood in Italy; Dallas Mavericks superstar and 2007 NBA MVP Dirk Nowitzki is German; All-Star Pau Gasol of the Memphis Grizzlies is from Spain; 2005 NBA Draft top overall pick Andrew Bogut of the Milwaukee Bucks is Australian; 2006 NBA Draft top overall pick Andrea Bargnani of the Toronto Raptors is from Italy; Houston Rockets Center Yao Ming is from China; Cleveland Cavaliers big man Zydrunas Ilgauskas is Lithuanian; and the San Antonio

Spurs feature Tim Duncan of the U.S. Virgin Islands, Manu Ginobili of Argentina and Tony Parker of France.

The all-tournament teams at the two most recent FIBA World Championships, held in 2002 in Indianapolis and 2006 in Japan, demonstrate the globalization of the game equally dramatically. Only one member of either team was American, namely Carmelo Anthony in 2006. The 2002 team featured Nowitzki, Ginobili, Peja Stojakovic of Yugoslavia (now of Serbia), Yao Ming of China, and Pero Cameron of New Zealand. Ginobili also made the 2006 team; the other members were Anthony, Gasol, his Spanish teammate Jorge Garbajosa and Theodoros Papaloukas of Greece. The only players on either team to never have joined the NBA are Cameron and Papaloukas. The only Japanese NBA player is Kenny Nakazawa.

Rules and Regulations

The object of the game is to outscore one's opponents by throwing the ball through the opponents' basket from above while preventing the opponents from doing so on their own. An attempt to score in this way is called a shot. A successful shot is worth two points, or three points if it is taken from beyond the three-point arc which is 6.25 meters (20 ft 6 in) from the basket in international games and 23 ft 9 in (7.24 m) in NBA games.

Playing Regulations

Games are played in four periods of 10 (international) or 12 minutes (NBA). College games use two 20 minute halves while most high school games use eight minute periods. Fifteen minutes are allowed for a half-time break, and two minutes are allowed at the other breaks. Overtime periods are five minutes long. Teams exchange baskets for the second half. The time allowed is actual playing time; the clock is stopped while the play is not active. Therefore, games generally take much longer to complete than the allotted game time, typically about two hours.

Five players from each team (out of a twelve player roster) may be on the court at one time. Substitutions are unlimited but can only be done when play is stopped. Teams also have a coach, who oversees the development and strategies of the team, and other team personnel such as assistant coaches, managers, statisticians, doctors and trainers.

For both men's and women's teams, a standard uniform consists of a pair of shorts and a jersey with a clearly visible number, unique within the team, printed on both the front and back. Players wear high-top sneakers that provide extra ankle support. Typically, team names, players' names and, outside of North America, sponsors are printed on the uniforms.

A limited number of time-outs, clock stoppages requested by a coach for a short meeting with the players, are allowed. They generally last no longer than one minute unless, for televised games, a commercial break is needed.

The game is controlled by the officials consisting of the referee ("crew chief" in the NBA), one or two umpires ("referees" in the NBA) and the table officials. For both college and the NBA there are a total of three referees on the court. The table officials are responsible for keeping track of each teams scoring, timekeeping, individual and team fouls, player substitutions, team possession arrow, and the shot clock.

EQUIPMENT

The only essential equipment in basketball is the basketball and the court: a flat, rectangular surface with baskets at opposite ends. Competitive levels require the use of more equipment such as clocks, scoresheets, scoreboard(s), alternating possession arrows, and whistle-operated stop-clock systems.

A regulation basketball court in international games is 28 by 15 meters (approx. 92 by 49 ft) and in the NBA is 94 by 50 feet (29 by 15 m). Most courts are made of wood. A steel basket with net and backboard hang over each end of the court. At almost all levels of competition, the top of the rim is exactly 10 feet (3.05 m) above the court and 4 feet (1.2 m) inside the baseline. While variation is possible in the dimensions of the court and backboard, it is considered important for the basket to be of the correct height; a rim that is off by but a few inches can have an adverse effect on shooting.

Violations

The ball may be advanced toward the basket by being shot, passed between players, thrown, tapped, rolled or dribbled (bouncing the ball while running).

The ball must stay within the court; the last team to touch the ball before it travels out of bounds forfeits possession. The ball-handler may not move both feet without dribbling, known as traveling, nor may he dribble with both hands or catch the ball in between dribbles, a violation called double dribbling. A player's hand cannot be under the ball while dribbling; doing so is known as carrying the ball. A team, once having established ball control in the front half of the court, may not return the ball to the backcourt. The ball may not be kicked nor struck with the fist. A violation of these rules results in loss of possession, or, if committed by the defense, a reset of the shot clock.

There are limits imposed on the time taken before progressing the ball past halfway (8 seconds in international and NBA; 10 seconds in NCAA and high school), before attempting a shot (24 seconds in the NBA; 35 seconds in NCAA), holding the ball while closely guarded (5 seconds), and remaining in the restricted area (the lane, or "key") (3 seconds). These rules are designed to promote more offense. Note: most high school games do not employ a shot clock.

No player may interfere with the basket or ball on its downward flight to the basket, or while it is on the rim (or, in the NBA, while it is directly above the basket), a violation known as *goaltending*. If a defensive player goaltends, the attempted shot is considered to have been successful. If a teammate of the shooter goaltends, the basket is cancelled and play continues with the defensive team being given possession.

Fouls

An attempt to unfairly disadvantage an opponent through physical contact is illegal and is called a foul. These are most commonly committed by defensive players; however, they can be committed by offensive players as well. Players who are fouled either receive the ball to pass inbounds again, or receive one or more free throws if they are fouled in the act of shooting, depending on whether the shot was successful. One point is awarded for making a free throw, which is attempted from a line 15 feet (4.5 m) from the basket.

The referee may use discretion in calling fouls (for example, by considering whether an unfair advantage was gained), sometimes making fouls controversial calls. The calling of fouls can vary between games, leagues and even between referees.

A player or coach who shows poor sportsmanship, for instance, by arguing with a referee or by fighting with another player, can be charged with a more serious foul called a technical foul. The penalty involves free throws (which unlike a personal foul, the other team can *choose* who they want to shoot the free throws) and varies between leagues. Repeated incidents can result in disqualification. Blatant fouls with excessive contact or that are not an attempt to play the ball are called unsportsmanlike fouls (or flagrant fouls in the NBA) and typically will result in ejection.

If a team surpasses a preset limit of team fouls in a given period (quarter or half) – four for NBA and international games – the opposing team is awarded one or two free throws on all subsequent fouls for that period, the number depending on the league. In the US college game if a team surpasses 7 fouls in the half the opposing team is awarded a one-and-one free throw (make the first you have a chance at a second). If a team surpasses 10 fouls in the half the opposing team is awarded two free throws on all subsequent fouls for the half. A player who commits five fouls, including technical fouls, in one game (six in some professional leagues, including the NBA) is not allowed to participate for the rest of the game, and is described as having "fouled out".

After a team has committed a specified number of fouls, it is said to be "in the penalty". On scoreboards, this is usually signified with an indicator light reading "Bonus" or "Penalty" with an illuminated directional arrow indicating that team is to receive free throws when fouled by the opposing team. The number of free throws awarded increases with the number of fouls committed. Initially, one shot is awarded, but after a certain number of additional fouls are committed the opposing team may receive (a) one shot with a chance for a second shot if the first shot is made, called shooting "one-and-one", or (b) two shots. If a team misses the first shot (or "front end") of a one-and-one situation, the opposing team may reclaim possession of the ball and continue play. If a team misses the first shot of a two-shot situation, the opposing team must wait for the completion of the second shot before attempting to reclaim possession of the ball and continuing play.

If a player is fouled while attempting a shot and the shot is unsuccessful, the player is awarded a number of free throws equal to the value of the attempted shot. A player fouled while attempting a regular two-point shot, then, receives two shots. A player fouled while attempting a three-point shot, on the other hand, receives three shots.

If a player is fouled while attempting a shot and the shot is successful, typically the player will be awarded one additional free throw for one point. In combination with a regular shot, this is called a "three-point play" because of the basket made at the time of the foul (2 points) and the additional free throw (1 point). Four-point plays, while rare, can also occur.

Common Techniques and Practices

Positions and Structures

Although the rules do not specify any positions whatsoever, they have evolved as part of basketball. During the first five decades of basketball's evolution, one guard, two forwards, and two centers or two guards, two forwards, and one center were used. Since the 1980s, more specific positions have evolved, namely:

— *point guard*: usually the fastest player on the team, organizes the team's offense by controlling the ball and making sure that it gets to the right player at the right time

— *shooting guard*: creates a high volume of shots on offense; guards the opponent's best perimeter player on defense

— *small forward*: often primarily responsible for scoring points via cuts to the basket and dribble penetration; on defense seeks rebounds and steals, but sometimes plays more actively

— *power forward*: plays offensively often with his back to the basket; on defense, plays under the basket (in a zone defense) or against the opposing power forward (in man-to-man defense)

— *center*: uses size to score (on offense), to protect the basket closely (on defense), or to rebound.

The above descriptions are flexible. On some occasions, teams will choose to use a *three guard offense*, replacing one of the forwards or the center with a third guard. The most commonly interchanged positions are point guard and shooting guard, especially if both players have good leadership and ball handling skills.

There are two main defensive strategies: *zone defense* and *man-to-man defense*. Zone defense involves players in defensive positions guarding whichever opponent is in their zone. In man-to-man defense, each defensive player guards a specific opponent and tries to prevent him from taking action.

Offensive plays are more varied, normally involving planned passes and movement by players without the ball. A quick movement by an offensive player without the ball to gain an advantageous position is a *cut*. A legal attempt by an offensive player to stop an opponent from guarding a teammate, by standing in the defender's way such that the teammate cuts next to him, is a *screen* or *pick*. The two plays are combined in the *pick and roll*, in which a player sets a pick and then "rolls" away from the pick towards the basket. Screens and cuts are very important in offensive plays; these allow the quick passes and teamwork which can lead to a successful basket. Teams almost always have several offensive plays planned to ensure their movement is not predictable. On court, the point guard is usually responsible for indicating which play will occur.

Defensive and offensive structures, and positions, are more emphasized in higher levels in basketball.

Shooting

Shooting is the act of attempting to score points by throwing the ball through the basket. While methods can vary with players and situations, the most common technique can be outlined here.

The player should be positioned facing the basket with feet about shoulder-width apart, knees slightly bent, and back straight. The player holds the ball to rest in the dominant hand's fingertips (the shooting arm) slightly above the head, with the other hand on the side of the ball. To aim the ball, the player's elbow should be aligned vertically, with the forearm facing in the direction of the basket. The ball is shot by bending and extending the knees and extending the shooting arm to become straight; the ball rolls off the finger tips while the wrist completes a full downward flex motion. When the shooting arm is stationary for a moment after the ball released, it is known as a follow-through; it is incorporated to maintain accuracy. Generally, the non-shooting arm is used only to guide the shot, not to power it.

Players often try to put a steady backspin on the ball to deaden its impact with the rim. The ideal trajectory of the shot is somewhat arguable, but generally coaches will profess proper arch. Most players shoot directly into the basket, but shooters may use the backboard to redirect the ball into the basket.

The two most common shots that use the above described set up are the *set shot* and the *jump shot*. The set shot is taken from a standing position, with neither foot leaving the floor, typically used for free throws. The jump shot is taken while in mid-air, near the top of the jump. This provides much greater power and range, and it also allows the player to elevate over the defender. Failure to release the ball before returning the feet to the ground is a traveling violation.

Another common shot is called the *layup*. This shot requires the player to be in motion toward the basket, and to "lay" the ball "up" and into the basket, typically off the backboard (the backboard-free, underhand version is called a *finger roll*). The most crowd-pleasing, and typically highest-percentage accuracy shot is the *slam dunk*, in which the player jumps very high, and throws the ball downward, straight through the hoop.

A shot that misses both the rim and the backboard completely is referred to as an air ball. A particularly bad shot, or one that only hits the backboard, is jocularly called a brick.

Rebounding

The objective of rebounding is to successfully gain possession of the basketball after a missed field goal or free throw, as it rebounds from the hoop or backboard. This plays a major role in the game, as most possessions end when a team misses a shot. There are two categories of rebounds: offensive rebounds, in which the ball is recovered by the offensive side and does not change possession, and defensive rebounds, in which the defending team gains possession of the loose ball. The majority of rebounds are defensive, as the team on defense tends to be in better position to recover missed shots.

Passing

A pass is a method of moving the ball between players.

Most passes are accompanied by a step forward to increase power and are followed through with the hands to ensure accuracy.

A staple pass is the *chest pass*. The ball is passed directly from the passer's chest to the receiver's chest. A proper chest pass involves an outward snap of the thumbs to add velocity and leaves the defense little time to react.

Another type of pass is the *bounce pass*. Here, the passer bounces the ball crisply about two-thirds of the way from his own chest to the receiver. The ball strikes the court and bounces up toward the receiver. The bounce pass takes longer to complete than the chest pass, but it is also harder for the opposing team to intercept (kicking the ball deliberately is a violation). Thus, players often use the bounce pass in crowded moments, or to pass around a defender.

The *overhead pass* is used to pass the ball over a defender. The ball is released while over the passer's head.

The *outlet pass* occurs after a team gets a defensive rebound. The next pass after the rebound is the *outlet pass*.

The crucial aspect of any good pass is being impossible to intercept. Good passers can pass the ball with great accuracy and touch and know exactly where each of their teammates like to receive the ball. A special way of doing this is passing the ball without looking at the receiving teammate. This is called a *no-look pass*.

Another advanced style of passing is the *behind-the-back pass* which, as the description implies, involves throwing the ball behind the passer's back to a teammate. Although some players can perform them effectively, many coaches discourage no-look or behind-the-back passes, believing them to be fundamentally unsound, difficult to control, and more likely to result in turnovers or violations.

Dribbling

Dribbling is the act of bouncing the ball continuously, and is a requirement for a player to take steps with the ball. To dribble, a player pushes the ball down towards the ground rather than patting it; this ensures greater control.

When dribbling past an opponent, the dribbler should dribble with the hand farthest from the opponent, making it more difficult for the defensive player to get to the ball. It is therefore important for a player to be able to dribble competently with both hands.

Good dribblers (or "ball handlers") tend to bounce the ball low to the ground, reducing the travel from the floor to the hand, making it more difficult for the defender to "steal" the ball. Additionally, good ball handlers frequently dribble behind their backs, between their legs, and change hands and directions of the dribble frequently, making a less predictable dribbling pattern that is more difficult to defend, this is called a crossover which is the most effective way to pass defenders while dribbling.

A skilled player can dribble without watching the ball, using the dribbling motion or peripheral vision to keep track of the ball's location. By not having to focus on the ball, a player can look for teammates or scoring opportunities, as well as avoid the danger of someone stealing the ball from him/her.

Height

At the professional level, most male players are above 1.90 meters (6 ft 3 in) and most women above 1.70 meters

(5 ft 7 in). Guards, for whom physical coordination and ball-handling skills are crucial, tend to be the smallest players. Almost all forwards in the men's pro leagues are 2 meters (6 ft 6 in) or taller. Most centers are over 2.1 meters (6 ft 10 in) tall. According to a survey given to all NBA teams, the average height of all NBA players is just under 6 ft 7 in (2.01 m), with the average weight being close to 222 lb (101 kg). The tallest players ever in the NBA were Manute Bol and Gheorghe Muresan, who were both 2.31 m (7 ft 7 in) tall. The tallest current NBA player is Yao Ming, who stands at 2.29 m (7 ft 6 in).

The shortest player ever to play in the NBA is Muggsy Bogues at 1.60 meters (5 ft 3 in). Other short players have thrived at the pro level. Anthony "Spud" Webb was just 5 feet 7 inches (1.70 m) tall, but had a 42-inch (1.07 m) vertical leap, giving him significant height when jumping. The shortest player in the NBA today is Earl Boykins at 5 feet 5 inches (1.65 m). While shorter players are often not very good at defending against shooting, their ability to navigate quickly through crowded areas of the court and steal the ball by reaching low are strengths.

Variations of Basketball

Variations of basketball are activities based on the game of basketball, using common basketball skills and equipment (primarily the ball and basket). Some variations are only superficial rules changes, while others are distinct games with varying degrees of basketball influences. Other variations include children's games, contests or activities meant to help players reinforce skills.

Wheelchair basketball is played on specially designed wheelchairs for the physically impaired. The world governing body of wheelchair basketball is the International Wheelchair Basketball Federation [5]

(IWBF). Water basketball, played in a swimming pool, merges basketball and water polo rules. Beach basketball is played in a circular court with no backboard on the goal, no out-of-bounds rule with the ball movement to be done via passes or 2 1/2 steps, as dribbling is not allowed.

There are many variations as well played in informal settings without referees or strict rules. Perhaps the single most common variation is the *half court* game. Only one basket is used, and the ball must be "cleared" - passed or dribbled outside the half-court or three-point line - each time possession of the ball changes from one team to the other. Half-court games require less cardiovascular stamina, since players need not run back and forth a full court. Half-court games also raise the number of players that can use a court, an important benefit when many players want to play.

A popular version of the half-court game is 21. Two-point shots count as two points and shots from behind the three-point line count three. A player who makes a basket is awarded up to three extra free throws (or unlimited if you are playing "all day"), worth the usual one point. When a shot is missed, if one of the other players tips the ball in with two while it is in the air, the score of the player who missed the shot goes back to zero, or if they have surpassed 13, their score goes back to 13. This is called a "tip". If a missed shot is "tipped" in, but the player who tips it in only uses one hand, then the player who shot it is out of the game and has to catch an air ball to get back in. The first player to reach exactly 21 points wins. If they go over, their score goes back to 13.

Other variations include streetball, knockout, and one-on-one; a variation in which two players will use only a small section of the court (often no more than a half of a court) and compete to play the ball into a single hoop. Such games tend to emphasize individual dribbling and ball stealing skills over shooting and team play.

2

Basketball Court

In basketball, the basketball court is the playing surface, consisting of a rectangular floor with baskets at either end. In professional or organized basketball, especially when played indoors, it is usually made out of a hardwood, often maple, and highly polished. Outdoor surfaces used include plastic interlocking tiles (suspended athletic courts), asphalt, blacktop, or similar materials are used. Amateur players would typically use tarmac as the surface.

The object of the game is to throw the ball through the baskets at either end of the court. When the game was first invented, actual baskets were used. Dr. James Naismith's original rules specified that "A goal shall be made when the ball is thrown or batted from the grounds into the basket and stays there, providing those defending the goal do no touch or disturb the goal." However, because it proved to be inconvenient to continually retrieve the ball from the baskets, the baskets were soon replaced by metal hoops (usually with dangling netting attached to direct the ball straight down.) The hoops are attached to rectangular (or sometimes fanshaped) backboards.

The basketball court comes in different shapes and sizes. In the National Basketball Association, the court is

94 feet long by 50 feet wide (28.65 m by 15.24 m). Under International Basketball Federation (FIBA) rules, the court is slightly smaller, measuring exactly 28 m by 15 m, although national federations are allowed to use smaller courts, as long as they are at least 26 m by 14 m. A highschool court is slightly smaller, at 84 ft by 50 ft. In amateur basketball, court sizes vary widely. The baskets are always 10 feet (3.05m) above the floor (except possibly in youth competition).

Basketball Court and Backboard

Key

The free throw line, or the key is 12 feet wide and 15 feet long. The distance from the free throw line to the three-point line is 4 feet 9 inches. The bottom block to the baseline is 4 feet. Under FIBA rules, the lane is 5.8 m tall trapezoid, 6 m wide at the endline and 3.6 m wide at the throw line. *The lane* is also known as *the key* or *the paint*, especially in play-by-play calling or post-game analysis. A jump shot from around the free throw line is often called "from the top of the key," and the number of lay-ups, dunks and other short-range shots are often referred to as "points in the paint."

Low Post Area

Another important area of the floor is the area in the frontcourt, near the basket and on one side or the other of the free throw lane. This is known as the low post, and is fundamental in strategy in American basketball (in international basketball, the key is trapezoidal, so low post play is not as prominent). Skilled low post players can score many points per game without ever taking a jump shot.

Three Point Arc

The distance to the three point arc has changed several times in the history of basketball. The rules for the international, United States amateur, and National Basketball Association versions of the game each specify distinct distances. In the 1979-1980 season, the NBA adopted a three-point arc that was a variable distance, ranging from 22 feet in the corners to 23′9" behind the top of the key. The line was briefly moved in to a uniform 22 feet during the 1990s before being restored to its original distance.

In college basketball, as well as in most high school associations in the United States, the distance is 19′ 9". The international distance, used in most countries outside the United States and in FIBA competition, is 6.25m (20′ 6"). On May 26, 2007, the playing rules committee agreed on a new rule for men's college basketball which will move the three point line back one foot to 20' 9". This rule will go into affect for the 2008-2009 season. The three point line for women's college basketball will remain at 19' 9".

Half Court Basketball

During halfcourt basketball, where only half of the court is used, a player must return to the area beyond the free throw circle (or the three-point line, depending on playing preference) before his or her team can score. Most play with an exception to this rule, disregarding it if the ball is turned over without contacting the rim of the basket during a team's possession.

Court Dimensions & Product Selection

When evaluating a wall mount basketball system the main dimension information necessary to select a system is the distance from the baseline of the court to the mounting wall plus 4'. Most wall mount systems offered by manufacturers are cut to order so this measurement is crucial in selecting a wall mount system. Basketball-Goals.com offers three major manufacturers of wall mount systems; Draper, BPI and First Team. Of the three manufacturers only First Team offers telescoping mounting structures enabling them to be adjusted at time of installation. Their wall mount systems mounting structures come in three different telescoping lengths between 4 and 6 feet, between 6 and 8 feet, and between 8 and 10'. Both BPI and Draper cut their wall mount mounting structures to the exact size the customer requests.

In US, another key dimension for NBA/NCAA approved portable stanchion systems is at least an 8' runnout. This is the distance from the front of the base of the unit to the face of the backboard. For this reason only selected stanchions meeting this criteria are acceptable for these purposes. Basketball-Goals.com offers Spalding Hydra-Rb Gared and Schelde Models that meet these guidelines. If your facility does'nt conduct sanction tournament play then check out our other less costly models from First Team, Schutt, Gared, & Spalding Hydra-Rib.

Basketball Three Point Line Dimensions

Most commercial basketball court stencils do not contain three point lines. The reason for this is most commercially sold court stencils are for residential use and most residential applications are not large enough to accommodate a three point line. This coupled with the fact that adding the three point line to a court stencil would double or possibly even triple the cost to the customer. Below are directions on how you can make your own 3 point line.

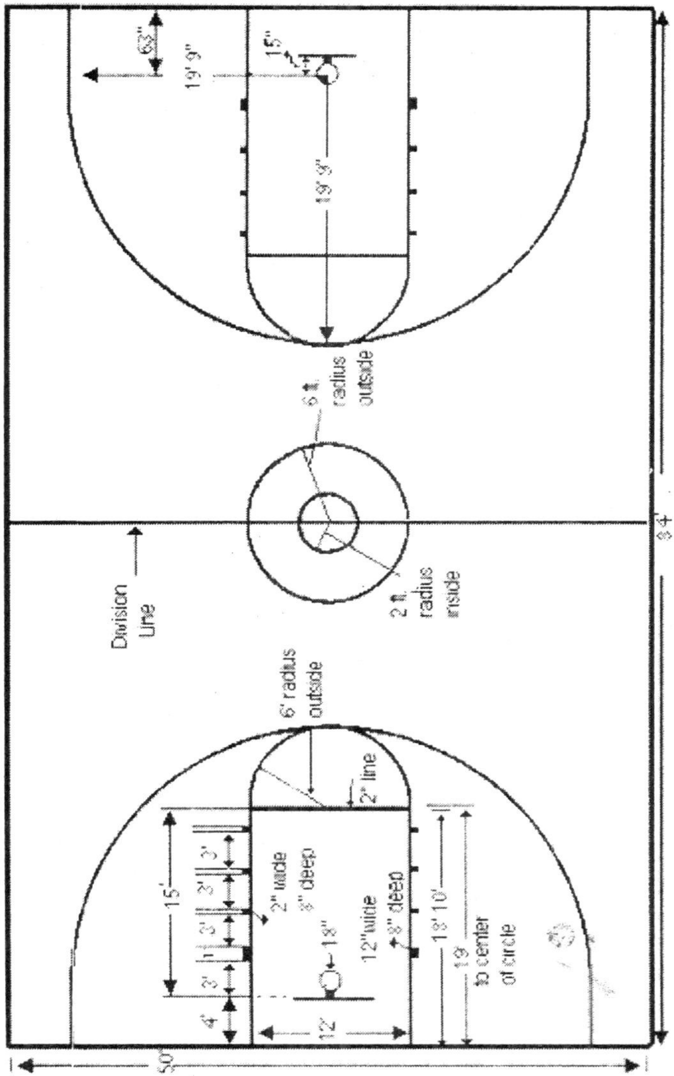

Basketball court lines

Three Point Line

To make a three point line you'll need the following items. (1) piece of Chalk, (1) roll of masking tape, 1 roll of string, (1) 1 plumb bob , (1) ladder (1) tape measure.

Same as above just substitute 19' 9" for the 23'9" shown above, and substitute 63" with the 5'3" shown above.

Installation Instructions

Layout

The first step to a gymnasium installation is to determine the proper layout. This is determined by measuring the dimensions of the area to be covered. Create a drawing showing length and width as well as any irregular areas to be covered.

Each tile is 12" x 12". You need a color layout showing which tiles go where, what colors and how many. By multiplying the length and width of each colored area, you can determine the number of tiles needed for each color. The length includes the four feet of space from the front of the backboard to the baseline.

Equipment: (Ideal conditions)

— 7' folding step ladder
— chalk line
— rigid putty knife
— 4' level
— duct tape
— plumb bob
— 25' tape measure
— razor knife

— 100′ tape measure
— construction crayon
— framing square
— table saw or circular saw
— power jigsaw

Site Conditions

Be sure to find out if any other contract work will be completed after the installation of the tile. If any other contractor needs to perform work on or above your floor after your installation, cover the tiles with a construction cover (plastic sheeting or some other protective cover). Make sure you coordinate access of the building with the building owner.

Generally, the tile and underlayment will be delivered to the job site on pallets. The easiest way to move the tile and underlayment is with a forklift of a pallet jack. In these cases, you will need doors large enough to accommodate the equipment. If a forklift or pallet jack is not available, a dolley can be used to move the tiles and underlayment.

Underlayment

A 3 millimeter rubber underlayment is recommended for inside gymnasiums and multipurpose areas which provides additional shock absorption as well as noise reduction.

Start the first row of underlayment by rolling it out the length of the gymnasium. Leave 1 inch between the wall and the end of the roll. For gym flo‿s which are longer than the roll of rubber, overlap the second roll by several inches and use a razor knife to cut through both layers creating a tight seam. This seam must be taped with duct tape.

The next row is lined up beside the first and unrolled. Do not overlap the sides of the rolls. The seams should be taped with duct tape. Repeat this process throughout the entire gymnasium.

Tile Installation

The installation of basketball court begins with finding the center of the basketball rims. The court installation is made between the two rims, not the squareness of the room or area.

Using a string and a plumb bob, drop a line from the front, dead center, of the basketball rims. Mark the floor under both rims. Snap a chalk line between the marks.

Using the plumb bob, make a mark on the floor from the front of both backboards, behind the rims. This mark will determine the location of the basketball keys.

Installation will be easier if you preassemble the tiles into in 3 x 4 sheets. Start the installation in the lane placing the 4 tile male side on the chalk line, using the appropriate color chosen for the lanes. Lay the male locks of the second sheet of flooring on top of the female loops of the first sheet laid down. Carefully step on the tiles, locking them into place. Continue in this manner until the tiles for the lane have been placed on the chalk line. Go no further than one sheet of tile from the chalk line.

Change to the color of tile chosen for the playing surface. Run this tile to the free throw chalk mark on the sub-floor at the opposite end. Switch back to the lane color and run more tiles. Some times the color change for the free throw lanes will not line up with your 15′ chalk marks on the sub floor. In a case like this, make your color change the same distance from the 15′ mark on the sub-floor. You can correct the actual distance when painting to make it regulation

Start the next row of tiles in the same manner as the first. Do not try to build out to the edge of the court, as it is easy to get mis-aligned at this stage. Be careful to make sure the first row of tiles has not shifted from the chalk line.

Pay close attention to your drawing to determine the point at which you will switch to the out-of-bounds color for the facility.

You are Halfway complete. Take a break.

The second half of the gym will be laid down in a different manner from the first half. You will be installing the width of the floor instead of the length of the floor.

Begin by laying out 5 sheets of flooring, this time toward the sideline, not down the center (remember to use the proper color chosen for the lanes, and floor color when necessary). You will work this five sheet width down the entire length of the floor. Attach these to the half of the floor already installed. Lay down five more sheets and attach them as well.

After you secure the first couple of rows of five tiles, there is a trick which can be used. Since lifting the floor after five sheets are down to tuck the loops under is very time consuming, we suggest you leave the loops on top of the half of the floor already installed. However, make sure your tiles line up even though they are not attached at the seam.

After 10 to 15 feet of the floor is down with the loops laying on the top, attach this to the rest of the floor. This is accomplished by lifting the floor already installed and allowing the female loops to fall beneath the male pegs. Then walk the line snapping them together.

After the first row of five sheets is installed halfway down the court you can start another person on the next row of five. Continue this method until you come to the point where the color is changed for the sideline/out-of-bounds area. Simply switch colors and continue until you reach the walls.

The field is now complete. The only tiles not installed are the cuts along the walls or around any fixed objects in the facility. The final step of the gymnasium installation process is to trim the edges. This step can be time consuming if you do not have the right tools and equipment for the job. Those tools are:

— band saw or table saw

— extension cords

— razor knives

— tape measure

When trimming the tiles keep in mind you have to allow for expansion and contraction of the floor. Sports/Expansion tile will expand and contract with temperature changes. There is a formula to calculate expansion and contraction, but generally leave a ½″ gap around the entire floor in an inside location, 3" to 4" for an outside location. Any time you trim a tile, the piece trimmed off may fit (snap on) the opposite side which can result in material savings.

3

Basketball Moves

Basketball moves are generally individual actions used by players to pass by defenders to gain access to the basket or to get a clean pass to a teammate.

Dribbling

Crossover Dribble

The crossover is a dribbling technique that involves a motion by which the player, before or while dribbling the ball, changes the dribbling direction by moving or bouncing the ball from one side of the body to the other. It is generally used quickly so the defender's momentum will not be able to stay with the player's new dribbling direction. This move provides the players a space to pass the defender.

Behind the Back Crossover

The behind the back crossover is a variation of the crossover, whereby the player, while dribbling the ball with one hand, bounces the ball behind his back to the other hand in order to switch the direction of dribbling. It is a more flamboyant way to evade the defender while protecting the ball, it can also be used to your advantage when the opposite player tries to steal the ball

Under the Legs Crossover

The under the legs crossover is yet another variation of the crossover. It is also known as the between the legs dribble. The move is done when the player dribbles the ball in between his legs from one hand to another. It's an effective way to change the direction of dribbling while protecting the ball from the defender.

Spin Move

A spin move is performed when a player spins his body in an effort to change the direction of the dribble or the layup while evading his defender. The spin move can be used while dribbling or in a post position. Post players usually use the move many times during a game in order to lose the opponent. Guards with better ball handling ability can use the spin move when dribbling (commonly known as a "Reverse Pivot").

The spin move gets the body in between the ball and the defender to prevent him from reaching the ball. The drawback of the move is that the ballhandler can be disoriented after performing the move. A slowly executed spin move can also allow a defender to position himself ideally to make a steal by surprising the offensive player, whose back had been momentarily turned.

Hesitation Dribble

The hesitation dribble is a dribbling action with an intentional change of pace or, like a stutter-step, intended to confuse or freeze a defender. The change makes it more difficult for the defender to predict the movement of the ball and so it is harder for him to make a steal. The move is often performed by street players. In the professional league, players like Allen Iverson are known to use this move in order to generate an easy layup or jump shot. The hesitation dribble is most effective in open-court situations, and is usually used in half-court sets to sucker a defender closer to the ball before the dribbler blows past him.

Passes

Bounce Pass

The bounce pass is a fundamental passing technique. The player passes the ball to a teammate by bouncing the ball off the floor. A successful bounce pass can easily result in an assist because a bounce pass is harder for defenders to intercept. At the same time, a bounce pass may still be intercepted due to its slower speed. Thus, a player is required to use his or her best judgment when determining whether or not to throw such a pass. The move has to be executed perfectly because a bounce pass just in front of the defender will result in a turnover or a hard catch for the receiver of the pass.

Chest Pass

This pass is performed by pushing the ball outwards from the chest with two hands while turning the hands over, ending with the thumbs pointing down. It is best used in the open court and on the perimeter.

Overhead Pass

An overhead pass is another fundamental passing technique. It is used by snapping the ball over the head, like a soccer throw-in.

Baseball Pass

The baseball pass is a pass where the passer throws the ball with one hand, as it were a baseball or a football. It is infrequently used, mainly only to set up last second plays off a baseline inbound.

Jump Pass

A jump pass is a pass performed while the passing player's feet are off the floor. When done intentionally, it can sometimes confuse the defender, causing him to believe that the passer is shooting instead of passing. However, it at times is done as a result of the player having their shooting lane blocked and often leads to the player turning the ball over to the opposing team. This kind of pass is strongly discouraged in all levels of basketball, as it leaves the offensive player very vulnerable to turnovers.

Blind Pass

Also known as a no-look pass, the blind pass is performed when a player looks in one direction but passes the ball to his target in another direction. blind passes are risky and as a result are not often performed. However, when done correctly, blind passes often confuse the defender(s).

Behind-the-back

Behind-the-back passes are passes dealt to a target behind the passer's back. Usually done to confuse the defender, behind the back passes can either be bounced off the floor or passed directly to a teammate. However, most behind-the-back passes are direct.

Elbow Pass

Introduced to much hype by Jason Williams, the Elbow Pass is one of the most difficult trick passes to execute. The Elbow Pass serves as a devastating compliment to the Behind-the-Back pass and can be used with varying no-look elements. Most effective on a fast-break, the Elbow Pass entails what appears to the defender as a simple Behind-the-Back pass, but as the ball crosses the passer's back, the passer hits it with his elbow, redirecting the ball back toward the side it started on and hopefully leaving the defender(s) flatfooted. Williams was able to pull off this pass at a full sprint during a Rookie All-Star game, but most amateurs have trouble hitting the ball with their elbow while standing still.

Two Person Game

Give and Go

"Give and Go" is an offensive play that involves passing the ball (give) and then running (go) to an open spot to receive the ball back, usually near the basket, for an easy score. This play can be effective when the defender pays too much attention to the ball instead of the player who moves after passing the ball.

Pick and Roll

"Pick and Roll" is an offensive play in which a player stops to screen (block) a defender for the teammate handling the ball and then slips behind the defender to accept a pass as the handler makes a move towards the basket.

Back Door

A back door play is when a player without the ball gets behind the defense and receives a pass for an easy score. This can be executed if the defenders are unaware of the open space behind them. Also, when a defender overcommits on defense (e.g. tries to steal or deny a pass), they are vulnerable to a backdoor play.

Finger Roll

A finger roll is performed when a player holds the ball with one hand during a layup and then lifts his fingers, rolling the ball into the basket. The rolling motion provides the ball with a soft touch, and the ball will roll around the rim and then drop into the basket.

Tear Drop

The tear drop, also called a runner or a floater, is usually performed by undersized players (mainly point guards). A player usually starts the layup procedure from a distance further away from the basket. The ball is generally released earlier and in a higher arch then the normal layup. The ball is usually away before the taller defender has the chance to block it. It is so named because the ball drops down from the high point of the arch like a falling tear drop.

Power Stop/Drive

Power drive is a continuation move in which a player stops dribbling and makes a huge leap forward, in the mean time securing the ball from the dribbling hand to both hands, then making a layup. The move is generally used as a layup because the huge movement coming from the forward leap provides the momentum for the player to jump forward for a layup. The move is a great way to squeeze the player under the basket for a fast layup.

Bank Shot

A bank shot in basketball is a shot that relies on the ball bouncing off backboard and into the basket. It is mostly used for mid-ranged jump shots from an angle (usually at the elbow) and layups. It is less used for long-ranged shots or shots from the middle. The purpose of using the backboard is to try to hit the backboard at an angle, thus slowing the speed of the ball and increasing its chances of falling into the hoop.

Putback and Tip-in

A putback describes a situation where a player secures an offensive rebound then immediately scores a basket. If the player secures the rebound while in the air, to be considered a putback the player can land on the ground before shooting, but cannot dribble before taking the shot. If the player does not secure the rebound but instead taps the ball into the basket, it is considered a tip-in. There is a point where a putback and a tip-in are a matter of subjective difference (eg, a one-handed rebound in the air followed by a score before touching the ground). A putback jam is a spectacular alternative to the tip-in where the ball is slam-dunked off the rebound in the same motion.

Triple Threat Position and Related Moves

Triple threat is the position when a player facing a defender receives a pass but has not dribbled yet. The offensive player's feet are slightly wider than shoulder width, his knees flexed, with both hands on the basketball in front of him, presenting the defender with an opponent able to move in any direction. One foot is held as the pivot. From this, the player can choose from three options: to shoot, to dribble past the defender or to pass it to a teammate. There are also options to get the defender out of his defensive stances by using jab steps and pump fakes.

Jab Step

Jab step is performed when a player holds onto the ball before dribbling while his non-pivot leg performs a routine jabbing. This move is used to test defender's defensive weaknesses and stance. A combination of the pump fake, the drive, the shot and the crossover drive can be performed along with the jab step to lure the opponent out of his defense. Denver Nuggets forward

Carmelo Anthony is well-known for taking the jab step. When he does this, the defender falls off from his defensive stance, creating a space between him and the defender, allowing him to take a quick mid-range jumper, a three-pointer, or a drive "to the lane".

Pump Fake

A pump fake is a fundamental move in basketball, used to cause defenders to jump (known in basketball slang as "lifting" the defender), or be shifted off-balance. Its main applications are in the low post area, where a player is much more likely to have his or her shot blocked. Two well known practitioners of low post fakes are Kevin McHale and Al Jefferson. On the perimeter, it is useful in creating open lanes to the basket by "showing" the ball enough to entice a defender to attempt to block or steal it, allowing the dribbler to penetrate easily. Tracy McGrady is an excellent example of this, and often gains extra free throw attempts due to his skill in ball faking.

Drawing Contact

An offensive move intended to produce a foul call on the defensive player. A typical strategy is to drive into a defensive player whose feet are not stationary. When the two players make bodily contact, a foul can be called on the defensive player. If the defensive player has a set position (ie, both feet are stationary and arms are not in a downward motion) the contact can result in a charging foul against the offensive player.

Post Up, Related Moves and Shots

To "post up" is to establish a position in the low post, the area near the basket below the foul line, usually in order to take advantage of a smaller defender. The offensive player usually faces away from the basket, so that his body can protect the ball from the defender. From this position, options such as spinning or backing down the defender to close in to the basket for better scoring opportunities become available to him.

Up and Under

The up and under is a move consisting of two parts, a shot fake (the up) and a step-through (the under). First the player with the ball fakes a shot by thrusting the ball above his head as if to take a shot, then when the defender jumps in an attempt to block the shot, the offensive player steps by him and attempts a clear, unguarded shot. Generally used by post players, Kevin McHale was considered a master of this move.

Hook Shot

The hook shot is one of the most effective inside moves, but it is also quite difficult to execute. A hook shot begins when the player puts his body between the ball and the opponent. He then releases the ball towards the basket with his outside hand in a "hook" motion. The hook shot and variations such as the jump-hook and skyhook are effective because they are very difficult for the defender to block, although it is harder to hit the shot with precision. The advantage hook shot offers is the space between the offensive player and his defender. This extra space can reduce or eliminate the advantages enjoyed by a taller defender. The hook shot is most often used by post players because it is difficult to make the shot from a distance.

Turnaround Jump Shot

When a player posts up, in order to shoot he has to turnaround to face the basket. This can be done by turning in the air, timing the jump shot when the defender is not likely to jump and challenge the shot.

Fade Away

A fade away shot is variation on a set jump shot in which the shooter attempts his shot leaning backward, creating the effect of "fading away" from his defender. This makes it more difficult for the defender to contest the shot. The fadeaway usually has less range than a regular jump shot, because the footwork required makes it somewhat tougher to project the ball over long distances. Michael Jordan, and Karl Malone were famous for their use of the fadeaway.

Drop Step

Also called a "reverse pivot", the drop step is a move in which the player posting up takes a back step on the side of a defender behind him and spins to that side to gain leverage. Afterwards he can shoot, pass, or drive to the basket.

Double Pivot

The double pivot also called the "MJ move" by athletic trainer David Thorpe, is a move termed by Thorpe for a special move executed by Michael Jordan (MJ). Thorpe describes the move as follows, "Michael Jordan, for a time the best back-to-the-basket player in the game, used to fake a shot while moving in one direction, then instead of stepping in the opposite direction when his defender bit on the fake, Jordan would pivot again in the same direction as he was moving and finish right at the rim."

Alley Oop

An alley oop in basketball is an offensive play in which one player throws the ball up near the basket to a teammate (or, much more rarely, to himself) who jumps, catches the ball in mid air and immediately scores a basket, usually with a slam dunk. It is an impressive way to score and often electrifies the spectators. The alley oop combines elements of teamwork, pin-point passing, timing, and dunking. The alley oop was first used by Al Tucker and his brother Gerald at Oklahoma Baptist University in the mid-1960s. It was popularised during the early 1970s by North Carolina State University to take advantage of the 48-inch vertical leap of Wolfpack star David Thompson. Because dunking was illegal in college basketball at that time, upon catching the alley oop pass, Thompson would simply drop the ball through the hoop.

The most common alley oop is done by having a player other than the dunker throw the ball into mid-air. The play can be difficult to execute during a game because it requires unspoken communication between the passer and the recipient of the pass. The passer must be able to anticipate the recipient's movement toward the basket and then time the pass appropriately. Outside of official basketball games, such as in a slam dunk contest, this is not an issue, and the thrower has more choices as to how he/she can throw the ball.

A less common version of the alley oop is done by having the dunker himself throw the ball, often bouncing it off the floor or backboard. In official competition, this is incredibly difficult to do without either committing a traveling violation, or simply creating the needless risk of a turnover. Alley oops are often combined with other tricks, such as a tomahawk, or a 360° spin. Many halftime shows feature trick slam dunks, which involve spins, flips and alley oops.

The term "alley oop" derives from French *allez-oup*, the cry of a circus acrobat about to leap. The term "Alley Oop" was first used to describe what is now known as the Hail Mary pass in football, but that eventually the term became used in basketball. Alley Oop created by cartoonist V. T. Hamlin in the early 1930s, because sportscasters believed those throws looked like Alley Oop in action. Hamlin picked up the term "allez-oup" serving in the Army in France during WW I.

Fadeaway

A fadeaway in basketball is a jump shot while jumping backwards, away from the basket. The goal is to create space between the shooter and the defender, making it much harder to block. However, this benefit comes with a drawback. The shooter must have very good accuracy (much higher than when releasing a regular jump shot) and must use more strength (to counteract the backwards momentum) in a relatively short amount of time. Also, because the movement is away from the basket, the shooter has less chance to grab his own rebound. However, once mastered, it is one of the hardest methods of shooting for defenders to block. The threat of a fadeaway forces a defender to jump into the shooter, and with a pump fake, the shooter can easily get a foul on the defender. It takes many tries and practice to excute this perfectly but it is a great shot to use in a game.

Wilt Chamberlain was renowned for his fadeaway shot, which he used to great effect in the 1960s. Michael Jordan was one of the best fadeaway shooters in history. Another excellent fadeaway shooter was Larry Bird. Hakeem Olajuwon, the all-star center, also adopted it into his repertoire.

Free Throw

In basketball, free throws or foul shots are unopposed attempts to score points from a restricted area on the court (the free throw line; informally known as the "charity stripe" or foul line), and are generally awarded after a foul by the opposing team. Each free throw is worth one point, and normally more than one is awarded. The importance of free throws is nevertheless sometimes underestimated; games have been known to

period, a team commits more than a set number of fouls. Even if a player is not in the act of shooting, two free throws are awarded no matter when or where the foul occurs. An exception is when the foul occurs while the offensive player is shooting, in which case it is treated like a normal shooting foul.

The team foul penalty situation is slightly different in U.S. collegiate basketball. Once a team has committed its seventh foul of a half, the fouled player shoots a *one-and-one,* in which the player must make the first free throw in order to get a chance to shoot a second. Beginning with the tenth foul of the half, two free throws are awarded. Free throws are not awarded for offensive fouls (most often charging fouls), even if the team fouled is in the bonus. As in professional play, a foul in the act of shooting is a two-shot foul.

If a player is injured upon being fouled and cannot shoot free throws, the offensive team may designate any player from the bench to shoot in the place of the injured player in college; the opposing team designates the player to shoot. In all other circumstances, the fouled player must shoot his or her own foul shots. If a player, coach, or team staff (e.g. doctor, statistician) shows poor sportsmanship, which may include arguing with a referee, that person may get charged with a technical foul.

A technical foul results in one free throw attempt for the other team. In FIBA play, a technical foul results in one free throw if the offending individual is playing on the court, and two free throws if he or she is on the bench. The technical fouls result in two free throws in all situations. At both levels, the opposing team may choose any player who is currently on the court to shoot the free throws, and is then awarded possession of the ball after the free throws. Since there is no opportunity for a rebound, these free throws are shot with no players on the lane.

Finally, if a referee deems a foul extremely aggressive, or that it did not show an attempt to play the ball, the referee can call a more severe foul, known as an *unsportsmanlike foul* in international play. This foul is charged against the player, and the opponent gets two free throws and possession of the ball afterwards. Unlike technical fouls, the player fouled must shoot the awarded free throws.

Fouls "away from the ball" (fouls that do not occur on the shooter or near the ball) are handled like the second case above in most situations. Many times defenders hold their opponent to avoid them from catching an in-bound pass or fight through screens and thus are called for fouls. These fouls are almost always treated as normal personal fouls. When there are only two minutes left on the clock of either half, off-ball fouls when the fouling team is over the limit are rewarded with one free throw and possession of the ball.

It is therefore common for a losing team to deliberately foul players such as Ben Wallace or Shaquille O'Neal, a dominant player but a terrible foul shooter, up until the two-minute mark, and then play intense defense for the rest of the game. It is believed that this rule was instituted because of Wilt Chamberlain.

This motivated teams to chase poor free-throw shooters, such as Chamberlain, around the court in attempt to foul him in an effort to extend the game. To discourage this practice, the NBA changed the rule to award one free throw and possession of the ball to a player who is fouled in the last two minutes of the fourth quarter. This rule does not apply in international play.

Procedure

Free throws are organised in procession. The shooter takes his place behind the free throw line (15 feet, or roughly 4.5 meters, from the basket). All other players must stand in their correct places until the ball leaves the shooter's hands:

Three people from the defensive team and two people from the shooting team line up along the sides of the restricted area (keyhole, paint, lane). These players are usually the ones that rebound the ball. Three line up on one side and two on the other. A defensive player always takes the place closest to the basket.

The remaining four players, two from each team, must remain behind the three point line and the free throw line extended (an imaginary line extended from the free throw line in both directions to the sidelines).

Leaving their designated places before the ball leaves the shooter's hands, interfering with the ball, and (for the defensive team only) attempting to put off the shooter, are all violations. In addition, the shooter must release the ball within five seconds and must not step on or over the free throw line until the ball touches the ring. A violation by the shooter cancels the free throw; a violation by the defensive team results in a substitute free throw if the shooter missed; a violation by the offensive team or a shot that completely misses the ring results in the loss of possession to the defensive team (only if it is on the last free throw).

Under FIBA rules, if the shooter does not commit a violation, and the ball goes in the basket, the attempt is automatically successful, regardless of violations committed by the non-shooter.

Hook Shot

A hook shot, in basketball, is a play in which the

offensive player, usually turned perpendicular to the basket, gently throws the ball with a sweeping motion of his arm in an upward arc with a follow-through which ends over his head. Unlike the jump shot, it is shot with only one hand; the other arm is often used to create space between the shooter and the defensive player. Once the ball is in shooting position, the hook shot is one of the most difficult shots to effectively defend. However, prior to that point, as the ball is being brought up into position, it is very susceptible to being stolen from behind.

Sky Hook

A "hook shot" is more commonly known as a "sky hook." An athlete forms a hook as the basketball is released with one hand over the shoulder as the basketball is released. An athlete is airborne as the ball is released, which is why this is a "sky" hook, since they are "in the sky.""Sky hook" is a street expression that has become part of the basketball vocabulary gaining great acceptance across America.

Jump Shot

In basketball, a jump shot is an attempt to score a basket by jumping, usually straight up, and, mid-flight, propelling the ball in an arc into the basket. It is accomplished by the player bringing his or her elbow up until it is aligned with the hoop, then sent towards the hoop in a high arc. It is considered the easiest shot to make from a distance. The purpose of the jump is to make it more difficult for the defender to block. It is also usually accomplished with one hand by the players. It is the most effective in open play but can prove to be hard when there is a taller player in front of you.

The jump shot originated in the United States with players in the National Basketball Association (NBA). In the NBA's early days, most players attempted field goals with both feet planted on the ground, a technique now known as a "set shot". Paul Arizin, a Philadelphia Warriors player in the early 1950s, was the first to perfect the jump shot. Over time, many players starting copying his jump shot, and it has become the most prevalent technique for shooting from the field.

Today, the jump shot has many varieties, such as the "turnaround jumper" (facing away from the basket, then jumping and spinning towards it, shooting the ball in mid-air), the "fadeaway" (jumping *away* from the basket to create space) or the "leaning jumper" (jumping *towards* the basket to move away from a trailing defender). Because a defender often has to jump to block a jump shot, an offensive player can try to get his defender in the air at the wrong time by using a pump fake.

Layup

A layup in basketball is a field goal attempt made by leaping from below, laying the ball up near the basket, and using one hand to tip the ball over the rim and into the basket (layin) or to bank it off the backboard and into the basket (layup). The motion and one-handed reach distinguish it from a jump shot. The layup is considered the most basic shot in basketball.

An undefended layup is usually a high percentage shot. The main obstacle is getting near the rim and avoiding blocks by taller defenders who usually stand near the basket. Common layup strategies are to create space, releasing the ball from different spots or use an alternate hand. A player tall enough to reach over the rim might choose to perform a more spectacular and higher percentage slam dunk (dropping or throwing the ball from above the rim) instead. To play a safer layup, you can hold it with two hands, that way it is harder to block and you take two steps so that distinguishes it from the jump shot.

As the game has evolved through the years, so has the layup. Several different versions of the layup are around today. Layups can be broadly categorised into two types: the underarm and the overarm. The underarm layup involves using most of the wrist and the fingers to 'lay' the ball into the basket or off the board. The underarm layup is more commonly known as the finger roll. Notable current NBA players who rely heavily on the underarm finger roll are Mike Bibby of Sacramento, Allen Iverson of Denver and Jason Williams of Miami. Finger-rolls are considered to be a considerably higher percentage shot than dunking, which sometimes tends to bounce off the rim.

Finger-rolls today have many forms, including the Around the World which involves a complete circle around the player before the layup and a variety of faking in the approach to the rim. A classic example is a play by Jason Williams (currently of Miami) during his time with Sacramento, in which Williams brings the ball behind his back with his right hand, in a fake of a back pass, and then brings it front again with the same hand for the finish.

The other layup is the overhand shot, similar to a jump shot but from a considerably close range. Overhand layups almost always involved the action of the backboard. Players like Scottie Pippen (formerly from Chicago) and Karl Malone (formerly Utah) have used this move to great effect.

Slam Dunk

A slam dunk (or simply a dunk) is a type of basketball shot that is performed when a player jumps in the air and manually powers the ball through the basket with one or both of his hands, then often grabs the rim shortly after the ball passes through the hoop (a dunk is still being performed if the rim is not grabbed, as long as the athlete powers the ball through the hoop manually). This is a standard field goal worth two points. The term "slam dunk" was first coined by former L.A. Lakers announcer Chick Hearn. The slam dunk is one of the highest percentage field goals one can attempt in basketball as well as one of the most crowd-pleasing plays. Other terms for slam dunk include "jam", "stuff", "flush", "cram" or "throw down".

4

Coaching Methods

Coaching methods are closely related with the ability to teach. Do you, as a basketball coach, have a scientific approach in your coaching methods? Are you interested in research? These are a couple of questions often asked of prospective coaches in search of a job. Coaches, today, must be good teachers. Competition brings out the best in all of us. Due to the intensity of public interest in their work, basketball coaches are checked and double checked every week.

Educators often say that the best teachers are found in the coaching profession. Present-day coaches understand the learning processes better than we ever did in the past. Here are some of the steps you can apply to your method of coaching basketball:

1. Keep an open mind and the will to learn.
2. Separate parts of the offense and use them as drills.
3. Use simplified fundamental drills.
4. Use both the whole and part method in your coaching.
5. Learn from experiences.
6. Use progression in teaching fundamentals.
7. Be analytical and use corrective methods.

8. Use proper progression in organizing your team.
9. Use stimulating and interesting methods.
10. Make your drills competitive.
11. Repeat things over and over.

Philosophy of the Basketball Coach

During a game, basketball coaches are highly visible and close to the spectators packed behind in the stands. Quite often, away from home, loud-mouthed fans continuously hurl abusive words his way. The coach must leave such barbs fall on deaf ears; but things like this add to the sometime-pressure of the trade "to win at all costs", already heaped upon his shoulders. Do you still want to be a basketball coach? Good! Not only do you have to be a teacher, you must be a parent figure, confessor, psychologist, counselor, public relations expert, and a role model for the community.

Making a Good Coach

The basketball coach does not need be a star player; however, he should be a student of the game. Many great coaches who were mediocre players. On the other hand, many great players have made poor coaches. To become successful as a basketball coach you must develop a road map called 'philosophy". A coaching philosophy takes years to develop; but, like mine, yours began the first day you picked up a basketball. Your experiences as a player and observer will allow yours to develop just as Wooden developed his own. It becomes your own personal roadmap to success. Your philosophy continues to grow as you learn more about the game and dealing with players. In the beginning, your philosophy can be meager at best. To compensate for this and to make certain yours will be positive, study the philosophy of proven coaches.

Read their books and attend coaching clinics to broaden your knowledge.

What is philosophy, anyway? When you add up all your experiences as a player, observer, lessons learned from reading, ideas picked up at clinics, gab sessions with other coaches and your own personality, you have the beginnings of a coaching philosophy. Warning: Do not be misled! All this is no guarantee of success. The way you implement this philosophy is equally important. It will continue to evolve through the years.

The coach should select the offense and defense he wishes to use during the season. Next, he should must break the offense and defense down into fundamental drills and procedures. Then, you must convince your players your chosen offense and defenses will help them win games.

Most of all, as the coach, you must make practices fun. When practice sessions become monotonous, players lose interest and focus. In a game, be yourself. Don't try to be a John Wooden or Bobby Knight. What is your priority? Is it to develop your athletes as people, or simply basketball players? It's OK to adopt ideas from others, but if you try to be someone you're not, your players will catch on right away and you will not be the successful as could be. 'If you try to be someone else, the best you can do is be second best."

Occasionally rules change the game somewhat. The 3-point shot is a good example; however, one is always the core of a sound coaching philosophy and that is the fundamentals of the game.

When teaching the fundamentals, the coach must stress perfection. These should be repeated so often they become instinctive in game situations.` Balance is a prime requisite in a team offensive philosophy. Basketball is a team effort. The best shooters should take the most shots and the best rebounders should be in position when those shots are taken. The coach must put players in their proper position. The best ball handler, of course, should handle the ball most of the time. Being the team quarterback, his duties involve getting the ball to the shooter when he is in position to shoot. "If that shooter is the type who insists on taking the shot whenever he gets the ball, the quarterback must see that the good shooter does not get the ball in a poor shooting position."

Players should be allowed to take advantage of their individual skills; however, you must make certain it conforms to the overall team effort. Welfare of the team comes first. The coach must maintain a good team spirit, getting players up for each game. He must get the best from each player. Also, he must be aware of the players who need the most attention and understanding.

Coaches must use caution in his disciplinary measures; however, he must deal with such problems, should one occur during the season. He should stay on top of any situation that might cause team friction. At the first sign of conflict between players, they should be called in to talk it over. All such problems can usually be settled if they are not allowed to fester.

Be constructive with criticism. Any suggestion made to one player applies to all. Praise a player who makes an outstanding play. A player should understand that a coach wouldn't waste his breath if he did not like you. The coach usually criticizes players he plays the most.

The coach's relationship with his players is most important. One-on-one conferences with each player before, during, and after the season are worthwhile. Use these conferences to discuss his approach to the game, basketball progress, weaknesses, shortcomings, health, studies, outside problems, the player's contributions to the team, and selection of a college.

At the high school level the selection of a college is one of the most important subjects. The coach should evaluate the boy's ability and give an honest opinion of his capability. Advise him what level of competition he should seek. The player should be told that he will have to work harder, than in high school, to make a college team.

Practice Planning

Basketball coaches should map the road to success prior start of the school year. Most successful basketball coaches will organize each phase of the season for best results. Some coaches tend to practice too long. A practice session should only be long as players can work at their best ability. Only rarely, should a practice session be more than one and a half hour long. Typical divisions could be as follows:

— *Pre-season conditioning* - the period from the start of the school to the date of the first permissible basketball practice.

— *Pre-season practice* - the period from the first permissible day practice with the coach is allowed until the day before the first scheduled game.

— *In-season practice* - the period from the first scheduled game to the last game of the season.

Conditioning should be a year-round process for any athlete. A conscientious player never gets out of shape. An athlete at this level should participate in other sports throughout the entire year; however, most basketball coaches should set up off-season conditioning programs for his players.

At the end of each school year, the coach should meet individually with each player to review his, or her, written evaluation. At the same time that player should be given his own personal off-season workout. Issue him, or her, a Daily Summer Workout form. The coach should prepare his own standard forms. One for post players and another for perimeter players. To see a typical Post or Perimeter Player Daily Workout form click on the following links:

— Post Players

— Perimeter Players

Organizing Practice

An outline of a general practice for the entire season should be made long before the pre-season conditioning. School scheduling, weather, scouting reports, and the team's progress often determine the weekly schedule during the regular season. Usually a practice schedule should be made no more than one week in advance. Even then, a schedule sometimes must be revised during the week and occasionally on the day of the practice. A sound practice schedule makes the best use of the practice time. Daily practice plans should be posted so players can report to specified areas without delay.

In high school, pre-season practices usually cover six weeks. Each week must be outlined objectively. Each of the six weeks' objectives must be listed. Daily schedules list the number of minutes allowed to each drill, to each area, and the type of work expected each day. The weekly objectives are kept on a master schedule plan so that the coaches can tell at a glance what has been accomplished and what is yet to be done. These are kept within the framework of the coach's philosophy.

Selecting Players

On the opening day of practice, the coach should give a get-acquainted talk to the entire group, outlining what will be expected of them during the entire season. Everyone, including the new candidates, must feel it is possible for him to contribute. The players must have a desire to play the game. An aggressive team is always a dangerous team. Every player must be willing to pay the price for the opportunity to play. They should report in good physical condition and practice diligently so that they improve each day. The team's success is based on unity and unselfishness. Loyalty to the school, the coaches, and teammates is expected at all times.

The basketball court is a classroom, not a playground. All players are expected to work towards maximum possible improvement. They either improve daily or they regress; therefore, practice must be designed to bring out the best in every player. The first pre-season practice session is usually devoted to a discussion of the rules of the game and the rules that the team must follow. Then, quickly as possible, reduce his squad to about twenty-five players. Unless you are blessed with assistant coaches, it is nearly impossible to accomplish any effective group progress with a larger squad.

The coach should never do on the court, what can be done off the court. Furthermore, that good coaches should never work with only one, or two, players during the team practice time. Individualized instruction should come before, or after, daily practice.

Teaching Skills

The coach should not over-teach in the early pre-season practice sessions. You want your players to retain what is being taught. Players can and should work when physically worn out; however, they can't learn when mentally exhausted.

The most significant point to stress at all times in the importance of possession of the ball. Also, all players should be warned that bad shots are detrimental to the team. After an incorrect, or unrelated, maneuver the coach should always ask the players, "Why?" If necessary, replace that player in scrimmage for a brief individual conference. Coaches should do this frequently during the practice scrimmages, because the players should know the reason for everything they do on the court. "A coach should *criticize softly* and *encourage loudly,* informing the team often that practice makes playing habits permanent."

Players who practice bad habits should be corrected immediately. Even in a drill on passing, the coach should correct a player who makes a poor, or improper, cut. He should then briefly explain the proper technique. The coach should strive constantly for mental anticipation, instinctive reaction, and intelligent aggressiveness on the part of all players. These intangibles turn a good player a great one.

Developing Offenses and Defenses

After determining the best offensive and defensive patterns for the material at hand, the coach should be positive in their development. Do this in a way the players will have confidence. Do it in this order.

— Explain and diagram your tactics.

— Demonstrate the skills involved yourself, or by using a skilled player, or show a videotape.

— Walk the players through the various parts of the offense, or defense.

— Then, run them through at half speed.

— After that run through at full speed without opposition.

— Finally, implement the strategy at full speed with defenders; however, at this stage, the opponents should be weakest players.

Following the above enables the team to practice their strategy successfully, thus developing a positive attitude about their ability. Also, this erases any doubt a player may have about the coach's strategy.

Take advantage of individual abilities. On the other hand, never allow individual abilities to take over the team. The best coaches, however, do allow free-lancing that won't hurt the team. "The style of play that a coach incorporates offensively should blend with the material at hand. It should be based on good offensive floor balance, movement, proper execution of play patterns, and good timing"

Daily Coaching Duties

"For all daily practice sessions, the coach should arrive on the court dressed for practice at least a half hour before the beginning of practice. He, or she, should review the day's scheduled practice. The coach should be sure that the necessary materials are available. These include basketballs, scrimmage shirts, training aids, extra shoelaces, tape, and towels to be used for obstacles in a drill. Managers can carry an armful of towels and place them in the proper spot easily and quickly."

Before practice begins, the coach can give individual attention to players, discussing shortcomings observed in the previous practice session. He can work with one, or two, players.

"In early pre-season, before cutting the squad down to a workable size, a coach should give time to new candidates for on-the-spot evaluation, making players who are in the questionable category feel that he has given them sufficient time. This attitude and attention by the coach makes the selection process less painful for both coach and players who are dropped."

"The coach should be sure that the players begin before-practice workouts as soon as they arrive. He should make certain that all players are on time and that practice starts at the prescribed time. The organized practice time, in which the timing by the manager is all-important, should begin with a whistle. The manager, or assistant manager, should check the time allotted for each part of the practice session and inform the coach when the time is up for each segment."

Drills

Drilling is the secret of good performance in a ball game. Early pre-season practice should stress conditioning and fundamentals because the team must be in condition before the first game.

The importance of carefully conceived, skillfully organized, and well executed drills cannot be overemphasized. 20 percent of the practice time should be devoted to all aspects of shooting. "All drills should incorporate the ingredients of the team's planned defenses and offenses; however, do not drill initiative and motivation out of a good basketball player."

Drills for fundamentals, simulating game conditions as much as possible. An experienced coach will know what drills will be best for his team, both for teaching his offense, defenses, and conditioning his players. A new coach must decide what drills to use and how long to spend on them. Drills should be simple and competitive. They should cover as many techniques as possible. They should also be selective. Don't use too many, or too complicated, drills.

Drills are good only when they are completely absorbed by the squad. The coach must give the reason for each operation and explain the correct technique because:

— If players understand they gain confidence.

— It shows them there is a reason for everything.

Proper technique is learned because the coach can analyze any mistakes that the players make and allows him to compliment those players who do the drill well.

Selected drills allow for concentrated practice in specific areas. Pre-season conditioning drills must be efficient; therefore, they should include fundamental techniques. Early in the year, many necessary conditioning drills use running without involving the ball, or defensive techniques.

Some drills serve as a change of pace in the daily practice routine. They are also excellent for before practice, or pre-game warm-up. These should be simple, short in duration, and interesting. A variety keeps players interested in seeking perfection, preventing boredom and complacency. Too little time on drills, leaves a desire for more. This is more effective than too much time in drills. When drills become boring, there is a lack of enthusiasm and bad habits will form. "Drills should be spirited, evoking constant chatter and desire for perfection."

Drills should reflect the team's offensive and defensive philosophy. In fact, coaches should devise their own drills. The most adaptable and inventive coach is generally the successful. Three steps to learning are as follows:

The student must be interested and ready to learn. A competent coach who has the full attention of a receptive student can teach him the proper fundamentals of the game, stressing the acquisition of accuracy before speed.

Practice makes perfect. Once the player understands the techniques involved, he practices willingly for hours on end.

The final examination, in this case, is the actual playing of the game itself and not whether the team wins or loses the game.

To introduce team concepts early in the pre-season, the coach should use skeleton teams offensively and defensively. The concepts should be broken down and practiced in drills involving two-on-two and three-on-three groups. Much of the offense and defense to be used in the season should be broken down into drills.

The man-to-man attack and defense, zone attack and defense, pressure attack and defense, and combination attack and defense must be broken into parts if they are to be used. Drills should be repetitive so that reaction becomes instinctive. Players should not have to think about what they are going to do.

Every drill must demand perfect, or near perfect, performance from every player. Coaches must be constantly observant and highly critical, making corrections immediately. They must overcome a tendency to ignore or overlook slight irregularities or imperfections in a player's form or habits. Coaches should remember that practicing something incorrectly is just as habit forming as practicing something correctly. Perhaps the most important motto for drills is, "practice makes permanent."

Competitive drills hold player's interest. The use of rewards for winners and penalties for the losers creates incentive and enthusiasm. Winners could be given a reward, and the losers made to run suicides.

All drills should have short, definitive names so that players know exactly what to do as soon as the name is called. Teams develop unity through drills. Players become accustomed to the movements, attitudes, habits, and idiosyncrasies of teammates. New drills can be explained during a brief practice break one day, then incorporated into the practice for the next day. Drills should be scheduled so that a physically strenuous drill is followed by one that is easier. Several small groups in which all players work strenuously are more beneficial than one large group in which several players are not working. The coach should plan to use all his players in drill activities every day in early season. At the end of a hard practice, the coaches should incorporate a drill that the players enjoy. This implementation will leave the players in a good frame of mind. They will anticipate the next day's practice.

Selecting and Evaluating Players

Early pre-season scrimmages are necessary in order to help select the squad. At this time, scrimmage teams should be selected for balance. Good players should be scattered evenly among the teams. Daily evaluations of each scrimmage should be made and recorded. Many of today's coaches drill too much and scrimmage too little. The right amount of scrimmage for a team depends on the experience, and physical and psychological condition of the players.

After the squad has been selected in the early season, scrimmage sessions should involve five-man teams of varying ability. In selecting squads for early pre-season scrimmage practice, coaches should allow designated players of equal ability to pick the other members of their teams. A different selection order should be used each round until each designated player has made four choices. The selectors should be varied as often as possible. Allowing the best players to select their teams enables the coach to see how the players rate each other. He also gains insight into personality clashes, or cliques, within the squad.

If there are three teams, they should scrimmage for approximately five to eight minutes. The winning team stays on the court. With four teams, play a round robin tournament with winners playing winners and losers playing losers. This procedure should be followed until each player has run approximately twenty minutes of full-court scrimmage. These scrimmage sessions should be interrupted for criticism and analysis when necessary."

Following is an outline of the factors to be evaluated by the players. (Naturally, each evaluator cannot include himself in any of the Positive factors.)

Positive Factors

— Three players who always take good shots.
— Three best shooters.
— Three best rebounders.
— Three best drivers.
— Three best passers.
— Three best defensive players.
— Three best team players offensively.
— Three best team players defensively.
— Three best hustlers.
— Three quickest players.
— Three players with the best straightaway speed.
— Four players you most like to play with.

Negative Factors

— Three players who habitually take bad shots.
— Three poorest shooters.
— Three poorest rebounders.
— Three poorest drivers.

— Three poorest passers.
— Three poorest defenders.
— Three poorest players offensively.
— Three poorest players defensively.
— Three poorest hustlers.
— Three players who are least quick.
— Three players with the least straightaway speed.
— Four players you least like to play with.

The coach should collect the unsigned sheets, transfer the information to a master sheet, and destroy the individual sheets. It is best to destroy them with the manager present, so that he can assure the squad that the sheets are not kept. The coach and assistant coaches should also fill out evaluation sheets, keeping the results confidential.

The coaches should then assess the player-evaluation results against their own evaluation. Many times it will be obvious to the coaches that there are possible discrepancies, or inadequacies, in their own thinking.

Also, personality clashes, or conflicts, may be festering; therefore, evaluations by the involved players should not be taken seriously in the master evaluation. However, for harmonious team relationship the coach should try to resolve any conflicts. Any good coach should be able to meet any contingency; and flexibility is an asset. Coaches should be prepared to learn from these evaluations. The use of teammate evaluation sheets, and player selection of teams for early season scrimmages contributes a great deal toward development of team spirit and understanding of the squad."

Player Self-Evaluation Sheets

A self-evaluation sheet is also important to players. This sheet covers the intangibles as well as the qualities that coaches can observe. This sheet is as follows:

Factors to be rated:

— Basketball instinct.
— Attention to details.
— Ability to follow instructions.
— Alertness.
— Aggressiveness.
— Individual defensive ability.
— Team defensive ability.
— Individual offensive ability.
— Team offensive ability.
— Rebounding ability.
— Shooting ability.
— Shot selection.
— Ability to penetrate.
— Desire for the game.
— Physical condition.
— Selflessness.
— Dribbling ability.
— Passing ability.
— Catching ability.
— Quickness.
— Straightaway speed.
— Hustle.
— Leaping ability.
— Work ethic.
— Footwork.
— Ability to get along with teammates.
— Ratings of 4 for excellent, 3 for good, 2 for fair, and 1 for poor should be given.

Many times a coach will find that players are downgrading themselves. Other players may have an exaggerated opinion of themselves. Through individual talks, the coach may be able to help the players evaluate themselves realistically. Self-evaluation sheets should be destroyed after they have served their purpose.

Scrimmaging in Early Pre-season

While you may not be able to scrimmage much during the first week, candidates of dubious ability should scrimmage full court as often as feasible, with some of the better players so that they feel they were given every opportunity to become members of the squad. Coaches should remember that scrimmaging is 10 teaching situations at once. By scrimmaging, players react under game conditions. All scrimmages must be properly officiated. During early pre-season scrimmages clocks must be available, as well as all the statistical sheets that are used in scheduled games. The assistant coaches should record the positive and negative factors during a scrimmage so that constructive changes can be made in practices that follow.

The head coach should be on the court, using the double-whistle technique to stop practice when something is fundamentally wrong. All aspects of each scrimmage should be charted and recorded so that individual player analysis is complete. All pre-season scrimmage statistics should be recorded on a master copy for dissemination and use with the squad. Shooting percentages, foul shooting percentages, and all other statistical information should be available to the squad as a result of these scrimmages.

If there are enough players for four balanced five-man teams, run a tournament type of competitive scrimmage allowing two teams to play approximately eight minutes. Then, the next two play for eight minutes. The winners then play for third and second place. The losers play to determine third and fourth place. This brings an element of competition into the practice and motivates the players to play well in early pre-season to reach a visible goal. Scrimmaging in early pre-season enables the players to work under the pressure they will be under once the season starts. This type of scrimmaging should not take place until the team has learned the necessary offensive and defensive fundamentals.

These scrimmages should be handled by officials. An experienced basketball official should be present at the first early scrimmage to explain the rule changes and the rule emphasis for the coming season.

Pre-season Essentials

At the close of each session, there should be a post-practice coaches' meeting, twenty minutes to one half hour long. At this meeting the coaches should analyze the practice session and decide if it accomplished what was planned. The coaches should also analyze each player's basketball progress, attentiveness, and attitude.

Rate Each Player

Each player should be rated on a 4 for excellent, 3 for good, 2 for fair, and 1 for poor. Keep a record of this analysis. At the end of the second week, the coaches can discuss any apparent weaknesses with the players in a before-practice session.

It is imperative that the following areas be thoroughly covered so the players are completely prepared for the first game:

Offense

— *Fast-Break*: This could either be a side-line or conventional break.

- *Secondary Break*: This is the possible scoring opportunities that occur while getting into basic patterns.
    - Basic attack against man-to-man defenses.
    - Basic attack against zone defenses.
    - Basic attack against combination defenses.
    - Basic attack against pressing defenses.
- Out-of-bounds plays, both from the side and under the basket, first for possession of the ball and then for a score.
    - Free-throw alignment for a possible fast-break.
    - Semi-freeze and stall situations.
    - A one-shot play for late in the game.
    - Rebounding fundamentals for the individual and the team.
    - Last minute and late game situations when behind, with the score tied, and when ahead.

Defense

- The methods of stopping the fast-break at the defensive backboard, cutting off the outlet, and guarding the rebounder to delay the break.
- Full-court defenses: Both man-to-man and zone. (Aggressive and loose)
- Half-court defenses: Man-to-man, zone, and combination. (Aggressive and loose.)
- The defensive rebounding pattern for both individual and team.
- Last minute situations when behind, with the score tied, and when ahead.

Controlled Scrimmages

The coach must control the offense and defense used by the scrimmaging teams in pre-season practice sessions. For example, in a 15 minute scrimmage, Team A may use a 1-3-1 offense for the first 8 minutes and a stacked offense for 7 minutes.

Team B may use a man-to-man ball denial defense for the first 5 minutes, a 1-3-1 zone for the next 5 minutes, and a full-court pressing defense for the last five minutes. Similar assignments are made for Team A on defense and Team B on offense.

A manager should keep an offense pattern chart for such scrimmages, noting the number of possessions, the number of shots, and the baskets scored for each team from the offense used. For example:

Team A

— *One-Thee-One Set offense*: 30 possessions - 28 shots - 15 baskets

— *Stack Offense*: 20 possessions - 15 shots - 5 baskets

— *Fast-break*: 7 possessions - 6 shots - 5 baskets

— *Secondary break*: 50 possessions - 30 shots - 12 baskets

Using statistics like these will indicate the effectiveness of the offenses and defenses used when assessed against the offensive-defensive apportionment.

As a basketball coach you should map your road to success prior start of the school year. Organize each phase of the season for best results.

Many coaches tend to practice too long. A practice session should only be long as players can work at their best ability. Only rarely, should a practice session be more than one and a half hour long.

Planning Basketball Practice Sessions

How long should a practice session last? This is a question every basketball coach must answer. Your answer will directly effect failure or success of the coming basketball season. Other than your ability to lead, no other stage of basketball coaching is as important as well planned and conducted practice session.

The ideal practice is short and most successful basketball coaches lean in that direction. Some circumstances determine the length of practice:

— The time available.

— The coach's disposition.

— Type of material available

The following reasons call for short practice sessions:

— Basketball is a energetic sport.

— The season is long and played at a time when the body is subject to all types of colds and viral ailments and resistance is lowered..

— Long practices do not achieve the physical and mental edge required of basketball players..

— Physical and mental powers must reach their peak at tourney time.

— Enthusiasm and response to drills are greater in short practices.

— Lessens the chance of injuries.

Few teams suffer from lack of instruction when subjected to a well planned one-hour practice; however, most teams benefit from a two-hour practice sessions during the first half of a normal basketball season. Still, less time should be devoted to practice as the season progresses.

Some coaches excuse their starting players twice a week after mid-season to keep them fresh and eager to play. Some of you may be surprised at the results this little trick achieves. This provides the coach more time to develop the reserve players. On these two days, the reserves come in for intense work on their fundamentals. On the other days, they come for about as much work as the starting five; however, Tuesdays and Wednesdays should be hard days for the Varsity.

The coach should know the length of the daily practice before the season starts. The next step is to apportion so much time to offensive fundamentals, defensive fundamentals, offensive team organization, and defensive team organization.

Plan early-season fundamentals a week in advance; however, once the season opens revert to daily planning. This is needed to teach the type of fundamental most needed. Every player is not weak in the same fundamental. Become a good systems administrator, recognize the problems, divide the squad, and work on the deficient fundamentals of each member.

Here is an idea concerning the amount of time spent on daily practices:

— Monday - 105 minutes

— Tuesday - 100 minutes

— Wednesday - 105 minutes

— Thursday - 105 minutes

— Friday - 105 minutes

— Saturday - 90 minutes

If you expect to succeed as a basketball coach, you must learn to plan each phase of the basketball year. For purposes of this study the season is divided into three parts.

— *Pre-season practice* - the period from the opening of the school year until the first day formal practice is permitted State Basketball Associations.

— *Early season practice* - the period from the first day of permissible practice and first officially scheduled game.

— *Season practice* - the period from the first scheduled game to the last scheduled game prior to tournament play.

Outdoor practices are advisable because a basketball season is long. Delay going inside as long as possible. Four to six weeks of outdoor work does wonders in developing good physical condition. Outdoor conditioning will give your team a quick and safer indoors start, with fewer chances of early injuries. The outdoor work gives the players added confidence in themselves and their teammates because they will, most generally be better conditioned than their opponents.

Explain the program in detail at the first meeting. Discuss other points such as maintaining their studies, training, schedules, etc.

Complete physical examinations are given the squad and practice uniforms issued. The players report to the athletic field three or four times a week at 3:30 P.M., and leisurely take six to eight laps around the field.

The first week:

After the laps, the squad reports to outdoor volleyball courts. The skills of volleyball are closely related to those of basketball, such as jumping, timing, ball handling, use of fingertips, balance and team play. These skills provide a stepping stone to basketball.

The second week:

This second week takes on a change which provides more running of the basketball type. Basketball running is described as dashes, spurts, or short sprints, and change of direction.

Starting the second week of outdoor practice, the players take three warm-up laps and then take two laps of short sprints, Good running form should be stressed in order to improve speed. The players sprint for five to ten yards and coast to a walk. Repeat this until two laps are completed.

The last lap, or two, is a change-in-direction style of running. Stress and perfect good form in this basketball fundamental. After the running, players report to the volleyball courts.

The third week

The third week consists of the same type of running, with two laps of change of direction added. Bring basketballs out this week and cover many of the basketball fundamentals after the running program.

Use only the fundamentals that can be as effectively outside as inside, such as body balance, ball handling, and peripheral vision drills. Do not cover any shooting drills, outside. Games stressing offensive and defensive rebounding might be played.

The fourth week

The fourth week is a continuation of the third week, except during the last week, hold elimination races to determine the fastest guard, forward, center and the speed player on the squad.

The forwards run in a 50 yard dash to determine the fastest forwards. The guards run next and the centers run last. The players to finish first and second in each race, line up for the final race. Using this method allows the coach to actually know who are the fastest and slowest runners. besides giving fun and competition to the program.

You can sometimes overcome weaknesses in some players by giving them special assignments to meet during this early fall session. Big players are encouraged to skip rope and do rope climbing. The latter exercise will improve the use of their arms overhead.

When indoor work starts, your players will be eager to get started. Such eagerness is necessary to a winning team and should be nurtured and cultivated.

How to Coach Basketball Individual Defense

Good basic basketball defense does require speed and quickness; however, players make up for these physical shortcomings by out-hustling and developing a defensive attitude that is aggressive. It isn't necessary that a player be highly skilled to play effective, hard-nosed defense.

Too many athletes get the idea that defense is passive. Passivity creates negative actions. Aggressiveness is positive. You will find that all aggressive minded athletes will be the best defenders. Even while defending a goal, players should always be on attack. Most important is the fact that anyone through hard work, and attention to detail, learn to play good solid defense. It is a known fact in the basketball coaching circle that a player can learn basic defensive skills far quicker than he can learn to properly execute basic offensive skills. On defense, hustle, aggressiveness, and anticipation tend to make up for other deficiencies in a player's game.

The great defensive performer is ready to start guarding his man when he comes out of his dressing room, guard him if he goes into the popcorn stand, and until the final whistle. The opponent should go home with the feeling of being attacked by a wild octopus. He should have nightmares dreaming about the aggressive tactics that wild man inflicted, not giving him one minute of peace.

The current trend is toward defense. No team has a corner on the defensive game, today. All good teams are playing it more efficiently each year. The trend is pointing in that direction out of necessity. More time must be devoted in preparation of a way to stop modern offensive formations and patterns. Younger coaches are discovering something that Bob Knight and Dean Smith have known for years and always practiced.

In most cases the defender positions himself either between his man and the basket, particularly if guarding a player with the ball, or partially or wholly between his man and the ball. Both positions serve to reduce the action-reaction advantage favoring the offensive player, forcing the offensive player to work harder than normal to get the ball or move into scoring position.

Individual Requirements

Defensive team play can only be as effective as the individual ability and dedication of each player. Attributes to be sought individually are:

— *Desire and Pride*. Regardless of how sound a player is fundamentally, he can not be an effective defender if he lacks either these two qualities. Playing hard-nosed defense requires hard work and determination, while offering little praise or recognition. Hustle is the child of desire that includes determination to play defense well. A good defender works tirelessly and puts forth that extra effort even when tired. Pride is the satisfaction one feels when knowing he played the part to the best of his ability while receiving little, or no credit.

— *Mental Alertness and Aggressiveness*. The player who reacts immediately from offense to defense will be in position to cover unguarded opponents, prevent the surprise offensive maneuver, putting the offense at a disadvantage. These two requirements can often force an opponent into a defensive posture even though he has control of the ball.

— *Anticipation and Adaptability.* Anticipation is the ability to predetermine offensive patterns. To decide whether a pass can be intercepted or change offensive men with a teammate before the situation presents itself. Adjusting to changes with the correct defensive action indicates a player's adaptability. This is not based entirely on instinct, but upon an intelligent study of an opponent's individual and team offensive moves from the moment the game began.

— *Speed and Quickness.* Running speed enables a defender to move from one court position to another more quickly than other players. His speed and quickness allows him to recover from defensive mistakes, assuming a new defensive position with little danger to the team. Quickness of feet, hands, and arms enables a defender to keep the offense in a protective attitude by individual harassment. Quickness effectively neutralizes an opponent's superior speed. Because the normal defensive distance from the basket is between eighteen and twenty -two feet, quickness is probably a bigger asset than speed.

The objective of a basketball team defense is to stop the offensive team from scoring. We all know this is an impossible task. More practical is the attempt to take the opponent out of the offense they are trying to run. This can be done by:

— Forcing the ball toward low-percentage shooters, or scoring areas by fronting or overplaying the opponent's high scorer.

— Getting back quickly on defense to limit the fast-break opportunities
— Forcing shooters to alter their position, timing, release, or arc of their shot

From the above, you can see the entire purpose of a team's defense is to limit the opponent's opportunity to score by these three things. The coach must use several factors, the most important one is the available personnel.

A good team defense, this day and age, incorporates the strong points of both the zone and man-to-man defense. The primary focus in a man-to-man is the person and the secondary objective is the ball; however, teams that use person-to-person as a primary defense also use some zone principles as playing loosely away from the ball. They collapse weak-side toward the basket to prevent penetration, compacting the defense in the basket area.

Conversely, zone defensive players play the ball first and the person second, but must be able to defend against the opponent with the ball on a person-to-person basis. In the old days, a zone player covered a specific area. It isn't that way, today. Zones of today, flex with a person-to-person attitude at the ball, attacking the person with the ball and preventing a pass into the pivot.

Whatever Defensive You Choose

— Insist that players never allow the offensive team to advance the ball to their point of attack without strong defensive pressure.
— As a coach do not use a single defense in your overall preparation.
— Adapt to whatever defensive style is best suited to counteract the opponent's offensive moves.

— Understand the type of defense you choose to use and be able to teach it to your players.

Work hard at improving your team's defense. Any defense used must be:

— Sound, both individually and as a team.

— Flexible, adaptable to different offensive attacks

— Simple, enough for your players to learn.

— Complex, for the opponent's to solve.

Defensive ability is based is based on the following factors:

— Hard work.

— Determination.

— Dedication.

— Discipline.

— Concentration.

— Responsibility.

— Cooperation.

— Physical and mental coordination.

— Speed and quickness.

— Willingness.

— Pride.

When coaches scout their opponents, they preview each other's defenses. Showing multiple defenses allows a coach to employ a defense that will give his opponent difficulty. This forces the opposing coach to use practice time to prepare for each defense playing against reserve players who must be taught each defense in order to act as opponents.

A good coach should pressure teams holding the ball for a last shot at the end of a period or the game. The stalling team generally are so interested in maintaining possession, they usually do not look at the basket; therefore, it might be easy to force them into a violation. Teams who are ahead should not relax and become passive either on offense or defense.

All teams must be able to press to some degree, especially in the late stages of a game. Defensive aggressiveness will cause the opponents to move out of their normal pattern. Defensively, a team should change the game pace to its own advantage. You must surprise and confuse the opponent. Saving some practiced defensive variations for the second half that were not shown in the first half is generally another good surprise maneuver. You could also use a defensive variation in the last few minutes of the first half so that the opposing coach will use much of his valuable half-time period discussing methods of attacking a defense that will not be used again in that game.

The winning team in basketball is frequently the team quickest in transition from offense to defense; therefore, it is important that your team maintains defensive balance while attacking offensively. You must always keep a player in a defensive safety position so that he may hinder, or stop, the opponents from scoring an easy unopposed basket. A team should have:

— Three offensive rebounders.

— One person who is half offensive and half defensive, going to the ball only if certain of possession.

— One player at Safety Defensive position.

Preparation

Defensive preparation begins the first day. Team defensive fundamentals are essential and should be reviewed throughout the season.

You must practice double-teaming opponents, working on the double-teaming aspects from person-to-person, zone, or zone-press defensive alignments. You must teach baseline defensive techniques and how to play persons who do not have possession of the ball. If you want an aggressive defense, you must have your players to overplay. If not, let them play loose or sag back when the player is one pass away. It is best that you teach all your players to never allow an opponent to cut in front of them to the ball, especially a corner player who wants to cut to the keyhole area with the ball out front or on the opposite side.

Emphasize the need for a good defense by doing as follows:

— Insist upon attention to detail when implementing the defensive.

— Break the defense into fundamental parts.

— Practice group defensive techniques each session.

— Develop rules for each phase of the defense.

— Spread defensive drills discriminately through daily practice. For example: at the beginning of one practice session, halfway through another, and at the end on the third day.

-- Never allow improper defense by any player. Correct poor procedure immediately.

— Reward good defensive play. Give praise both public and private for outstanding defensive accomplishment.

Determining Team Defense

The basic makeup of your material must be considered. In general, a team will consist of one of the following groups:

— Five taller than average players - If you choose a person-to-person defense, it should be a loose defense. If the coach prefers a zone, a passive type might be best. In this type of defense your players can defend the goal area. Whenever pressure is needed, a type of half-court pressure should do the job. Have your quickest player force the ball up to the mid-court line and the entire team giving pressure in the half-court area.

— Four tall players and one small and quick player - Teach this group a loose person to person defense or a one-two-two zone where the smaller and quicker player is given freedom to anticipate and intercept. Whenever pressure is needed, a type of half-court pressure is best, with the small player forcing the ball up to the mid-court line and the entire team exerting pressure in the half-court area.

— Three tall players and two smaller players - The team could also use a two-one-two or a two-three zone, a combination defense, or a pressure defense that could be extended to a two-two-one full-court pressure.

— Two tall players and three small players - You can use any type of person-to-person defense. You could use a three-two zone, a one-two-two zone, a one-three-one zone, or a combination defense. Whenever a pressure defense is needed, this team can use any type pressure defense, be it half-court, three-quarter-court, or full court.

— One tall player and four small players - A switching person-to-person defense whereby the four small players switch on every lateral cross or movement toward the basket, staying with their player only on diagonal cuts. The best half-court zone would be either a two-two-one or a one-three-one. Leave the big player in the basket area at all times.

— *Five small players* - This team should use a tight person-to-person half-court defense with double or turn action taken on the outside dribbler. A full-court person-to-person would be OK, too. A zone press defense could be used, with all five players crashing the defensive boards, or an aggressive two-three zone defense in which pressure is put on the ball at all areas of the front court.

Team Principles of Basketball Defense

All good defenses, be it person-to-person, combination. or zone, are based on these six principles:

— Reduce the High-Percentage Shots.

— Decrease the Number of Shots under 18 feet.

— Limit you opponent's Second-Shot opportunities.

— Eliminate Turn-Overs.

— Attack the Ball with Controlled Aggressiveness.

— Discourage Opponents from Penetrating.

Secrets to Picking the Players

Over the years, as shooting, passing, and dribbling have become more sophisticated, offensive alignments have changed. They probably will continue. Rule changes often dictate this. For example, take the three-point shot. This has changed the philosophy of a lot of coaches. Previous to the three- point shot, big men dominated the game. Teams constantly looked for only a close-in shot. As a result, most defenses packed back in tight.

Changing the Game

The three-point shot has changed all this. This new rule has opened up the game. Defenses must come out. It is quite common to see coaches using 3 and 4 guard offenses. Some of them even have their offensive teams and defensive teams, substituting freely to suit the particular need. Fundamentals, however, remain much as they were 40 years ago. Things that worked then, still work today.

Terminology used today, to describe offensive alignments are different than they were 40 years ago. Some team offenses have evolved so that every player must be able to play at any and all positions. The flex offense is an example. Yet, this type offense is over 30 years old. Us old timers called it "the shuffle." In either offense, the center often finds himself out at a guard position. This type offense is well suited for today's rules; however, adjustments are made to fit the abilities of available players.

All coaches should appreciate the importance of the appearance of their team. A well dressed team is enthusiastic and happy. They even look like they want to play. A good state of mind is not likely to be present if the team is self-conscious because of ragged uniforms. Your team should be well-dressed but not exaggeratedly dressed.

Before the game

Don't over-coach. "A little learned well is better than a lot done poorly" is a good truism to follow. Most teams perform better a little under-coached than over-coached. The desire to play must be retained in order to have that natural gusto so noticeable in most younger athletes. It is also good psychology for the coach to have physical and mental behavior at all times. This calmness breeds player confidence. "Acting" by the coach weakens his judgment and causes players to lose confidence.

Basketball is an emotional game; however, players usually work harder under stress of emotion. A wise and observant coach will recognize the proper emotional pitch.

The coach's poise helps the players develop their confidence. This trait, in the right degree affects the mental condition and necessary relaxation of the athlete. The player possessing the right confidence will not be bothered with the two evils, overconfidence and lack of confidence.

Overconfidence, in addition to the fighting heart of the underdog, creates a lot of upsets. The former, overconfidence, robs the player of his mental and physical aggressiveness. This condition can only be fixed through a couple defeats. A coach can fight this condition by arousing a fear of defeat. You can accomplish this by using a bulletin board for clippings, write-ups, and statistics of opponent's best games. The coach could emphasize the opponent's strength where his team is weakest. Another way to meet this condition is to temporarily bench a player and let somebody play who wants to play.

If the team is in the favorable situation as underdog, the coach's problem is that of building confidence, hope, desire, and enthusiasm. Some coaches are masters of the art of getting the team at the right pitch, where they have diminished the proficiency of the opponents to the high opinion which shows his players tat defeating the opponent is not impossible. They are fired-up, yet under control, and can see the added standing of victory over that favored team. The players call on that physical and mental reserve which places them on another level of performance. This is accomplished through encouragement and good leadership.

At the half

Most coaches have a fixed policy for procedure between half-time. This should be established at the first game of the year in the interests of efficiency and organization. No one, except the squad and members of the athletic department, should be allowed in the dressing room . The players should immediately lie down and relax. It is important that everyone be quite for five or six minutes to permit complete relaxation. The trainer, or coaching assistant, should cleanse the faces and necks of players with cold towels.

This is a period of rest and not a egg on session. Meanwhile, coaches can be outside the dressing room discussing strategy for the second half. After the relaxation period, the coach can cover mistakes and the progress of the first half. Next, the coach should explain the plan for the second half, stressing no more than about two main points. If a coach asks his players to remember too may things, the team would have been better had the coach forgotten which dressing room his team was in. Be sure to give encouragement to the players who need encouragement and express confidence in the team before they go back on court.

Basketball is fun and should be played for fun. Sometimes coaches get wrapped up in the interests of the team and forget this fact. A burning desire to have his team just right for certain games often lends to over keying. This causes tenseness which is an enemy to good shooting and the team will not play as well as normal. If the team is composed of players who have the team's interest at heart, they will do a better job of keying themselves, than the coach.

After the game

If the team played a good game, but lost, tell them so with honest feeling. If they played a poor game, and won, tell them they were lucky and not to be too proud of their victory. Refraining from criticizing a player in defeat immediately after the game is good policy. Give the player time to settle down and think things over. You can cover things in detail the next day.

5

Basketball Training Skills

Strength Training

Strength training is an important part of becoming a better basketball player, especially during the off-season.

Be sure to check with your doctor, parents, or coach before beginning any strength training program or workout routine.

Strength training with traditional weights is an important part of any good basketball training program. But with all the new equipment, and new training techniques available today, weight training as it was done 15 or 20 years ago is truly a thing of the past.

In addition to the traditional weight lifting exercises, there are a variety of sport-specific exercises and techniques you should include in your strength training workouts.

Here is a list of some of the basic weight lifting exercises you will likely want to include in your training program:

— Bench press

— Incline bench press

— Bicep curl

— Tricep press downs
— Squats
— Lunges
— Shoulder press
— Leg extensions
— Leg curls
— Calf raises

But what is also very important, is how you do these exercises. The benefits of training for power and explosiveness:

Use power during the exertion part of the exercise

In otherwords, rather than go through the full range of motion very slow and methodically, power-out or up when doing the exercise. Always be under control and make sure to use good form, but using power in addition to strength during the exercise pays big benefits.

For example, say you're doing bench presses. Once you bring the weight down to just above your chest and are about to push the weight away from your body, do so with power. Don't just raise the weight, raise it like you are pushing against something, and trying to push it away as quickly as possible. Again, don't jerk the weights, but use a controlled, yet powerful motion to build strength and power.

Emphasize full range of motion

The best way to train your muscles, especially for a sport like basketball, is to train through a full range of motion. For example, if you're doing a shoulder press (where you sit in a workout chair, and raise either dumbells or a barbell from your shoulders to up above your head), you'll want to go through that complete motion. Don't stop short at the top or bottom of the exercise.

If you only go through part of the motion, you're not utilizing your muscles completely. The best way to strengthening your muscles, and keeping them lithe and flexible, is to train through the full range of motion.

Balance exercises

The new breed of professional trainers utilize balance-based exercises to effectively train athletes. Most sports, but especially basketball, require great body balance. Think about it: leaping to grab a rebound...lunging to tip a pass...sprinting out to grab a loose ball...all require great balance.

Doing certain exercises on an exercise ball (to help strengthen your abdominals and body balance), or using a BOSU balance trainer, are amazingly effective ways to help train your overall body (as a unit), and work on your balance. As your body adjusts, compensates, and focuses on keeping you on balance throughout the exercise, you're actually building strength and body balance.

There are lots of places to train, so you don't have any excuses for not training:

— A health club or fitness center usually has all the basic free weights and machines. In addition, most high-end clubs have things like exercise balls, BOSU balance trainers, agility bands, etc.

— Most high schools, junior colleges, and universities have training rooms for their athletes.

— Many of my clients train at home, with free weights, Universal machines, or even a Bowflex machine.

— If you don't have access to any type of training facility, you can do push ups, sit ups, and various other exercises to help build strength.

Agility Training

In sport, agility is characterised by fast feet, body coordination during change of direction and sports skill performance, and reaction time/ ability. It is an amalgam of balance, speed, strength, flexibility and coordination. Although a performer's agility relies heavily on the acquisition of optimum sports technique, it can also be enhanced by specific conditioning.

A variety of performance-enhancing agility drills, systems and items of equipment are available to the sportsmen of today and their coaches. The 'science' of agility (and speed and power) training has made rapid strides recently, especially in terms of its accessibility to the mainstream sporting world.

Dissecting a Sports Skill

Essentially, agility training dissects a sports skill: a skill like the fast-stepping ability required of a rugby player is broken down into its constituent parts, which are then specifically trained. It's all about patterning and conditioning a heightened physical, neural, sport-specific response.

A wide variety of running, hopping and jumping drills can be carried out in all directions, using the rungs of this ladder, which is laid flat on the ground. Such drills enhance foot speed and upper body agility, just like any other aspect of sports performance, by progressive overload. England rugby wing Ben Cohen has been specifically singled out as a player whose feet have been rendered especially fleet by means of extensive use of the rope ladder and other agility training methods.

Speed through a floor ladder can indicate much about a player's quickness. A time of less than 2.8 seconds (male) and 3.4 seconds (female) for running the length of a 20-rung ladder, one foot in each rung at a time, is regarded as 'excellent' for college athletes.

Agility training also utilises numerous other drills and items of specialist kit; these include balance drills, slaloming in and out of cones and stepping over and around small hurdles. To make the transference of the agility skill even more sport-specific, an actual sports skill can also be introduced. This could take the form of dribbling a football in and out of cones, or receiving a rugby pass while stepping through a foot-ladder.

SAQ

Obviously, companies like SAQ International claim their systems get results and improve players' agility. But is their confidence justified? Polman and associates looked at the effects of SAQ techniques on female footballers over a 12- week period. The players were divided into three groups, two performing SAQ training, while the third carried on with their normal conditioning programmes. The results were as follows:

— All three interventions reduced the participants' body mass index (-3.7%) and fat percentage (-1.7%), and increased flexibility (+14.7%) and VO2max (+ 18.4%);

- However, the SAQ groups showed significantly greater benefits from their training programme than the other group on a sprint-to-fatigue test, a 25m sprint, and left and right side agility tests.

— Working to improve the agility of a dynamic sports performer by means of SAQ and similar techniques seems highly appropriate, relevant and valuable. But will the same principles apply to endurance athletes? After all, quick-as-a-flash agility is not a prerequisite for triathlon or marathon running.

— Alricsson and associates carried out a study to evaluate whether dance training had any effect on the joint mobility and muscle flexibility of the spine, hip and ankle and on the speed and agility of young cross-country skiers. Cross-country skiing is a not a sport renowned for quick dynamic movement, but shaving seconds off on every turn and jump could add up to significant time savings. Dance training was selected for this task because of its potential contribution to agility and flexibility.

The study involved 20 élite cross-country skiers, aged 12-15, with half of them (five girls and five boys) receiving weekly dance training and the rest serving as non-dancing controls for a period of eight months. Joint mobility and muscle flexibility of the spine, hip and ankle were measured before the study period and at three and eight months. Two sport-related functional tests – a slalom test and a hurdle test were carried out at the same times.

The researchers found that the dance group had increased their speed by a total of 0.3 seconds over the slalom test after eight months. They also improved their speed and agility on the hurdle test by 0.8 seconds after three months and by a further 0.6 seconds after eight months. Furthermore, they increased flexion-extension of the thoracic (upper) spine by 7.5° after three months and by a further 1.5° after eight months, while lateral flexion improved by 0.04mm and a further 0.03mm over the same periods. Meanwhile, the non-dancing controls did not show any improvements in any of the studied variables.

Dance Training

Dance training has a positive effect on speed and agility and on joint mobility and muscle flexibility in flexion-extension and lateral flexion of the spine in young crosscountry skiers'. Had his subjects made use of more sport-specific agility training, the chances are that their gains would have been even greater.

Marathon runners do not have to dart sideways, backwards and forwards with lightning speed over the course of their 26-mile effort, so could they have anything to gain from agility training? To answer this question, we need to consider the interplay between agility and power training.

Research indicates that, despite prolonged running training, runners' leg muscles may not actually be that efficient at returning energy to the running surface. In fact, at certain speeds these muscles may be working at only 50% efficiency because of the 'natural' energy return effectiveness of the foot arch and Achilles tendon.

It's a bit like having an engine turbocharger that works in reverse. Your Achilles and foot arch are the turbo: they cut in automatically when your foot strikes the ground, producing a burst of power but leave the running muscles (quads, hamstrings and calf muscles – the engine) working at less than their full potential. Unless you target these running muscles with specific power conditioning drills, your ability to drive up running speed can be compromised.

Such exercises as hopping on and off of a low box and spring jogging (virtually straight leg movements, where the performer propels himself forwards primarily by means of feet and ankles) not only develop 'harder', and therefore more effective, running muscles through their plyometric effect, but also improve agility.

Plyometric exercises enable muscles to generate huge amounts of force in a split second, when a concentric (shortening) muscular contraction immediately follows an eccentric (lengthening) contraction of the same muscle.

These agility and power moves can 'sharpen' foot/ ground contact and result in a more economical and powerful running stride, regardless of running distance.

Backwards and sideways running can also 'prehabilitate' against injury, providing a further reason why endurance runners (and those involved in running-based sports) should perform agility training.

As mentioned above, conditioning exercises, such as a plyometric drills, can develop both agility and power. However, these drills may not exactly match what is required in a playing situation. To ensure they do, it is essential for coaches to analyse in real detail the agility and movement patterns required for their sport and to use this information to construct the most relevant conditioning programme. In this respect foot positioning can be crucial.

Kovacs and associates looked at the relevance of foot positioning, particularly foot-landing positions, in athletes performing plyometric depth jumps drills involving stepping off a box then immediately springing upwards, sideways or forwards. Specifically, the researchers were interested in comparing the force generated by flat-footed and forefoot ground contacts.

Ten male university students performed two types of depth jump from a 0.4m high box placed 1m from the centre of a force plate. They were instructed to land either on the balls of their feet, without the heels touching the ground, or on their heels. The researchers discovered that the two different jumping styles generated force in very different ways. Using specific measuring equipment, Kovacs' team demonstrated that a forefoot landing depth jump produced significantly more power at impact and at the transition into the jump than a flat-footed landing depth jump.

Depth Jumps and Power

Kovacs' findings have crucial implications for optimum agility and power conditioning. Even though a flat-footed-landing depth jump will develop power, this may not channel optimally into enhancing the agility and power of a player in a specific sport. For example, a sprinter would probably benefit more from forefoot-landing jumps, as the sprint action is performed from a similar foot-strike position, whereas a basketball or volleyball player is likely to develop greater vertical spring – a key requirement of the games – by using flat-footed landings. Muscle firing patterns are very specific, and conditioning drills must mirror sports skills for optimum results.

Finally here's an example of an even more specific agility/power conditioning drill, designed for a tennis player. The player should perform a depth jump with a forefoot – but non-aligned – landing position, which will enable him or her to rotate and sprint, in 3-5 strides, to a designated target to the left or right. This drill mimics and conditions the typical agility (power and speed) required in a game situation – eg to reach a drop shot. And it can be made even more specific if the player holds a racket and 'ghosts' a shot on reaching the designated target.

Choking Under Pressure

Choking has been defined as 'performance decrements under pressure circumstances' and is thought to occur when a performer focuses in a conscious way on skills that have become automatic, with a detrimental effect on performance.

In the Australian study, 66 student basketball players completed questionnaires designed to measure self-consciousness and sport anxiety before completing 20 free throws under two different conditions: 1. Low pressure – observed only by a research assistant with no consequences attached to performance; 2. High pressure (about one hour later) – videotaped, observed by an audience and with a performance-contingent financial incentive.

The hypothesis was that performance would decline under pressure and that performers displaying high self-consciousness and/or trait anxiety would be most susceptible to choking. In fact there was an overall decline in performance from the low pressure to the high pressure condition, with a mean score (successful shots out of 20) of 13.56 under low pressure, falling to 12.53 under high pressure.

Of the 66 participants, 35 had a lower score under pressure, seven scored the same and 24 scored better. When analysing the relationship of selfconsciousness and sport anxiety ratings and free throw scores, the researchers made the following findings:

— As expected (but contrary to some previous research) high self-conscious participants were more likely to choke than their low self-conscious counterparts;

— This tendency was particularly evident for the private self-consciousness sub-scale (where attention is directed inwards, to private thoughts and feelings, as opposed to public selfconsciousness, where attention is directed to the self as the object of others' awareness);

— In terms of trait anxiety, only somatic trait anxiety (measuring physical feelings, eg jitteriness) was a significant predictor of choking.

Because a significant minority of the participants actually improved their performance under pressure, the researchers believe that a good deal could be learned by studying athletes who are 'choking-resistant'.

'Finally,' they conclude, 'intervention studies are needed to examine whether athletes can be inoculated to choking effects and to test the efficacy of choking recovery strategies. Specific techniques to ameliorate choking would most likely benefit the many athletes who experience choking and hence suffer diminished enjoyment or social anxiety.'

Pre-conditioning

'Pre-conditioning' is a relatively new 'buzz' word in the world of sports training. It is about 'training to train' rather than training to compete; and it resembles the preparatory processes followed in numerous manufacturing industries, whereby tolerances and tests are painstakingly devised for materials and structures, so that when they are finally incorporated into the product the risks of failure are virtually nonexistent.

The start of the training year would seem an ideal time to pre-condition. Indeed, many coaches would say that's what they are already doing by emphasising general training methods to build a foundation of strength for more specific work. In many ways these coaches are engaged in preconditioning, but in others they are not.

As a model, let's look at how Formula 1 racing teams prepare. They work meticulously on their cars and drivers during the off-season as well as the Grand Prix season. They don't, for example, simply fit the biggest engine they can find into their cars but rather work out just how much stress the chassis can take and what the cornering forces and breaking implications will be. A huge amount of data is generated to make this process as successful as possible.

The sports coach should adopt a similar approach for optimal pre-conditioning, determining, for example, the nature of the weaknesses in the athlete's performances over the previous season, what injuries occurred, and when, and what the athlete's body can handle.

Pre-conditioning should be seen as an ongoing process, operating continuously in the background of the main training programme to keep the athlete in prime training condition all year round. For example, bouts of eccentric calf training to 'protect' sprinters and endurance runners against Achilles strain should be used periodically throughout the training year to keep this potential injury at bay.

Ultimately, pre-conditioning underpins all aspects of training. But its effectiveness depends on a broad range of determining factors.

Understanding how muscles contract to produce sporting motion is one such factor. Most sports rely on a combination of concentric and eccentric muscular actions. A concentric contraction occurs when a muscle shortens as it contracts to move a limb – eg the biceps movement during the lifting part of a biceps curl; an eccentric action occurs when a muscle lengthens as it contracts – eg the biceps movement during the lowering phase of the curl.

Eccentric Contractions

Eccentric contractions create more short- and long-term muscular damage than the concentric variety. Many runners will be all-too-familiar with the delayed onset of muscle soreness (DOMS) that occurs in the thighs after a workout involving downhill running. This results from the thigh muscles having to stretch on ground strike to control the speed of the descent. More serious strain injuries can also result from downhill running and similar eccentric activities.

Although the key aim of pre-conditioning is to minimise injury, if an athlete does sustain an injury it is important to understand why and take remedial steps to avoid a recurrence, and this goal will form a significant part of future preconditioning programmes. In this respect, selfdiagnostic tests can be used throughout the training period to predict potential injury.

With regard to learning from previous injuries, Brockett and associates investigated hamstring injuries in elite athletes, hypothesising that those with a prior history of hamstring muscle strain were at increased risk of sustaining similar injuries in future. Using specialised equipment, the researchers compared the torque that the hamstring muscles were able to exert. (Torque is a force that produces a twisting or rotating aspect: in a muscle, torque places increased strain on muscle fibre, creating greater potential for strains.) They found that torque peaked at much shorter muscle lengths in the injured athletes. In order to condition them against further injury, they recommended a combined programme of muscle testing and eccentric exercise.

Not all coaches have access to equipment like isokinetic machinery that is required to test muscular strength, but this should not be seen as a huge impediment to successful preconditioning (and injury prevention) as there are numerous other methods available.

The following general pre-conditioning advice can be used by coaches working with athletes from many disciplines:

— Use 'home-grown' tests to determine muscular weaknesses and imbalances. For example, onerepetition weight training maximums (1RM) and/or plyometric (jumping) bests can be very useful pre-conditioners that can also act as periodic points of reference during conditioning. If, for example, there is a great discrepancy in strength between legs, the coach could instigate training designed to promote greater parity. In so doing, he or she will also increase an athlete's general power expression and reduce injury risk.

— Develop a repertoire of relevant preconditioning exercises – and know when to use them.

— Establish 'norms' for required sport specific range of movement (ROM). Injury is likely if insufficient ROM is available in key muscle and tendon groups, such as the hamstrings and Achilles tendons for sprinters. This process will be subjective to some extent, particularly for novices with no training history, but the process of working out where muscular tightness could at best impair performance and at worst cause injury are key to successful preconditioning.

— Analyse sporting technique. From a preconditioning standpoint, the emphasis should be on looking for muscular imbalances rather than focusing on ways to enhance performance. When filming a runner on a treadmill from behind, for example, the focus should be on hip alignment, the recovery phase of the running action, foot strike and back and shoulder position. From study of the film it may be possible to discern such problems as poor left leg hamstring and hip flexor muscle strength, identified by a 'lazier' lower left leg return phase during the running cycle. The coach can then design a training programme to counteract this technical deficiency in time for the start of the season.

— Self-test for potential injury on an ongoing basis. Numerous self-diagnostic trigger point (TP) tests are available to coaches and athletes, although these should not be regarded as substitutes for sports medicine/physiotherapy interventions. TPs can flag up potential 'problems' before they become acute, allowing the coach to attempt to condition them out and/or seek appropriate professional help.

— Use eccentric training. This is recognised as a conditioning method in its own right due to its ability to recruit fast twitch muscle fibre and improve the 'elastic' properties of muscles. Here are some pre-conditioning suggestions:

Controlled bouts of eccentric exercise to induce minimum muscular soreness – eg 4 x 100m of downhill running at 70% effort. There is much evidence to suggest that one bout of eccentric exercise will 'inoculate' against further eccentric muscular damage caused by the same activity for a period of up to six weeks afterwards;

Eccentric pre-conditioning drills. For example, those involved in running sports could perform drop/depth jumps where the emphasis is just on the 'landing and hold' from the drop. Another example is eccentric weight training, where you concentrate on the lowering phase of a movement, such as controlling the weight as it is lowered to the chest during a bench press.

In terms of pre-conditioning, weight training is a must, since it can reduce the incidence of injury by strengthening soft tissue (muscles, ligaments and tendons). This is a very important consideration for endurance athletes, who may be wary of weight training because of its theoretical potential to 'interfere' with endurance training. However, this should not be a problem if the 'right' exercises are selected.

Coaches tend, quite naturally, to prefer exercises that have the capacity to develop their charges' playing power. Invariably, they look at how power is generated – for a basketball jump shot, for example, or a tennis serve

– then design a progressive conditioning programme to enhance that capacity. Although this is obviously crucial in terms of performance, thought must also be given to the muscles not directly involved in performing the relevant skill.

It is vital for a coach to gain a full understanding of the muscular dynamics of all relevant sporting actions. For example, shoulder and elbow problems often occur in racket sports players, who tend to have very powerful internal shoulder rotation muscles and much weaker external rotators – the result of years of hitting. There are numerous exercises that can be used to balance shoulder rotation strength, such as the cable or pulley external shoulder rotation described below. Whatever their sport, coaches need to consider including such 'balancing' in their pre-conditioning and conditioning programmes.

The role of weight training in pre-conditioning, let's consider the use of heavy weight eccentric calf raises as a means of combating Achilles tendon injury. This and similar exercises can be used by a coach to 'shore up' an athlete's body before the main training programme and to reduce the risk of injury during training. Tendinosis is the technical term for degeneration of Achilles tendon tissue, while achilles tendinitis refers to inflammation of the soft tissue. Most Achilles pain is now believed to be a consequence of the former, particularly in athletes who are mature in training terms. Alfredson and associates discovered that heavy weight eccentric calf lowering exercises were a great treatment in research on two matched groups of 15 recreational athletes, both suffering from long-term Achilles tendinosis.

The first group performed the heavy calf raises with an emphasis on the eccentric phase, while the other received 'normal' physiotherapy treatment. At the end of the 12-week training programme, the weight training group were able to run at pre-injury levels. By contrast, the controls did not respond to physiotherapy and ultimately needed surgical treatment. The eccentric calf exercise is basically a normal calf raise, with an emphasis on the lowering phase, when the athlete lowers the weights very slowly.

As is probably becoming apparent, preconditioning is an incredibly complex phenomenon, and coaches need to have a full understanding of their sports (biomechanically, physiologically and in terms of injury risk) and match this to the abilities and limitations of their athletes. Only when completely armed with this knowledge will they be able to optimally precondition (and condition) them.

To add to this complexity, it is also more than likely that no two athletes in the same squad or team will have exactly the same specific preconditioning (and conditioning) needs. Gender differences must also be considered. There are significant biomechanical differences between men and women that could lead to injury if not taken into account. This is not prejudice but physiological/biomechanical fact. For example, female athletes are at 4-7 times greater risk of anterior cruciate ligament (ACL) injury than their male counterparts playing at similar levels in the same sports. This is because of gender differences in hip and lower limb alignment which can lead to increased knee joint torsion in women.

SOCCER FITNESS TRAINING

Some studies have also shown that Soccerers tend to cover less distance and work at lower intensities during the second half of games than during the first half. The logical interpretation of these findings is that fatigue is limiting the players and that if they were fitter they would perform more effectively in the latter stages of their matches. None the less, until now no investigation has clearly shown that improving aerobic capacity and overall fitness boosts performance on the Soccer field.

Their new study involved 19 male players from two Norwegian junior lite teams - 'Nardo' and 'Strindheim' - all of whom had been playing Soccer for at least eight years. Both teams had been among the most successful in Norway over the past five years and six of the participants were members of the Norwegian national junior team. The players had an average age of 18 and mean mass of 72kg (158lb).

Aerobic Interval Training v Extra Technical Training

Players within each team were randomly assigned to either a training group or a control group, so that each team had members in both groups. In addition to their regular Soccer training and play (four 90-minute practices and one game per week), members of the training group performed aerobic interval training twice a week for eight weeks. Each interval workout consisted of four discrete four-minute work intervals at 90-95% of maximal heart rate, with three-minute recoveries at 50-60% of max heart rate.

Technical and tactical skills, strength and sprint training were emphasised in most practice sessions, and about one hour of each practice was devoted to mock Soccer games. While the training group members carried out their four-minute intervals, control soccer players engaged in extra technical training, including heading drills, free kicks and drills related to receiving the ball and changing direction.

At the beginning and end of the eight-week study period, all players were tested for VO2max, lactate threshold, vertical jumping height, 40m sprint ability, maximal kicking velocity and the technical ability to kick a Soccer through defined targets.

After eight weeks of twice-weekly interval training, the players in the training group had improved VO2max by almost 11%, from 58.1 to 64.3 ml.kg-1.min-1; meanwhile control group players had not upgraded VO2max at all! Similarly, lactate-threshold running speed improved by 21% and running economy by 6.7% in the training group, while controls again failed to improve at all. Clearly the players in the training group were gaining tremendous physiological benefits from just two aerobic workouts per week!

Furthermore, after eight weeks of interval training the number of involvements with the ball per game increased by 24%, from 47 to 59. (Involvements were defined as situations in which a player was either in physical contact with the ball or applying direct pressure to an opponent in possession of the ball.) Interval training also boosted the athletes' overall ability to play at high intensity; after eight weeks of interval work, they were able to perform at an average of 85.6% of max heart rate during their games, compared with just 82.7% beforehand. Training group members also spent 19 minutes longer than controls in the high-intensity zone (ie above 90% of max heart rate) during an actual game.

Of course, interval training isn't a panacea, and sprint speed, squatting strength, bench-press strength, jumping height, kicking velocity and the technical shooting and passing test were unchanged by the aerobic work, as you might expect. None the less, this very simple interval training programme produced some dramatic improvements in overall play. Put simply, boosting VO2max, lactate threshold and running economy with interval routines gave the players an enhanced ability to cover longer running distances at higher intensities during games and to be involved with the ball more frequently and thus play a greater role in deciding the outcomes of competitions.

No Soccerer can argue that he/she does not have enough time for such additional training, which should be included in all overall programmes. Interestingly enough, the VO2max ultimately attained by the interval-trained players (64.3 $ml.kg^{-1}.min^{-1}$) is above the average VO2max reported for experienced international Soccerers, suggesting that a large number of Soccer players could benefit from aerobic training.

Athletes in many other disciplines which are not traditionally viewed as endurance sports might also benefit from the kind of interval training carried out by the Norwegian Soccer players. In particular, interval work should offer advantages for those involved in rugby and basketball. Recent research carried out at the Victoria University of Technology in Australia revealed that basketball places huge demands on the cardiovascular system, suggesting that aerobic capacity improvements might upgrade the quality of play(4). In this study, eight players (three guards and five forwards or centres) from the Australian National Basketball League were monitored during league competition and practice games. Each competition consisted of four 12-minute quarters, with a 15-minute break at half time and two-minute breaks between quarters. Maximal aerobic capacity (VO2max) was determined for each player.

When the ball was in play, there was a change in movement category (for example, from medium-intensity shuffling to sprinting) every two seconds, and 'very intense' activity accounted for almost 30% of court time. This translated into a heavy load on the players' cardiovascular systems, with heart rate during play averaging 89% (compared with 86% of max for the interval-trained Norwegian Soccer players and 83% for the Norwegian controls). Basketball players' heart rates were above 85% of max for at least 75% of court time.

Even more impressively, cardiac beating was in the 95-100% of max range for 15% of court time and in the 90-95% range for 35% of total time. During free-throw shooting, heart rates recovered to around 70-75% of max.Interestingly, blood-lactate levels were also quite high in the basketball players, with average lactate concentration at 6.8 millimolars (mM)/litre. Somewhat surprisingly, lactate levels as high as 13 mM/litre were recorded in some of the athletes, comparable to those seen in top-level sprinters after 400m races. These findings suggest that lactate-threshold improvement might benefit basketball players' performances.

Overall, there were about 105 'high-intensity' efforts per player per basketball game, and each such exertion (whether it involved fast running or intense side-to-side shuffling) lasted for about 14 seconds. Thus, a basketball game was a bit like carrying out an interval workout with 105 14-second reps. Recoveries between repetitions were short, since intense efforts occurred every 21 seconds.

As it turned out, the Australian basketball players had average VO2max readings of 61 $ml.kg^{-1}.min^{-1}$, compared with 64.3 in the interval-trained Soccer players and 59.5 in the control group. This suggests not only that basketball itself boosts VO2max but also that improvements in VO2max might foster better play, just as it does in Soccer.

What other interval workouts besides the Norwegians' 4x4-minute scheme might be beneficial for Soccer and basketball enthusiasts? Clearly, some of the renowned French scientist Veronique Billat's 'v VO2max' sessions would be helpful, since they are very intense in nature and lead to enhancements in VO2max, lactate threshold, and running economy.

Two of Veronique's Workouts

— *The 30-30*. To perform this workout, athletes should simply warm up effectively, then alternate 30 seconds of running at close to max intensity with 30 seconds of easy ambling. Initially, they should go for 10 reps, but as aerobic capacity improves they can simply keep going until fatigue kicks in;

— *The 3-3*. This is like 30-30, except that athletes alternate three minutes of hard running with three minutes of loping. The pace for the strenuous three-minute intervals should be determined by the best-possible speed achieved during a six-minute test. (Naturally, 're-tests' of six-minute velocity will be needed every 4-6 weeks-or-so, since running capacity should improve.) Few athletes should try to complete more than five three-minute intervals per workout.

In several key ways, Soccer and basketball count as 'endurance sports', since they place a high demand on the cardiovascular system, and since performance ability appears to hinge on physiological variables such as VO2max, lactate threshold and running economy. Thus, performing the types of interval workouts used by endurance athletes should be helpful to players of both sports.

Skills Based Fitness Training

Fitness Training for Female Games Players

Strength, power and speed are just as important for female as for male games players, yet many females are uncomfortable in the traditional strength-training environment. The answer, according to James Marshall, could be skill-based fitness training. Female games players in sports such as soccer, rugby, tennis, netball, hockey and lacrosse, who wish to perform at a high standard, need high levels of fitness. Aerobic capacity, power, speed, agility and strength are all required in varying degrees to enable players to excel at these sports. Technical and tactical skills also play a major role in games players' success; a team sport player has to work on the interactions with their team-mates as well as his or her individual skills.

With coaches having limited time to access their players, and with a host of things to work on, combining skill training with fitness training seems an ideal way to maximise contact time with the players. This is commonplace practice in male soccer and rugby league environments.

However, female games players are slightly different for two reasons; firstly, many female athletes are uncomfortable in the strength-training environment, because they regard it as more of a 'male' mode of training; secondly, the female body is obviously different from the male – specifically the biomechanics of the lower limb can make females more susceptible to lower limb injuries (females are 2-8 times more likely than males to suffer knee injuries).

In order to provide a positive environment that encourages female games players to improve their fitness and also reduce their risk of injury, integrating skills and fitness sessions could be beneficial. This article looks at creating an injury prevention-based warm-up, and then at the research on skill-based conditioning games and how to apply them. Although strength training for female games players is not addressed here, the need for an adequate strength base before starting speed or power training cannot be emphasised enough.

Warm-up in Team Training

Warm-ups in team training environments should be used to prepare the players for the activities to follow. If the sport requires jumping, then jumps should be included, sprinting requires sprint drills, contact sports require contact etc. Where possible, a ball should be involved for ball sports, and game- related drills performed so that the players can then get warm physically, technically and mentally.

This may also be the ideal time to introduce a basic routine that helps players develop better landing mechanics in order to prevent anterior cruciate ligament (ACL) injuries. The players are fresh, the progression is suitable for warm-ups and they are supervised. The ACL is at significantly higher risk of injury in females than males. When looking at non-contact injuries, the factors are either internal (joint laxity, hormonal differences, ligament size and femoral notch width) or external (landing mechanics, muscular strength, level of competition, muscle recruitment activities), with landing mechanics being responsible for many of these differences.

A recent study of female soccer players in the USA looked at introducing a commercially available warm-up package designed to train landing mechanics over an eight-week period. The authors of the study wanted to see whether the Sportsmetrics 'Warm-up for Injury Prevention and Performance (WIPP)' training programme improved the landing mechanics of the soccer players compared to a control group who did normal soccer training without the WIPP programme.

After eight weeks of training, both groups improved their vertical jump scores and their landing mechanics, indicating that soccer training in itself has a training effect. However, no difference was shown between the groups in their landing mechanics. The subjects in this study were young (average age 10 years) so it could be that any training that they did may have improved their landing mechanics. Studies isolating specific exercises that improve the function of the lower limb compared to normal training in trained female soccer players are required.

BALANCE VS. PLYOMETRIC TRAINING

Another study looked at older female volleyball players (average age 15 years) who had all been training for a minimum of four years, and compared a seven-week balance programme to a seven-week plyometric programme on lower limb mechanics. Both groups also performed a concurrent strength and speed programme on alternate days between their neuromuscular training. The researchers wanted to test the premise that both dynamic stabilisation and plyometric activity can enhance the neuromuscular activity in the lower limb, and therefore help prevent ACL injuries.

The plyometric group performed exercises that required maximal effort in sport-specific ranges of motion. Jumping and landing with a quick turn, single-leg bounding, landing and responding to a command to provoke an unplanned change of direction were all included, with the movements becoming more complex over the seven weeks. The balance group performed cushioned landings, with knee flexion and avoiding lateral movement of the knees. This progressed from stable surfaces to unstable surfaces such as the BOSU ball and Swiss ball, and also from double-leg to single-leg landings.

Both groups showed an improvement in their vertical jump, their hamstring strength and their hamstring-to-quadriceps strength ratio. They also showed an improvement in knee stability on landing. The balance group showed a significant improvement in their ability to reduce the force of impact during a single-leg jump, whereas the plyometric group didn't. This was almost certainly because the balance group had practised this landing technique.

Both of these training protocols were effective, but they were done in conjunction with a strength-training programme. Isolating a single set of exercises that will help reduce ACL injury risk is difficult. Instead, a combination of strength work, plyometric exercises and dynamic stabilisation exercises seems best.

BOSU Ball Training

The use of the BOSU ball is becoming more commonplace in commercial gym environments, but does it have any place in sports conditioning programmes? Using it may help you improve your balance on unstable surfaces, but if it doesn't help you improve your sporting performance, then why bother?

One recent study showed that using the BOSU for four weeks not only helped improve balance performance, but it also reduced time of completion in a multi-directional shuttle run compared to a control group(7). No difference was found in the vertical jump of the control and test groups, but then balance training was not theorised to have an impact on power performance. Follow-up tests two weeks after the end of the BOSU training period showed that while balance on the ball was maintained, shuttle time had increased again. The bottom line is that balance training is likely to have an impact on injury prevention and agility, but little impact on power and speed, and that the training must be continuous. Including it as part of a warm-up protocol throughout the season is recommended.

Skill-based conditioning games

If balance training has little impact on speed and power, or on anaerobic conditioning, then can skill-based conditioning games have such an impact? Good coaches can integrate skills training into small games and drills that require a game-related physical effort, making them fun and hard work.

Other coaches see skills and fitness training as two very different areas; I have witnessed sessions consisting of hours of technical drills with no physical fatigue (but a lot of mental fatigue) followed by 10 minutes of all-out fitness at the end of the session – none of which is game specific, with the players rapidly losing interest. If female games players have a negative perception of fitness training to begin with, then these types of drills will only exacerbate the problem.

An example of how skill-based training affects physical parameters is found in research on junior volleyball players in Australia. Here the authors measured the results of three skill-based sessions taking place each week over eight weeks. The targeted skills were passing, setting, serving and spiking. Physical parameters measured included 5 and 10m speed, agility, body mass, skinfolds, aerobic power and vertical jump ability.

At the end of the testing period, the players' ability to set, pass, and spike had all improved significantly. Physically, their 5 and 10m speed and agility had also improved, but no other physical changes were apparent. Surprisingly, not even vertical jump performance increased, despite hundreds of repetitions of jumps in the spike and serve training. The speed and agility may have improved due to the sheer volume of practice of these movements in the skills training sessions.

The authors of the study recommended that additional physical training take place to induce physiological changes in the players. However, what if the drills taking place had then moved into smaller games to replicate the game situations? Could the coaches structure the practice differently to allow the skill and physical abilities of the players to develop concurrently? What sorts of game practices are specific and which physical parameters do they affect?

Aerobic/anaerobic training effects of 'small games'

Soccer and hockey are good examples of sports that monitor their games with heart rate monitors (HRMs) to see the aerobic/anaerobic effects of the games sessions. A recent study looked at comparing different variables of soccer games, with player numbers and pitch size changing in each drill, and using HRMs to assess the training effect.

Drills varied from 2-a-side for 2 minutes work with 2 minutes rest period, for 4 sets over a 30x20 yard pitch to 8-a-side for 10 minutes work, 1.5 minutes rest for 3 sets over a 70x45-yard pitch. Average heart rates for the smaller-sided games were 90-95% HR max, ideal for improving VO2max in conditioned players. With more than 5 players per side, HR averages were 85-90% HR max, more suitable for improving lactate threshold capabilities in these professional players.

Depending on the level of conditioning of your players, manipulating the size of the pitch and the number of the players will help induce different training effects. Obviously, the more players involved, the greater the similarity to the real game tactically, but the same set of technical skills will be used to a large extent, even in the 2-a-side games. As an aside, the successful use of HRMs needs some education of the athlete, especially as most female recreational exercisers tend to use a self-selecting perception of exercise intensity, rather than heart rates.

Speed, power and agility and 'small games'

Aerobic and anaerobic conditioning can be affected with the use of small-sided games, but what about speed, power and agility? As was shown in the volleyball study, speed and agility can be improved as a result of pure technical training with enough repetitions.

A study on rugby league players compared two in-season training methods and their impact on 10, 20 and 40m sprint times, aerobic power, vertical jump ability and agility. The first group of players performed traditional running activities without a ball for their conditioning, while the second group of players played various games from 2-a-side to unequal defence vs. attack games.

Both groups improved their 10m speed and maximal aerobic power, but the games conditioning group also increased their 20m and 40m sprint performances, and their vertical jump ability. Perhaps more importantly for the coach, whilst both groups had the same win-loss records in their matches, the games conditioning group scored more points in attack, and had a greater points differential than the traditional running group.

Increase Your Jumping Ability

Jump to it – why and how you should improve your jumping ability. Being able to jump well is crucial for performance in a number of sports, requiring good conditioning and technique. John Shepherd examines the theories and practical strategies that can help you maximise your vertical and horizontal jumping ability and so enhance your sporting prowess

The standing long jump and sergeant jump measure the ability to jump for distance and for height respectively (from a standing two-footed position), and are often used as tests of sports ability. At first sight, this type of jump appears pretty straight forward; the athlete simply bends their knees, whilst swinging their arms back and forward, before making their leap into the pit. However, even this relatively simple jump can be improved technically in one training session, perhaps adding 10cm or more to the distance jumped.

A study by Australian researchers focused on the optimum take-off angle for standing long jumps. They discovered that jumping distance was strongly influenced by the jumper's take-off speed and take-off angle. High take-off angles resulted in poor jump distances, as the athlete was unable to generate sufficient horizontal velocity to propel their bodies forward. The researchers discovered that take-off angles of 19-27 degrees optimised jumping distance and that this was actually lower than the jumper's preferred angle of take-off (31-39 degrees).

Role of Arms in Jumping

The use of the arms and free leg (when jumping from one leg) are, like angle of take-off, equally important determinants of jump distance. In an effort to discover exactly how much contribution the arms make to standing long jump distance, researchers from the University of Texas used computer modelling to investigate what effect free and restricted arm movements had. They found that simulated jump distances were 40cm longer when arm movements were free. Arm movement allowed for a 15% increase in jump velocity of the centre of gravity.

More specifically, this was attributed to an additional 80 joules of propulsive work done by the shoulder muscles. In order to benefit from this extra energy during sports activity, you need to vigorously swing your arms back and forward as they rise and fall with your thigh movements, timing the arm swing past your legs to coincide with the leg drive into your take-off. This will maximise jump speed (provided of course you aim for a take-off angle of between 19-27 degrees). Arm action is crucial to optimum performance, whatever the jump.

The high jump is the ultimate test of vertical jumping ability. The men's world record stands at an incredible 2.45m and was set by Cuba's Javier Sotomayor in 1993. Researchers from John Moores University in the UK, have looked specifically at how the free limbs are used by elite high jumpers in generating vertical velocity.

Six elite male high jumpers were subject to tests that enabled the researchers to determine the power and speed of the jumper's joint motions at take-off. It was discovered that the arms had a greater influence on take-off performance than the free leg. This seemed to be as a result of the limited ability of the free leg to drive further 'into' the jump once the take-off foot was grounded and extending into the jump, and was in contrast with the ability of the arms to drive more forcibly 'through' into the jump.

In all it was estimated that the free limbs contributed 7.1% of whole-body momentum at take-off. The researchers concluded that in order to maximise the contribution the free limbs can make to performance, the arms should have a vigorous downward motion at touch-down (take-off) to make the most use of the high (but little changing) relative momentum of the free leg.

Foot contact

Such detail can even be extended to foot contact when

jumping. Researchers looked at the relevance of foot positioning, and in particular foot-landing positions, when athletes performed depth jumps drills. These exercises develop plyometric leg power and require the performer to step off of a suitable platform and on landing, spring immediately upward, sideways or forwards. Specifically, the researchers addressed the force generated from flat-footed versus forefoot ground contacts.

Ten healthy male university students performed two types of depth jump from a 0.4m high box placed 1m from the centre of a force plate. They performed jumps down onto either the balls of their feet (without the heels touching the ground during the subsequent vertical jump), or onto their heels (flat-footed). The researchers discovered that the first (landing) and second (subsequent jump) peaks in force generation were 3.4 times greater and 1.4 times lower respectively for flat-footed landings as opposed to forefoot landings.

For athlete and coach this type of research has some important implications. Specifically, the nature of jumping foot-strike (ground contact) should be carefully analysed for particular sports and the most appropriate jumping exercises performed that have the greatest sports match. For example, while a flat-footed landing depth jump will develop some jumping power, it may not optimally transfer into the specific performance requirements of an athlete in a specific sport. To give some examples:

— A sprinter may benefit more from forefoot, single-leg-landing depth jumps, as the sprint action is performed from a similar foot-strike position;
— A basketball or volleyball player may derive greater vertical spring (a key requirement of their games) by using flat-footed, single- and double-leg-landing depth jumps.

The free-limb actions also have to be carefully considered and training drills designed to replicate these. Thus high jumpers, when performing depth jumps, should employ a double-arm shift action (where both arms are driven back and forward and 'up' into the jump at take-off) to mimic the specifics of their event. They should also emphasise single-leg landing jumps. Doing this will maximise the transference of the conditioning drill into actual event performance.

Leg Stiffness

The long jump is ultimate test of horizontal jumping and long jump research provides equally prescriptive and detailed findings. For example, researchers from Germany looked at the athlete's centre of gravity during the take-off phase. The researchers focused on a number of contributory factors, one of which was the 'leg stiffness' of the jumpers' muscles.

Leg stiffness refers to the tensile properties of muscle. Using an analogy, suppose that a long jumper's legs were made of plasticine. Even if the athlete could make it down the runway, the take-off leg would instantly buckle under the forces required to launch the athlete off the runway.

However, now suppose our athlete's legs were made of carbon fibre; there would now be little if any yielding and the jumper would very efficiently transfer their horizontal velocity into the jump. Obviously, long jump athletes (and other jumpers) do not want plasticine legs, but would they benefit from carbon fibre-like stiffness? The German researchers concluded that while there is a minimum standard of leg stiffness required for maximum long jump performance, further increases in stiffness do not lead to longer jumps.

Leg stiffness can be enhanced by weight training and plyometric drills, power combination training and jumping itself. However, from a more technical perspective, researchers have advocated increasing the touch down velocity of the take-off leg to improve jumping distance. This is something that is also recommended, by George Dintimen, one of the world's leading speed coaches. He argues that the faster a plyometric drill is performed (the long jump take-off is a plyometric movement) the greater, everything else being equal, will be the power transference into the jump. Using another analogy, the harder a ball is thrown against a wall the further and quicker it will fly back.

Thus, the faster the foot makes contact with the ground during jumping and running movements, the quicker the reaction will be. However, despite this, athlete and coach need to realise that certain jumping movements require more ground contact time than others (see table 2, opposite). If a high jumper attempted to use the same amount of approach speed as a long jumper, then optimum vertical lift would be sacrificed, as there would not be enough ground contact time to generate vertical lift. It is important that these take-off times are replicated in training, as well as the foot-strike position, and that free limb movements are optimised (as outlined above) for maximum jumping power.

Training to Improve Jumping Ability

How can athletes utilise these findings to enhance their own training performance? As indicated, plyometric drills are the main weapon in the training armoury when it comes to enhancing jump ability. Here's how to get the most out of them:

— Plyometric exercises must replicate the movement patterns and speed of movement of the jumping activity as closely as possible.

— Athletes should be fresh and rested when performing plyometric exercises, especially if they perform in immediate anaerobic pathway activities such as long and high jump and the gymnastic vault.

— For sports involving fatigue, where jumping is required, such as football and rugby, quality jumping power should be developed, in ways similar to immediate anaerobic pathway athletes, but also in separate workouts, under conditions of fatigue. Exercises should also be performed on the surface that the player will normally encounter, ie in the case of a field sports player, soft to hard turf.

— For field sports (as for immediate anaerobic activities) the mechanics of the jumping skill must be optimised. For example, footballers must be made aware of the importance of using their free limbs to aid height and distance. However, due to the nature of these sports, perfect technique will not always be possible. To this end practices should be employed that work on balance, kinaesthetic awareness and proprioception. These will maximise jumping potential and reduce the chances of injury, as the player is able to better control the position of their body in space, their proximity to other players and their landing.

— Power combination training that combines weights and plyometrics in the same workouts should be utilised throughout the training period. Research indicates that both exercise modes affect the other in a way that enhances the power generation of fast-twitch muscle fibre.

Depth Jump

Muscular action

The depth jump is a plyometric exercise. Plyometric

exercises work on the principle that a concentric muscular contraction is much stronger if it immediately follows an eccentric contraction of the same muscle. (Eccentric muscular action occurs when a muscle lengthens under load – eg the lowering phase of a biceps curl. Concentric muscular contraction occurs when a muscle shortens under load.)

The effect of a plyometric exercise is a bit like stretching out a coiled spring to its fullest extent (the eccentric contraction), then letting it go (the concentric contraction); large amounts of energy are released in a split second as the spring recoils.

Conditioning benefits

The depth jump provides a great base of dynamic power for the majority of sports. This is because it closely matches the sport specific speeds of movement and muscular action. Most standard weight training lifts, even when performed as quickly as possible, take 0.5-0.7 seconds to complete, whereas during a depth jump your feet may only be in contact with the ground for between 0.2 and 0.3 seconds.

Sport specific – Although the basic depth jump is very sports specific in itself, it can be made even more so by adaptation and variation (more later).

Start position

Stand on top of a strong platform 0.5-0.8m high (the greater the height, the greater the strength component, the lower the height the greater the speed component).

Action

— Step slightly forward off the platform. Land toward your forefeet;

— React as quickly as possible to the ground and spring immediately back up into the air;

— Use your arms to add to your speed by drawing them back prior to stepping off the platform and swinging them vigorously upward as your feet hit the ground;

— Keep your back in neutral alignment, ie not arched or rounded;

— Focus your gaze straight ahead of you.

Training tips

— Maintain neutral posture and a balanced elevated chest position throughout the exercise. Do not attempt to absorb the landing on impact, rather react as quickly and as fast as you can, even if this sacrifices height gained;

— The faster a muscle is forced to perform an eccentric contraction, the greater the concentric force it can generate. To help your understanding: think of a rubber ball being thrown against a wall. What happens when the ball is thrown harder? It springs back even faster and further. This is the effect you are looking for when performing plyometric exercises, like the depth jump;

— Always warm up thoroughly before performing depth jumps;

— Don't perform more than two workouts a week and allow at least five days before important competitions;

— Monitor the number of jumps performed. Depth jump volume is measured in ground contacts; avoid more than 60 in a session. Start with 3 x 6 repetitions;

- To allow your power-producing fast-twitch muscle fibres to be at their most effective, take 30 seconds recovery between exercises and two minutes between sets;
- Perform depth jumps on a non-slip flat surface – a sprung gymnasium floor or an all-weather athletics track are ideal surfaces;
- You need to be in 'the right frame of mind' to get the most out of depth jumping. Going through the motions will not turn on sufficient neuromuscular input to optimise their performance.

Sport specific exercise progression

Single-leg depth jump (hop) for distance

This variation will up your leg muscles' power and is a great exercise for field and racket sports players, sprinters and jumpers (where all movements are performed with an independent leg action). Note the single-leg depth jump places greater potential strain on the legs and back, as such this exercise should only be performed by those with a high degree of prior plyometric training experience.

Assume the same starting position as for the first exercise, but this time drive forward to land about 1m in front of the platform, on the same leg. React as quickly as possible to the ground and hop forward as far as you can. Maintain an upright posture and cycle your hopping leg under your body whilst in the air. Coordinate your arms with your legs, ie in a running, 'opposite arm to leg' style. Try 3 x 5 repetitions, alternating left and right leg sets.

Complex Training

Complex training describes a power-developing workout that combines weights and plyometric exercises. About 10 years ago, these workouts were greeted with great acclaim as research indicated that they could significantly enhance fast-twitch muscle fibre power and, therefore, dynamic sports performance. However, more recent research has highlighted a number of questions about complex training as well as some new potential benefits.

The key physiological vindication for these workouts is the 'potentiation' effect – ie the enhancing effect one training mode can have on another. Initially, research focused on the potentiation of the plyometric exercises by the weights exercises (note that the exercises involved are 'paired' and work the same muscle groups). More recently, though, researchers have turned their attention to whether weightlifting power could be enhanced by the prior performance of a plyometric exercise.

Fast-twitch muscle fibre holds the key to increased dynamic sports performance, since these fibres can contract 2-3 times faster than their slowtwitch counterparts. Type IIb fast-twitch fibres are the turbochargers of the power athlete's engine (as opposed to type IIa 'transitional' fast-twitch fibres, which can be modified for either power or endurance purposes). But these turbochargers are notoriously difficult to activate fully, since there can be as many as 1,000 of these fibres to every one motorneuron in their muscle motor unit.

A motorneuron acts as a sort of ignition key to its bundle of power-producing fibres. Under normal training and competition situations, 'turning the key' requires a highly focused mental approach. Simply going through the motions will not excite type IIb fibres enough to achieve a PB weight lift or series of bounds.

In fact, it is argued that even when an athlete is 'psyched' – ie applying great mental pressure to unleash the might of their fast-twitch fibres, this may still not be enough. It is because of this that power combination workouts, with their seeming ability to fully potentiate fast-twitch fibre as if by magic, have become very appealing.

The way plyometric and weights exercises are ordered into a power combination workout can have a significant effect on training adaptation and potentiation. There are two basic approaches:

— *Complex training*. This involves performing sets of weight training exercises before sets of related plyometric exercises – eg three sets of 10 half squats, before three sets of 10 jump squats. Such combinations of sets are known as 'complexes';

— *Contrast training*. This involves alternating sets of first weights then plyometric exercises – eg one set of 10 half squats followed by one set of 10 jump squats, repeated over three sets.

Complex training effects

It is argued that the weights exercises for both complex and contrast training workouts should be in excess of 70% of 1 repetition maximum (1RM), since lighter loads are considered inadequate for activating type IIb fibres and setting off the potentiation effect.

Although a great deal of research points to the success of power combination workouts and *PP* 125 Nov 99), a number of questions have been raised – not least over the potentiation effect itself. Jones and associates, for example, looked at complex training and the effect heavy squats had on counter-movement jump (CMJ) and depth jump (DJ) height, and on muscle activity, as measured by electromyography (EMG), in the subsequent plyometric exercise.

Eight strength-trained men were involved in the research under two conditions:

Complex training, performing five squats at 85% of 1RM, followed by the first set of jumps, with the second, third and fourth sets performed three, 10, and 20 minutes after squatting;

Control condition

The team found no positive potentiation for any CMJ performance variable or EMG activity, regardless of muscle or phase of jump; nor were there any significant effects of the squats on DJ performance. However, EMG activity in the biceps femoris (hamstrings) during the propulsive phase of the DJ was found to be significantly higher after squatting (although this did not improve jump performance). The researchers concluded that complex training did not enhance plyometric muscular activity.

There are a number of potential explanations for these findings. First, it is possible that greater exposure to the complex training workout could have produced greater improvements in plyometric performance: the fact that higher EMG activity was discovered in the hamstring muscles during depth jumping indicates that more fast-twitch fibres were being recruited, which in time could have provided more propulsive power.

Order of exercises

Secondly, the order of the exercises could have affected the outcome, and the results might have been different if a contrast methodology had been used.

Research by Duthie and associates examined jump squat power in complex, contrast and 'traditional' training workouts. Eleven women with varying strength levels completed three randomly ordered testing sessions, as follows:

- *Traditional* – completing sets of jump squats before sets of half squats;
- *Complex* – sets of half squats before jump squats;
- *Contrast* – alternating sets of half squats and jump squats.

The researchers found no significant enhancement of jump squat performance with any method in the subjects with lower strength levels. However, the stronger women demonstrated superior jump squat performances with contrast training, and the researchers concluded that this method was more effective for increasing power output in athletes with relatively high prior strength levels.

Other research, such as that by Gourgoulis et al, has also pointed to the importance of prior strength levels on power combination workout outcomes. They found that pre-squatting significantly enhanced the vertical jumping ability of stronger participants by 4.01%, but of weaker ones by just 0.45%.

In practical terms, this means that coaches must be mindful of individual strength levels, and be prepared to vary the ordering of power combination workout training elements accordingly in order to achieve the most significant adaptations. They should also be prepared to vary the loading of the weights exercises (between 70 and 90% of 1RM) and the number of repetitions. Recording the results will highlight which workouts produce the best results and the physical attributes performers may need to work on to produce the best potentiation gains.

Training maturity should also be taken into account as an important potential variable in the success of power combination workouts – particularly when it comes to the order of exercises. Research by the Soviet sports scientist Yuri Verkhoshansky (the so-called 'father' of plyometric training) showed that novice track and field athletes developed less explosive strength when they performed heavy weights exercises before their plyometrics (rather than vice versa) over a 12-week training period. This may simply be because the heavy squatting tired the athletes' relatively untrained muscles to an extent that impaired subsequent explosive performance.

The length of rest periods between exercises is a further matter for debate in connection with power combination workouts. A complex training workout in its 'purest' form is designed to create an almost immediate potentiation effect. The rest between exercises and sets is normally kept to about two minutes – long enough to minimise fatigue but short enough to create and maintain potentiation, therefore optimising power output throughout the workout. (Note, though, that some power combination workouts are designed to deliberately develop power endurance and use shorter recoveries and greater numbers of exercises. These workouts, applicable to such sports as basketball and rugby, inevitably generate greater fatigue that can inhibit potentiation.)

Plyometrics and Weights Exercises

Plyometrics and weights exercises on the same day but, crucially, not during the same workout. This group performed the weights exercises first, followed by plyometrics some three hours later.

The team found that, although all training methods improved vertical jump and squat performance, the athletes combining plyometrics with weights experienced the greatest performance enhancement – a maximum squat improvement of 36kg, compared with 16.4kg for the weight training group and 28kg for the plyometric group.

This research has positive implications for those embarking on power combination training. Separating the two training elements on the same training day with a longer recovery time could avoid fatigue yet still maintain potentiation.

Most power combination training research has focused on the potentiation of plyometric exercises by weights work. However, research by Masamoto looked at the effects of plyometrics on weight training, particularly on 1RM squat performance. Twelve trained men participated in three 1RM testing sessions, separated by at least six days of rest. In the first session, they performed a series of weights sets with increasing loads until 1RM was determined; in the second and third sessions, they performed either three double-leg tuck jumps or two depth jumps 30 seconds before each of three 1RM attempts, interspersed by at least four minutes' recovery.

The researchers discovered that performing a plyometric exercises before going for a 1RM best had a positive effect. Tuck jumps upped the average squat performance to 140.5kg, and depth jumping boosted it to 144.5kg, compared with 139.6kg with no prior plyometrics. This is obviously very encouraging news for power and weight lifters and anyone else looking to increase general muscular strength via weight training.

Can power combination workouts enhance competitive as well as training performance? Research by Matthews looked at the effect of pre-squatting on 20m sprint performance. During the control condition, participants performed two 20m sprints separated by 10 minutes' rest. During the experimental condition, the second sprint was preceded by five squat repetitions with a load equal to each participant's five repetition maximum (5RM). While the researchers found no improvement between the first and second sprints in the control condition, there was a mean improvement of 0.098 seconds when the second sprint was preceded by the squats.

Squats and Sprint Cycling

Similar findings were made by Smith et al, who looked at

the effect of squats on a very intense 10- second bout of sprint cycling. In this study, involving nine men, the time between squatting and sprint performance was varied over three conditions, as follows:

— Control – a 1RM squat attempt immediately before the 10-second cycle sprint;

— 10 squats at 90% of 1RM five minutes before the sprint;

— As for 2 but with a 20-minute rest before the sprint.

The researchers noted significant increases in average power and average power relative to body weight with the second condition and concluded that this protocol could be useful in enhancing sprint performance.

The implications of this research are obviously immense, although in practice it may be difficult to schedule in five minutes of squatting before a 100m sprint final! However, you may be able to get away with performing the following potentiating exercises to be completed five minutes before competition – as long as you experiment with them in training first:

— *Sprinting/jumping/throwing* – perform three single leg-squats on each leg;

— *Sprinting/jumping/throwing* – perform five squats with a willing training partner/team-mate on your back;

— *Weightlifting* – perform five throw-and-catch medicine ball chest passes against a wall as fast as possible and/or complete three tuck or depth jumps.

Power combination training, despite some of the reservations expressed earlier, seems to offer a great deal for those in search of increased fasttwitch muscle power. However, coaches need to take careful account of prior strength levels, training maturity and the types of power combination workouts most appropriate for their athletes, in order to get the most from them.

Fitness Testing

Four simple ways to keep a check on your overall fitness. Whether you are a ball player, a cricketer, an endurance runner, a triathlete or a serious practitioner of some other sport, it is important for you to improve your fitness steadily over the course of your training year or competitive season, because fitness upgrades should improve your ability to perform well in your sport. Trouble can come, however, when you try to assess your current state of fitness. Competitions can be poor arenas for fitness assessment because of variations in environmental conditions, playing surfaces and the quality of opponents. It makes sense to carry out standardised tests of your fitness which, when repeated later, can give you a valid estimate of your progress. Such tests can be invaluable: if you find your fitness is not improving, you can make key adjustments to your training to enhance your speed and/or endurance in time for the most important competition of the year.

On the other hand, if your fitness is improving progressively you gain confidence from knowing that you are on the right track with your training. Some standard fitness tests which work well for a variety of different sports, but you should bear in mind that it is extremely important to carry them out under relatively uniform conditions. You would not want to perform the six-minute run (our first test), for example, on a cool, dry day which is perfect for running and then repeat it six weeks later when the weather has turned hot and humid. Similarly, you would not want to compare the results of a test carried out when you were feeling tired and overtrained with those of a test performed on a day when you felt great. At least one day of rest or very easy training should precede each fitness test, and you should always feel fresh and ready to perform at a high level on a fitness-testing day.

Here are four simple ways to assess your fitness:

1. The six-minute test

Warm up thoroughly, run as far as you can in six minutes, then carefully measure the exact distance you have covered in the allotted time (this test works well on a track). If you are doing the right things in your training, the distance covered in six minutes should steadily advance over the course of your season. The average speed you employ in this test will be very close to your vVO2max – your running velocity at your maximal aerobic capacity – which is known to be one of the very best predictors of endurance performance. Not an endurance athlete? vVO2max will still predict your fatigue-resistance on the football pitch pitch, cricket pitch or basketball court, so it is a worthwhile variable to monitor for a variety of athletes. Non-runners can use the test, too: cyclists can cycle as far as they can in six minutes, swimmers can go all-out for six, rowers can heave-ho on the oars for six minutes, and so on; for each sport, the six-minute test will provide a good estimate of vVO2max. Incidentally, if you find that your vVO2max is not improving over the course of your season, one of the best ways to enhance it is to complete three-minute intervals at your current vVO2max (the one you established in your most-recent six-minute test).

2. The hopping test

Most athletes who run in their sports don't realise that one of their legs is almost always stronger than the other, in the sense that it produces a longer stride than the other and is more injury-resistant. Fortunately, this can be corrected fairly easily, with pleasing results: as the weaker leg comes up to par with the stronger, you should become faster and less injury-prone. First, though, you must identify the weaker leg, and our hopping test is great for this purpose. Simply find a hill with an inclination of about 4-6% and a length from bottom to top of at least 40 metres. Starting from the bottom (after a thorough warm-up) begin hopping up the hill very quickly on one foot only. Take 100 hops – or, failing that, as many as you can manage, and mark your progress; jog down to the bottom of the hill, then when you feel sufficiently rested, repeat the exercise on the other foot (with the same number of hops as the first leg if you didn't make it to 100), again marking your progress. Anecdotally, over 90% of athletes find a consistently significant difference in the distances covered by their legs, a finding which should not be considered depressing since it actually represents good news: performances can be improved simply by shoring up the poorly-performing limb. To do so, complete the hopping test a couple of times a week, performing extra reps on the 'bad' leg. Cyclists can perform a similar test on a cycle ergometer by cycling as fast as possible for one minute, using one leg at a time; the poorer-performing leg can then be put through extra one-leg exertions.

3. The gut check

Proper strength in the 'core' of the body – or, more specifically, the abdominal and low-back areas – is incredibly important in almost every sport, because core strength maintains stability of the upper body during movement. If core strength is poor, the torso tends to move unnecessarily during motion, wasting energy; if core strength is good, an athlete can move with high efficiency. You can test your core strength as follows:

— Assume the prone 'Chinese-push-up' position, with full body weight supported only by your forearms and toes. Your body should be absolutely linear as you do this and your pelvis tucked (for proper tucking, tighten your butt muscles so that the bottom of your pelvic girdle moves forward or – in this case – towards the ground);

— Hold the basic position (weight on forearms and toes) for 60 seconds, then lift your right arm off the ground for 15 seconds, supporting your full body weight on your left arm and the toes of both feet (keeping your body linear and your pelvis tucked);

— Return your right arm to the ground and raise your left arm for 15 seconds, again keeping your body in the proper alignment;

— Return your left arm to the ground and raise your right leg for 15 seconds, then return it to the ground and repeat on the other leg;

— Finally, elevate your right arm and left leg simultaneously for 15 seconds, then your left arm and right leg simultaneously for 15 seconds more (don't try lifting both legs or both arms at the same time!);

— Return to the basic position, and hold for 30 seconds to finish your core test.

If you don't pass, work on the routine four or five times a week until you do – and then monitor yourself on a regular basis. Once you can gut-check with aplomb, you will notice something very nice: your movements will be much more coordinated and stable, and you should be able to run faster.

4. The flying 50

Speed is important in nearly every sport, and this test is all about speed. It's also a very simple check-up: all you need to do is warm up properly and then – after a running start of about 20 metres – cover 50m as fast as you possibly can (it will be helpful to have a friend or training partner time you with a stop watch). Over the course of your season, your 50m time should gradually improve. If it doesn't, you will need to add high-speed running drills to your overall programme, along with running-specific strengthening routines and plyometrics.

Longevity

Regular exercise extends life, and the effect is so powerful that even people who wait until they are middle-aged to begin exercising gain extra days on earth. Overall, starting exercise in one's middle years lowers the risk of death by 23 per cent over the next two decades or so

Excellent—or even good—athletic ability is not necessary to get the extra time. In fact, research tells us that college nerds who take up exercise in mid-life live longer than topflight collegiate athletes who later become sofa spuds. When it comes to exercise and longevity, persistence wins out over innate ability.

How much extra time can exercise buy? In the well-known Harvard Alumni Study, which examined mortality rates over a 22- to 26-year period in more than 17,000 men who had attended Harvard University, life expectancy was about two years longer for those who expended 2,000 calories per week during exercise, compared to individuals who were sedentary. Since 2,000 weekly calories can be consumed during just 15 miles of jogging, it's clear that a fairly modest investment in exercise can bring a large return.

Within limits, exercise's protective effects tend to expand as you increase your quantity of exercise. Jogging just 10 miles per week improves your chances of living longer rather dramatically, compared to completing no exercise at all. Covering 25 to 30 miles each week lowers your risk of dying even more. Beyond 30 miles, though, there's little evidence that more miles limit the grim reaper's activities any further.

Ralph Paffenbarger, M.D., one of principal investigators in the Harvard Alumni Study, summarises the benefits of exercise with a neat formula: For each hour that a person exercises, he/she gets roughly two extra hours of life! Paffenbarger's proposition is true only for reasonable amounts of exercise, though (probably for up to 30 weekly miles of running). Otherwise, immortality could be 'purchased' simply by exercising for slightly more than 12 hours each day, which would 'buy back' the lost 24-hour period.

"Run-play" Training

Run-play workouts can be altered to suit the needs of different athletes, and specific weaknesses in an athlete's fitness (in speed, stamina, or leg power, for example) can be corrected by accenting various portions of the overall run-play format. Individuals who need more speed can emphasize the speed- training units, while those who lack stamina can focus on speed endurance, and so on

Run-play workouts can be especially helpful during the general-preparation or base-building phases of training. However, periodic use of the run- play format can give you much-needed variation in your training during the pre-competitive and competitive phases of training. All run-play activities, including warm-ups, running, sprinting, bounding, and various drills, should be performed on a soft, resilient surface away from the track and roads, so the best site for run-play training is an outdoor trail, a park, or a level, grassy field.

Run-play training can be carried out by individuals or groups; with groups, run-play can be incorporated into a game of 'follow the leader' which increases camaraderie and helps build team unity (especially when used with young athletes). Coaches can easily add new activities to the run- play format to keep the programme interesting and fun. Run-play sessions are typically scheduled near the end of a training week (on Saturday, for example) and are followed by a day of rest or light training to allow for complete recovery and the restocking of energy stores

The actual number of exercises, drills, and activities in run-play training is virtually limitless, but the basic pattern of training units (for mobility, power, speed, and endurance) is organized in a way that emphasizes the specific characteristics of an athlete's particular event. For example, in the case of runners, since a sprinter is looking for greater leg power, acceleration, and maximal speed, a middle- distance competitor is primarily trying to improve basic speed and speed endurance, and a distance runner is hoping for better speed endurance and aerobic endurance, the actual composition of a speed- play workout is different for each type of athlete.

Speed Training

These questions can't be answered simply. To really understand how hills work to improve running capacity, you need first to understand that the movement of the human body during running is similar to the bouncing of a ball. Running involves a bouncy gait in which energy is absorbed passively by muscles and tendons in a leg whenever a foot hits the ground, so that the body can be momentarily slowed and lowered.

Much of that absorbed energy is then used to lift and accelerate the body during the latter part of footstrike, so that toe-off can be accomplished and an athlete can 'fly' through the air towards an eventual collision of the other foot with the ground. Such flight can be considered a 'budget special', since it is accomplished at low cost; that is to say, the energy stored when the foot strikes the ground furnishes the majority of the propulsive force necessary for the ensuing flight. Mechanically, muscles and tendons stretched during impact simply recoil like rubber bands - without additional metabolic cost - to push the body upwards and forwards.

A ball behaves in the same sort of way: when a ball hits the ground, its surface deforms (just as the human leg does by flexing at the ankle, knee and hip), absorbing energy in the process. As this deformation occurs, the ball decelerates and its centre of mass moves lower - the precise actions of the human body during the initial stage of footstrike. Of course, the ball's absorbed energy is released as its surface springs elastically back to its normal configuration, and the resulting push on the ground lifts and accelerates it. Like the running human body, the ball flies upwards and forwards toward its next impact with the ground.

Naturally, the human body also functions in ways balls never even dream about! Specifically, when the human foot is on the ground during running, some leg and trunk muscles must actively expend energy to provide the force necessary to support the body, keeping it upright in an efficient running posture; a ball's 'posture', on the other hand, is maintained without cost - through internal air pressure and the ruggedness of its 'shell'.

Interestingly, the supportive role played by muscles when the foot is on the ground is usually the result of isometric - or nearly isometric - muscle actions. These are the actions in which muscles exert force without actually shortening. If you have trouble picturing this process, think about what would happen if you placed your hands under a 600lb rock and tried to lift it from the ground; the muscles of your arms and legs would produce tremendous amounts of force, but they would not shorten since the rock would not move!

Isometric Actions in Running

It might seem odd that isometric - or nearly isometric - actions play such a key role during running, given the dynamic nature of the activity. However, think for a moment about the movement of your trunk as you run: if all is going well and you are running efficiently, your trunk - or upper body - will remain in a fairly stable position as you move; if it waggled back and forth precipitously, you would be a very inefficient runner. This relative motionlessness of the trunk is a result of isometric contractions of your abdominal and low back muscles; if those muscles' actions were concentric (ie involving actual shortening), your trunk would flap around a lot, pulled one way by the abs and the other by the sinews of the lower back.

This knowledge that forward movement is accomplished mainly by storing and then releasing the energy of impact, while stability is attained via isometric muscular contractions, can be used to help athletes who want to enhance their running economy - ie run more efficiently. Such athletes should try to minimise their cost of producing force as they run by letting the stretch and recoil of tendon and muscle 'springs' do even more of the work needed to bounce their bodies forward; at the same time, they should not waste too much energy keeping their bodies stable. Furthermore, as running speed increases, and the amount of work carried out per step rises in consequence, these runners should be able to let 'recovery energy' (the non-costly 'recoil' energy) shoulder an increasing proportion of the required work, while actual muscular work is limited.

Practical Hill Training

Athletes can use hill training throughout the year, but it is best to delay emphasising it until you have already completed a circuit-training base to build overall body strength and coordination and until you have also become very familiar with running-specific strength training which mimics the movements required for running. (Such training would include one-leg squats, lunges, bicycle leg swings, one-leg heel raises, runners' poses, etc.) This progression will help to ensure that hill work does not increase the risk of injury and that hills are run with a high degree of coordination and at decent intensities. During a hill-emphasis period, hill workouts can be completed 2-3 times a week.

The following are the hill-session favourites:

1. Warm up by jogging easily for 10-15 minutes, and then carry out repeats on a hill with an incline of about 10% (one foot of elevation for every 10 feet of horizontal movement) and a length of at least 50m (anything between 200 and 800m would be ideal). Run at an intensity that feels rougher than 5k racing on your ascents, maintaining a rapid stride rate as you climb. Recover by jogging easily back to the bottom (for very steep slopes or distances over 600m, you'll need someone to taxi you down in a car or on a bike) and surge up again as soon as you feel ready. Start with about four reps for your first session (more if the hill is really short) and gradually increase the number of reps over time. If you can't find a 10% slope, you'll simply have to use a treadmill for this workout.

2. On a more modest hill (about 2-3% incline), run aggressively for 1,000-1,600m, trying to stay as close as possible to 10k race pace, then recover by jogging back to your starting point. Start with just two reps, building up to four as your power and overall fitness increase. Make sure you maintain your usual rapid stride rate. If a hill like this is unavailable, go for a treadmill workout consisting of three-minute work

intervals at 10k pace on a 3% incline, with three-minute jog recoveries. In this case, start with four reps and build.

3. Over very hilly terrain, ramble for about an hour or so, working very hard on all ascents and recovering by going easy on the downslopes and/or flat areas in between hills.

4. To complete a very special hill workout which we call 'Shane's mill-hill tempo run', begin by jogging very easily on a treadmill for about 10 minutes. Once you are feeling loose and ready to work, set the treadmill inclination at 4%. For your first stab at this workout, simply set the treadmill speed at a level which permits you to work fairly comfortably. The workout then proceeds - without break - as follows:
   — Five minutes at 4%
   — 10 minutes at 5%
   — 10 minutes at 6.5%
   — 10 minutes at 7.5%.

This will give you 35 minutes of running 'under pressure', with the treadmill inclinations within the rugged range of 4-7.5%. Naturally, you should then cool down with 10 minutes or so of easy jogging. As mentioned, choose an apparently easy pace for your first stab at this latter workout. If you can complete the 35 minutes without excessive discomfort, up the treadmill speed by 0.5mph for your next session, which you should aim to complete about a week later. For example, if you chose 7mph for your first session and things went pretty well, step up to 7.5mph for the next effort, and so on. Out of our four recommended sessions, this last is actually our favourite. It is similar to the workouts used by top Kenyan runners when 'sharpening' themselves before their most-important competitions. As well as boosting strength and power, this session will raise your VO2max and lactate threshold quite convincingly. Athletes who use it achieve quite high heart rates - even above those achieved during interval and fartlek sessions - for extended periods of time.

The bottom line? If you want to be a more powerful athlete, hill training can be an extremely valuable training asset. Use the workouts described above a couple of times a week for five weeks-or-so, move into a programme of 'explosive' training for another five weeks, and you will emerge with a higher max running velocity and greater overall fitness. These enhanced capacities should, in turn, translate into improved performances on pitch court or track.

6

Fundamental Plays in Basketball

Throughout time, there have been a total of eight basic plays in basketball.

Play #1 (One-On-One)

Stationary Moves

After a player catches the ball and squares up to the basket in the triple-threat position, he is in ready to attack his defender. This is so called because the player makes the move from a stationary position, before shooting, passing or putting the ball on the floor. All players should practice one-on-one moves every practice session.

Strong-Side Drive

After catching the ball in the triple-threat position, your attacker should execute a jab step. The purpose is to get the defender to react. This step should be made with the right foot by right-handers and the left foot by left-handed players.

The jab step should be short and quick, only about six inches. If the defender does not react quickly enough to the jab step, the offensive player takes a longer step with the same foot, attempting to get his head and shoulders past the defender. The player then should close the gap and explode to the basket with one dribble.

While teaching stationary moves, emphasize the advantage of using the fewest dribbles possible. Keep the head up and pass-off to a teammate, should the defenders collapse on the drive.

Crossover Step

In the course of making a jab step, the defender responds by sliding in that direction, teach your players to react with a crossover step in the opposite direction with a weak-side drive.

For example, a right-handed offensive player catches the ball, jabs with his right foot, forcing his defender to react, taking away the strong-side drive. The offensive player then crosses the right foot over to the left, stepping by the defender's foot thereby, putting that defender on his right hip. Teach the importance of keeping the body and ball close to the floor as he brings his shoulders through and steps past the defender and puts the ball on the floor with his left hand.

Once again, the offensive player should always attack the defender by going in a straight line to the hoop. Teaching the fundamentals of effective dribbling of keeping the head up, ball low, and closing the gap is as important in the crossover drive as it is in the strong-side drive. When executed properly, either of these moves can lead to an open jump shot or a lay up.

Jab Step to Jump Shot

Defenders usually adjust to the jab step by taking a step backward to prevent a drive to the basket. This retreat gives the offensive player room to go straight up with a jumper if within his shooting range. Every player has his limits, but they don't often know what it is. As their coach, it becomes your duty to tell them their limitations. This is the best way the coach know to end losing streaks and start winning games.

To get his shot off, the offensive player must maintain good balance after executing the jab step. He can do this only by keeping the feet shoulder-width apart and staying low. This is why it is important to keep the jab step short (no more than 6 inches). Too long of a jab step forces the offensive player to reset which allows the defense time to recover and block the shot.

All these stationary moves should be part of every practice session. Coach McCutchan always started every practice with players spending 10 minutes between several stations scattered about the gym. On his whistle, every minute, his players quickly moved to the next station. That guy won 5 Division II National Championships and got him in the hall of fame.

Drills for PLAY #1

There are many team drills for the One-on-One Play. The coaches like to use it in conjunction with the Two-Step Drills given in the following examples. Some are strictly instructional; however, most can be put in competitive drills which can be run many different ways. "Make it – take it" is a good method. That is, if the offense makes the basket, he or the team remains on offense. If the offense fouls, it is a turnover. If the defense fouls, the ball remains with the offense. A specific number of "turnovers" can be set up for the offense with score kept. Losers can do push-ups or laps.

Use both sides of the court for drills. You can reverse the procedure and have the guards use the two-step rule.

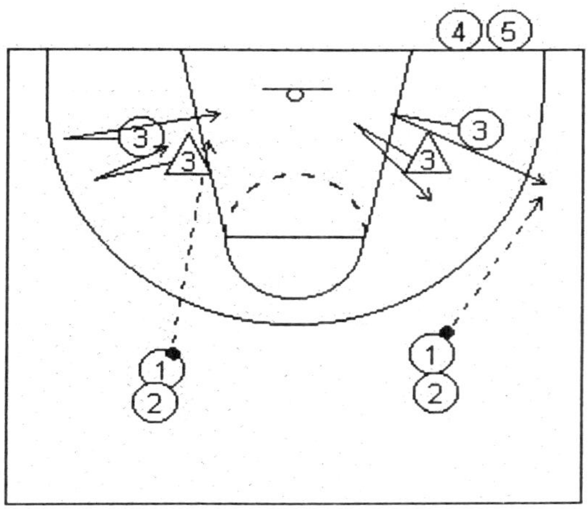

The Two-Step Moves by Forward to receive the ball

Rule: When mal ing a cut without the ball, take two steps away from the direction you are planning to go and then either cut toward the basket or com back to the ball.

Always demand your guards pass-fake to the two-step to freeze the defense. You may add a defensive guard to this drill.

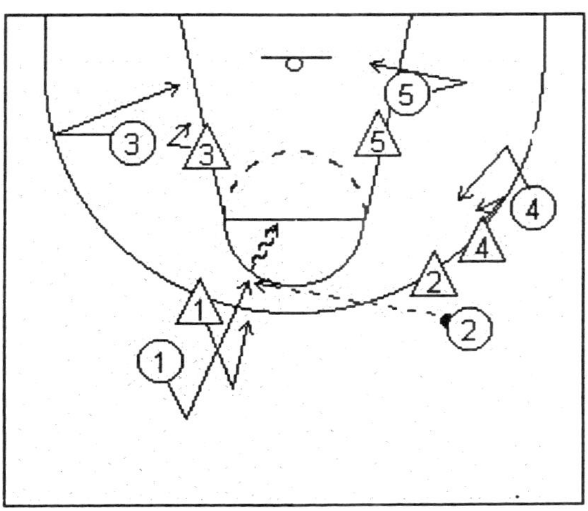

The Two-Step Moves by all five players.

In this case, the Guard is open to receive the ball for an high-percentage open shot.

Rule: When making a cut without the ball, take two steps away from the direction you are planning to go and then either cut toward the basket or com back to the ball.

Always demand your players pass-fake to the two-step to freeze the defense.

Too often, players tend to stand around. The two-step rule teaches them to move without the ball and helps them to understand what you mean when you tell them to read the defense.

Play #2 (Give and Go)

The second fundamental play, like the first, is as old as basketball itself. Again, every one of your players should be fundamentally strong in this play. The following diagrams illustrate Play #2 used in six different offensive sets.

The give-and-go, often called pass-and-cut, is a basic offensive play in which a player simply passes (gives) to a teammate and cuts (goes) to the basket, attempting to break free of his defender and expecting a return pass from his teammate. If the defender moves with the first pass, or turns his head, the ensuing cut should be quick and straight; however, a fake, feint, change of direction, or change of pace may be necessary in order to draw a reaction from the defender.

When they see the give-and-go maneuver initiated, other offensive players must decoy their defenders from the basket area and passing lane. If free to receive a pass, the cutter should raise his hand nearest the basket as a passing signal and target. The pass can be a straight pass, a bounce pass, or a lob pass as the situation warrants.

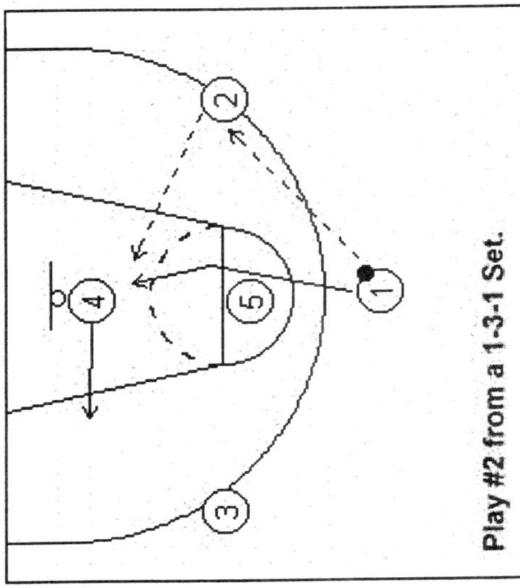

Play #2 from a 1-3-1 Set.

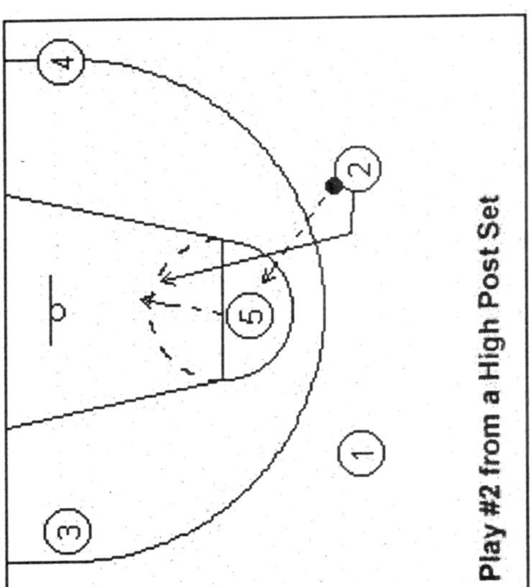

Play #2 from a High Post Set

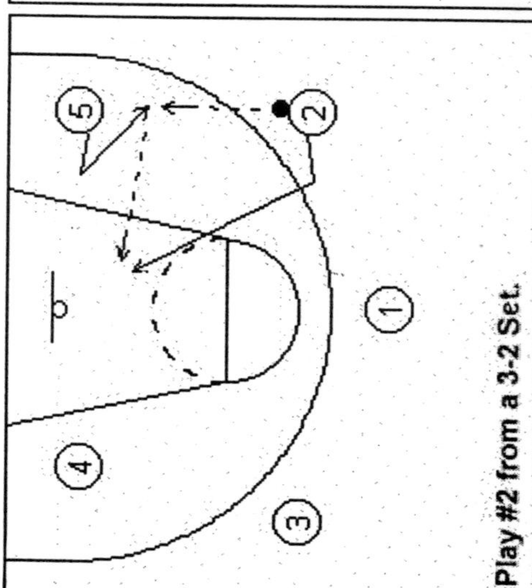

Play #2 from a 3-2 Set.

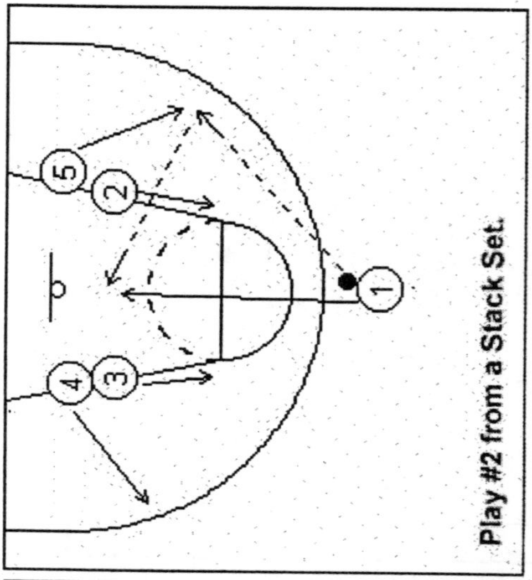

Play #2 from a Stack Set.

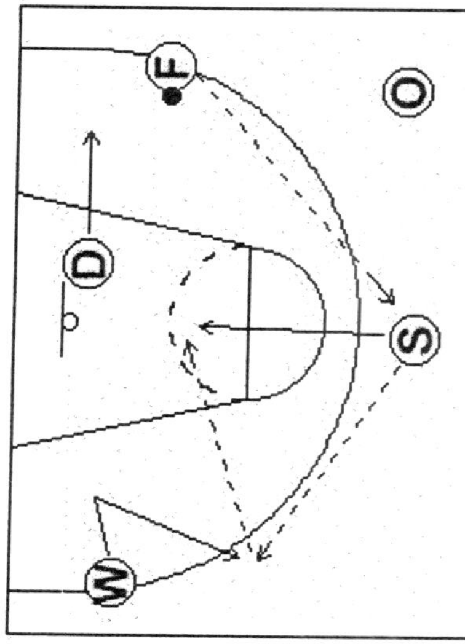

Play #2 as a transition into any offense from a Sideline Fast Break attempt.

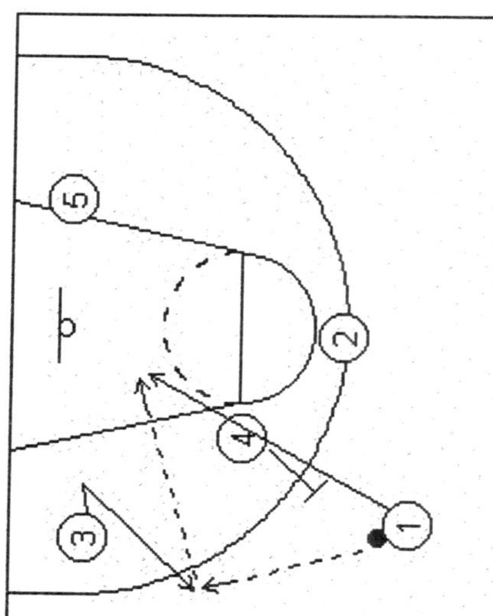

Play #2 from an Overload Set.

One thing that when scouting an opponent was to see what the guard did after passing to a wing. Even today, most coaches key their offense this way, but fail to utilize one of the easiest ways to score in basketball. The guard brings the ball down court, passes to the forward and cuts through the defense to the opposite side; however, the guard rarely looks for a return pass, because he is simply getting the offense started. What a waste! Any coach who allows his players to do this is passing a great scoring opportunity. Let's always look for a scoring opportunity and put it in the hoop. I'm sure many coaches call this their first option, but the ball seldom ends up in the cutter's hands. When the first cutter is a definite threat, defensive help on the other options is lessened.

Drills for Number 2

There are many more drills for the give and go than is shown here. Some are strictly instructional; however, most can be put in competitive drills which can be run many different ways. "Make it – take it" is a good method. That is, if the offense makes the basket, he or the team remains on offense. If the offense fouls, it is a turnover. If the defense fouls, the ball remains with the offense. A specific number of "turnovers" can be set up for the offense with score kept. Losers can do push-ups or laps.

Play #3 (Pick and Roll)

Go to any playground and watch pick-up games. You will see the best two-man play in basketball. It is a play that most every kid understands; however, this does not mean it is always done right. A good coach makes certain the every fundamental play is executed properly. The pick & roll is no different.

The Basics

If you want to give each of your players a chance to do their best thing, play #3 fits right in. The forward, or guard, can call the screen, either verbally or with hand signals. Signaling is important. Here is the law:

> If you desire a pick, call for it. If you are picking for a teammate, signal your intention, either by raising three fingers or calling number "3."

In structuring your patterns, you must understand the pick & roll works best when there is less congestion on that side of the floor. Players on the other side should follow this law:

> If #3 is being executed do not bring your defender into the area; however, keep him occupied so he cannot sag and congest the play area. Look for a shot to be taken and try to be in a good rebounding position

Guard-Forward or Guard-Center #3

The guard with the ball should always call this play. He may continue with the ball and use the screen himself, or pass to another guard, or wing, for a pick and roll on their specific side of the floor. In the next page, the diagrams show the guard with the ball in various sets in a position to call, play #3.

Fundamentals of Pick and Roll

Before you can execute any of these eight fundamental plays, you must understand all the fundamentals of the play. Many teams use the pick and roll, yet fail to get decent shots. There are others, but here are seven reasons this play fails:

— The screen is not set on the correct position on the floor.

— Improper setting of the screen.

— The screen is not held long enough.

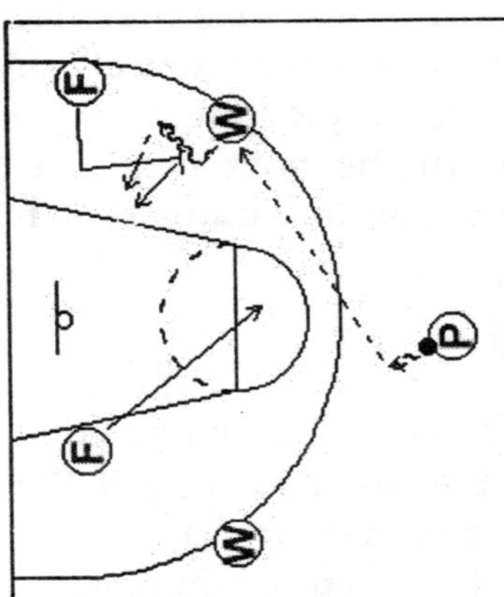

Play #3 from a three-guard set

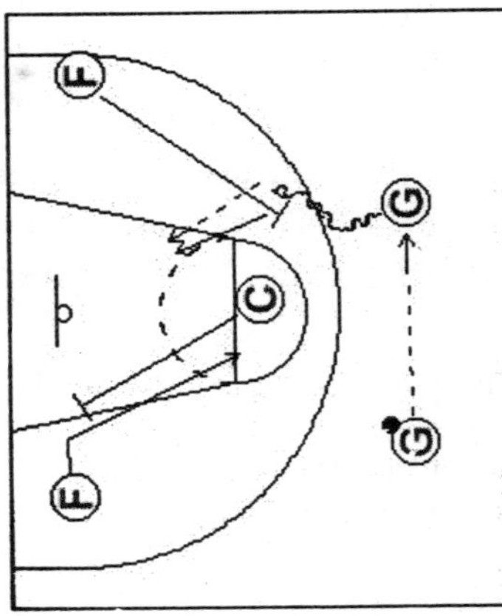

Play #3 from a two-guard set

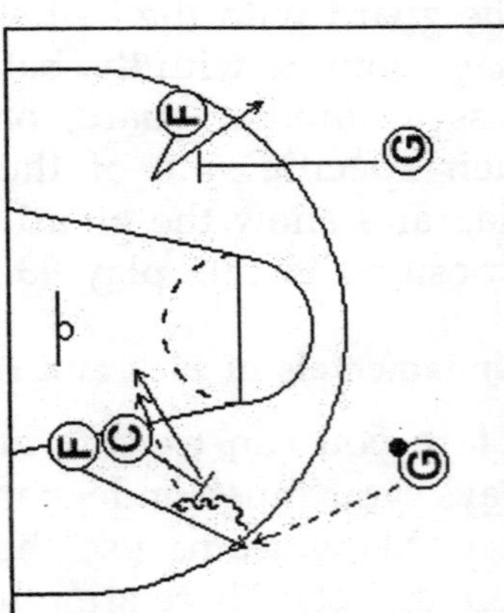

Play #3 with a low-post stack.

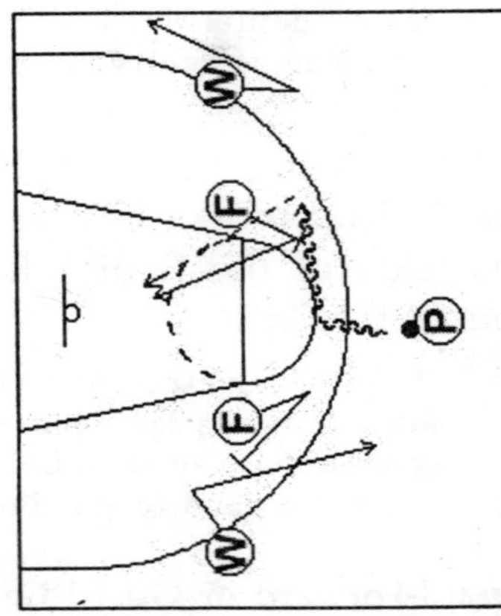

Play #3 in a one-four high set

- — Failure of man with the ball to maneuver his defender into the screen
- — The roll is made incorrectly.
- — The pass is deflected or intercepted.
- — One, or both players, fail to take advantage of shifts made by defense.

Setting a Good Screen

The front screen is the most basic and should be taught first. In setting this, the player faces the defender to be screened. The rules allow the screener to set his screen as close as possible as long as the defender can see him. Set the screen to his peripheral side.

The legs of the screen should be wide with knees flexed an arms raised in a defensive stance. This makes your body big and allows the referee to see your hands. Too many players set screens like a telephone pole with hands protecting the crotch. This is wrong. Have the hands in the air, ready to catch the ball once the roll is made.

Making a Good Roll

If the legs are wide at the screen, it is easier to make a wide roll. This helps to screen out the defender on a switch. Make the pivot on the foot nearest the basket throwing the outside elbow toward the basket with hand extended as a target for a pass. The butt should make contact with the defender being screened. This puts the defender on the roller's back should a switch occur. Contact is necessary for best results. Even if the player with the ball shoots, the roller is in excellent rebounding position because he has the man on his back.

Guard Runs the Defender into the Screen

Success or failure of the pick and roll depends largely

upon the player with the ball. There must be an inside maneuver to set up the execution. He must master these five fundamental moves with the ball:

— The cross-over step

— cross-over dribble

— behind the back dribble

— reverse dribble

— between the legs dribble

Rule: The player with the ball is responsible to run his defender into the pick once the screen has been set.

Improper Placement of the Screen

If the screen is not set in the proper place on the floor, the defense can easily adjust or does not need to adjust at all. When set in the middle of the floor, the roll is into a congested area. The defense can help and recover too easily. When a pick is set outside, or on a clear side, the defense must make more adjustments, or give up a shot. If the screen is set too far outside, the guard may have a shot beyond his range, then no switch is necessary.

Rule: If the guard is dribbling, let the guard make an inside move first, before setting the screen. Then, let the guard drive his defender into the screen.

Setting a Wide Screen

Another reason the pick and roll fails is because the screen is not wide enough. The screen, whether it be a front or back screen, should be set wide. The feet should be wider than the shoulders, yet the knees should be flexed to take the contact. If the screen is not wide enough, the defense can go over the top or slide through too easily.

If the screen is wide, the screener will take his first step wide to the basket. This also prohibits the defense from switching well enough to cover the roll. The long step produced by the wide screen keeps the defensive guard and the offensive forward's back. The short step allows the defense to front the roller with less difficulty.

Hold the Screen Long Enough

The screen must be held long enough that the defending guard is screened out of the play. Too many times the forward rolls before the guard is screened and no switch is needed to defend the play.

> *Rule*: The screen should be held until the offensive ball handler is past the screen. The guard should be out of the peripheral vision of the roller before he executes his roll.

Release too early and the play fails; however, if the screen is wide and the switch is made, it really makes no difference when the roll is made. The offense should have the advantage because a guard will now be defending a forward. Even if a shot is taken from the outside, the offense has a better advantage of rebounding a missed shot. If not, the guard can take the ball to the corner and the forward can post up down low with a small defender on his back.

> *Rule*: If the switch is made, especially a jump switch, the guard should try to take the defensive forward to the corner and the offensive forward should post his smaller opponent.

The Incorrect Roll

For some reason, many players turn rather than roll to the basket. A "turn" is a front pivot rather than a reverse pivot. A front pivot turns the offense into the defensive guard causing a moving pick. Also, the forward takes his eyes off his teammate who has the ball. The roll gets you to the basket quicker because the first step is toward the basket. The roll causes the defensive guard to be behind the forward rolling toward the basket. Players must be drilled early in the proper execution of Play #3.

The Incorrect Pass

Whenever a player passes through a defender on any offensive situation, either of two passes may be executed, a bounce pass or a high pass.

> Rule: Use only the high pass or a bounce pass in executing the pick and roll.

Defending Play #3

There are four basic ways to define the pick and roll:

— No switch

— Jump switch

— Slide through

— Help and recover

— No Switch

Whether this method is used or not, it should be practiced, especially early in the season. Aggressive players are necessary. Players should be talking constantly on defense and the guards must be quick and have the ability to change directions quickly. Defensively, the "no switch" is the best because the defense never gets involved in a mismatch.

The defensive guard must learn how to beat the screen. To go over the top: step-up, belly-up, and go over the top. Whenever the defensive forward sees his man going to set a screen, for example, he should, instead of calling "screen left," he should shout, "step-up left." This helps to remind the guard to step-up with his left foot in order to beat the screen. This generally takes a couple of short quick steps to get in front of the screen. Then, the defending guard throws his hip and stomach forward and slides over top of the screen. Using the hand nearest the screen also helps him to find the screen.

Rule: Call out screens when your man is setting a screen. Use "step-up right" when the screen is on the right and vise versa.

If your opponent's offense isn't strong, you can beat many screens this way, especially if the defense is communicating properly. Talking on defense is one of the most important factors in any good defensive team. Players must be drilled on this and penalties assessed to players not conforming, especially early in the season. Bench time, or laps, usually work.

Jump Switch

If you choose to switch, the jump switch, if executed properly, is best. If properly executed, you may draw a charge, trap the ball, or cause a turnover.

For example, say you have been going over the top, usually the defense tries to adjust. Sometimes a change to the jump switch will often catch a very good offensive player off guard and cause an error.

The jump switch is just that. The defensive forward, or guard, makes a quick sideways move in front of the dribbler. The most common mistake is that the jump fails to make the dribbler alter his direction. In fact, they have accomplished what they wanted – a mismatch or a defensive player out of position. If the switch is made properly, the offensive guard must stop, change direction, or charge.

Rule: If you jump switch, jump completely to the outside of the dribbler.

Most dribblers do not come close enough to the screen because they are driving hard to the outside. If a switch is made, they continue hard, but may have to move farther outside. Very few dribblers come back to the pick side when a screen is set for them. If the jump switch is hard and far enough, an error generally happens the first time.

This defensive action works better if the ball handler is weak; however, even good ball handlers are usually best with their strong hand.

Rule: If it is a guard to guard pick, always jump switch.

The Slide Through

Some coaches prefer to defend against the pick and roll by having the defensive forward step back and help the defensive guard through. Unless the guards shoot from the outside, this is not the best defensive option against the pick and roll.

Help and Recover

This is a combination of the no switch and jump switch defensive options. No switch is really involved. The defensive move made by the guard is "belly-up and over" while the forward uses the "helping" move. Do not teach this one until the no switch and jump switch has been taught.

The defensive forward should be outside as if ready to jump switch. This forces the offensive guard to go outside a little farther off the screen and helps the defensive guard to "belly-up and over.

Drills for Number 3

There are many more drills for the pick and roll than is shown here. Some are strictly instructional; however, most can be put in competitive drills which can be run many different ways. "Make it – take it" is a good method. That is, if the offense makes the basket, he or the team remains on offense. If the offense fouls, it is a turnover. If the defense fouls, the ball remains with the offense. A specific number of "turnovers" can be set up for the offense with score kept. Losers can do push-ups or laps.

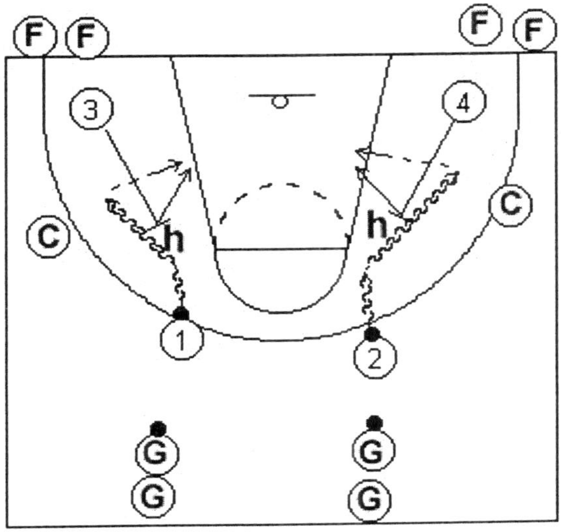

Pick & Roll Chair Drill for Forwards

- The forwards line up along the baseline
- Guards line up near center line. The two front guards have a ball in the position as shown.
- The two front forwards (3 & 4) are in their starting position.
- A coach is on both sides of the floor and chairs are placed as shown in the diagram near the free throw line.
- The coach calls for the forward to come up and set a screen.
- The forward must wait for the guard to drive before rolling.
- The coach has guards to alternate timing, checks, and corrects any faults.
- All faults must be eliminated before using any defense.

— The screen must be set close to the chair so the "turn" is prohibited.

— A good pivot is produced. In the beginning no balls are used, just the pivot on the chair.

How to coach and teach the basketball pick-opposite play (aka the backdoor and flex cut)

Play #4 (Pick Opposite)

Back about 1959, Pete Newell used the backdoor trap. Later, Ed Jucker of Cincinnati fame refined it by swinging the pattern from side to side. Cincinnati's Backdoor Trap series had one purpose: to give his big men at the forward and post position tremendous scoring power in close to the basket. We all know the easiest way to score is to get a player open under the basket and give him the ball. All eight fundamental plays have this in common; however, one of the most popular moves in the past century was this backdoor trap which later evolved into the flex offense.

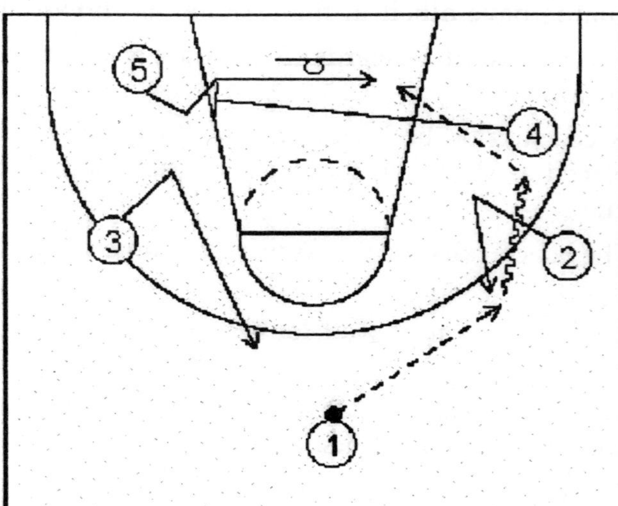

Play 4 from a 3-2 Offensive set

It gets players moving without the ball on the weak side of the court and helps players in receiving a pass while in motion. The screen often causes mismatches when the defense switches to counter the movement. This play can be run from any offensive formation. Only a few are shown here:

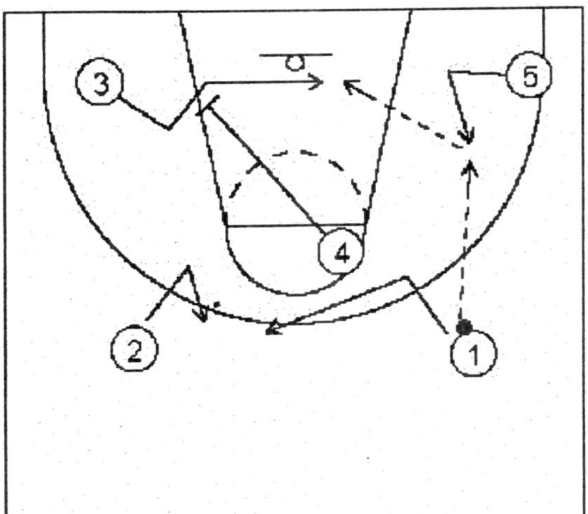

Play 4 from a High Post Offensive set

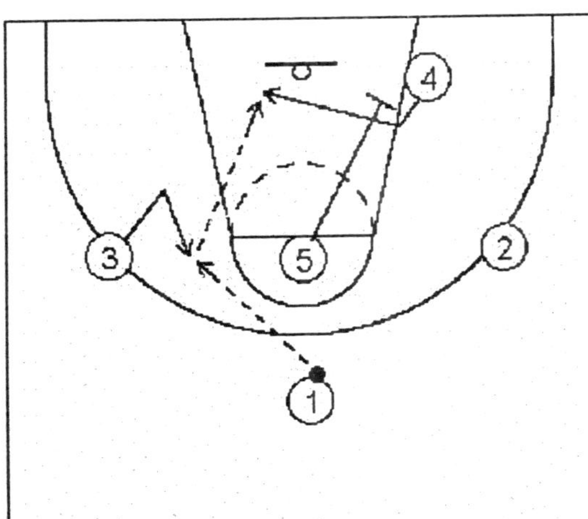

Play 4 from a 1-3-1 Offensive set

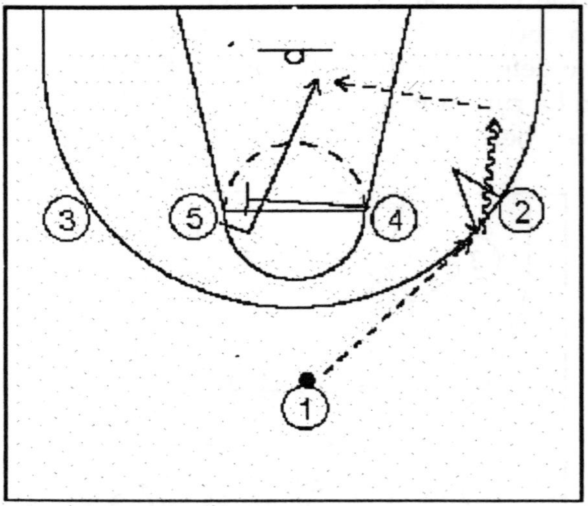

Play 4 from a High 1-4 Offensive set

Setting a Good Screen

Many of the same fundamentals for plays #2 and #3 are the same for play #4. The screen must be wide and must be set on the defensive player, no matter where the offensive teammate is on the court. Since the screener will be facing the defensive man, he can set the screen as close as needed without touching him. The screener's knees should be flexed and ready for contact.

Use a roll to widen the screen. The roll can be a reverse pivot in the direction taken by the defensive man. This gives the screener good rebounding position or leaves him open for a return pass. Whenever the screen forces a switch, you know a good screen has been set.

Play #4 Options

Players may receive the ball at the low post, medium post, or high post. Different shots must be mastered from all three positions, even though it is designed primarily to get the ball to a man at the low post.

When breaking off a #4 or flashing to the post players must come to the ball hard and come to a jump stop. This way, either foot can be the pivot foot. The screener should always open toward the ball as he, more often than not, is the most often open for a good shot

Drills for play #4

Close-out pivot chair drill

Use a chair to practice close-out pivot to open up for a pass. As the players break to chair, reverse or close-out pivot, and break back for the pass. Note: two steps should be taken.

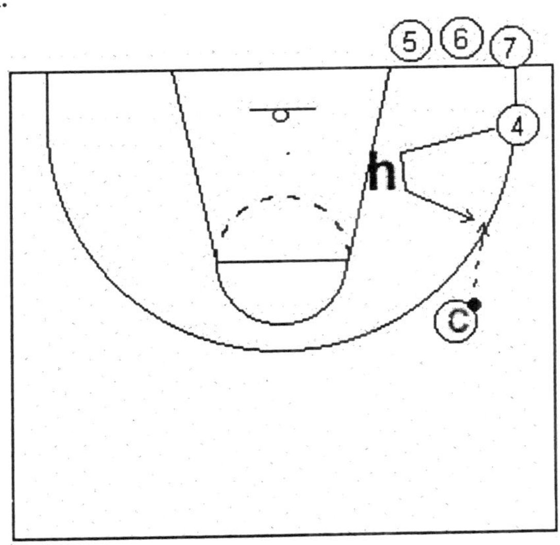

Forwards dribble & close-out pivot

Give all forwards a ball to practice the dribble-up and close-out pivot. All dribble and come to a jump-stop. On command they all step toward the coach and prepare to hand off.

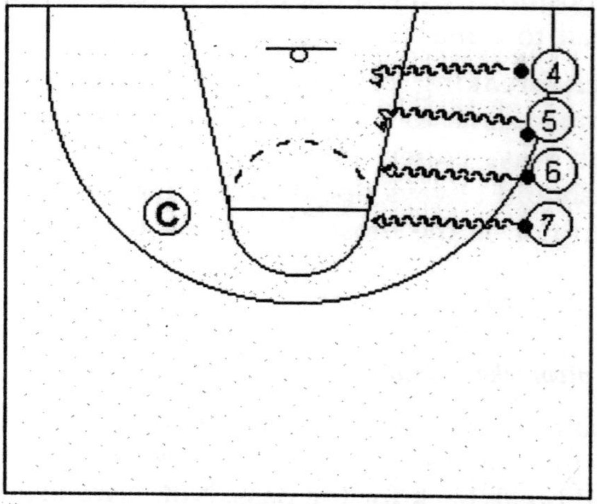

Two-man close-out pivot Drill

Forward starts with ball and dribbles to the free throw area and comes to a jump stop.

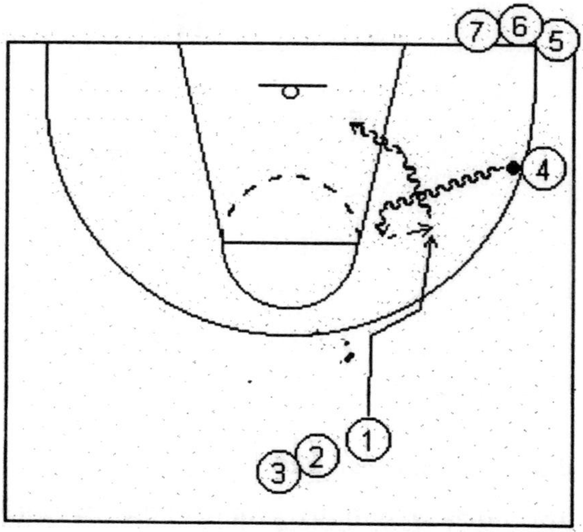

1. Guard goes outside
2. Guard goes inside
3. Guard goes either way
4. Add defense on guard
5. Add defense on forward

PLAY #5 (SCISSORS CUT)

The most common three-on-three play in basketball is splitting the post, scissoring off the post, or first cutter and second cutter. This play utilizes an inside screen and a rear screen. It involves the high post man and both guards, or a medium pivot player with a forward and guard on the ball side of the court

The high pivot man moves into a position in the outer half of the free throw circle. As he reaches the position, the ball is passed to him by either guard. The pivot man moves toward the ball, catching the ball with both feet in the air and landing on both feet simultaneously and facing mid-court, his back to the basket, with well balanced foot spread. In this manner either feet can be the pivot foot. This player should be extremely protective of the ball. it's a good idea to tuck the ball under his chin and spread the elbows wide. It's most always crowded in this area. Hesitating slightly, the passer cuts first following his pass, cutting close off the pivot man. The second guard cuts closely behind the moving first cutter in the opposite direction, timing his cut so that his defender is impeded in the crossing maneuver.

Scissor 1 - Basic Movement

This play involves two guards 1 and 2 and the center, 5. Guard 1 passes to 5, cutting to the outer half of foul circle and cuts to the right. Player 2 fakes a step toward the right, then cuts to the left. The passer is always the first cutter, going to the outside of the pivot. The other cutter cuts behind the first cutter in a scissors movement.

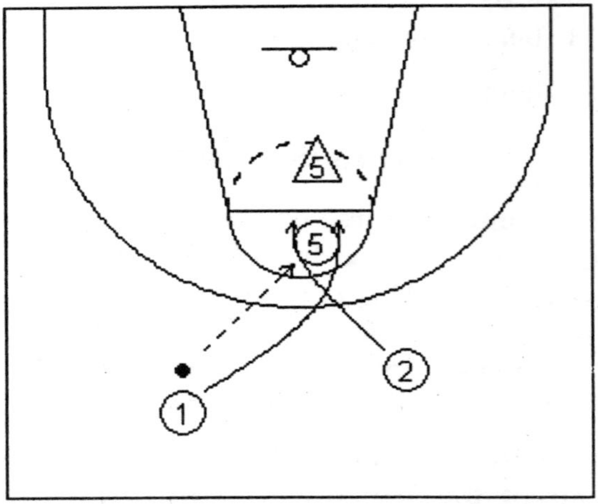

Scissor 2 - Basic Movement (used with a shot over double screen)

Player 5 receives a pass from player 2, who moves in his normal scissors movement to the outside of his pass.

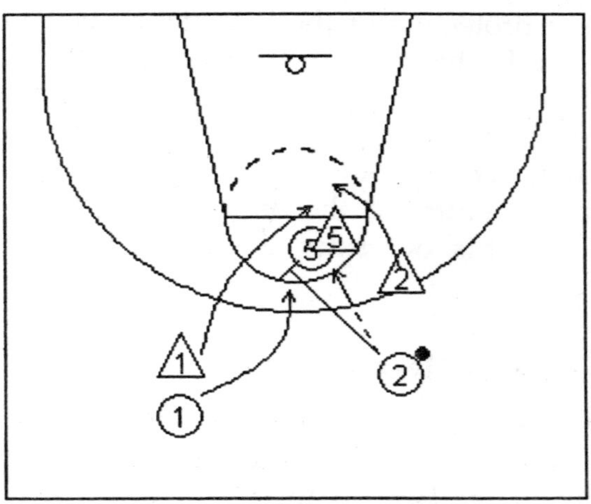

Teammate 1 fakes a cut to his left and completes the scissors. Defender 1 slides back behind offensive player 2 to negate the effectiveness of 2's cut. Teammate 1 stops, receives a pass from teammate 5 and shoots an 18 foot jump shot over the double screen set by teammates 2 and 5.

Rule: Pivot players must always catch the ball with both feet off the floor and land simultaneously on both feet comfortably spread. This way, either foot can be the pivot foot. Also, they should pass with both feet on the floor.

The pivot player must be quick to read the defensive reactions to determine whether the first cutter, or the second cutter, will be in the better scoring position. Also, he must be aware of his own defender's reaction.

After handing off to either guard, the pivot player should step toward the basket with the foot to the side of his hand-off and move quickly toward the basket. This step opens his body toward the ball side, allowing a quick return pass if his defender switches to the cutter. It also brings him into good rebounding position in case the cutter, or man in possession of the ball shoots.

It is easy to neutralize opponent's defensive tactics used to upset the scissoring action by using optional splitting the post maneuvers. Some defensive post players will overplay to the side where the play is initiated, expecting the second cutter, who will come this way to receive the pass. The post defender can step in and draw the charge. The offensive pivot player should see this defensive shift with a slight turn of the head and peripheral vision. A good fake handoff and a drop step with the foot opposite the defenders position and a one bounce dribble will usually get the post player an easy layup.

Scissor 3 - Basic Movement (Shows pivot technique)

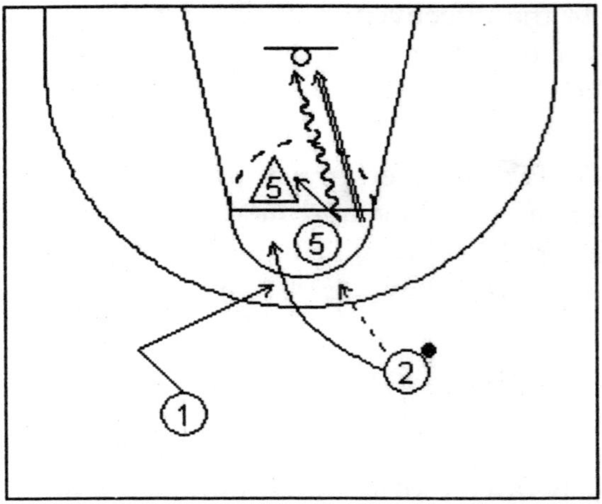

Player 2 has passed to 5 and started his cut. The pivot man, 5, observes his defender move to the right in anticipation of 2's cut. Upon seeing this defensive manuever, teammate 1 delays his cut. Player 5 pivots on his right foot and steps toward the basket with a long left stride. He may either (1} dribble in for a lay-up or (2) take a jump shot.

Many guard defenders in a scissors attack will drop back about a step in front of the post player and switch on the crossing guards. To neutralize this tactic, the second cutter can change direction immediately after starting his cut behind his teammate and go through on the same side of the first cutter. Or the first cutter can stop in front of a defender on the same side as he passed instead of crossing, and the second cutter can stop behind the double screen formed by the post player and other guard for a medium range jump shot.

Scissor 4 - Movement (When defenders anticipate and switch prematurely)

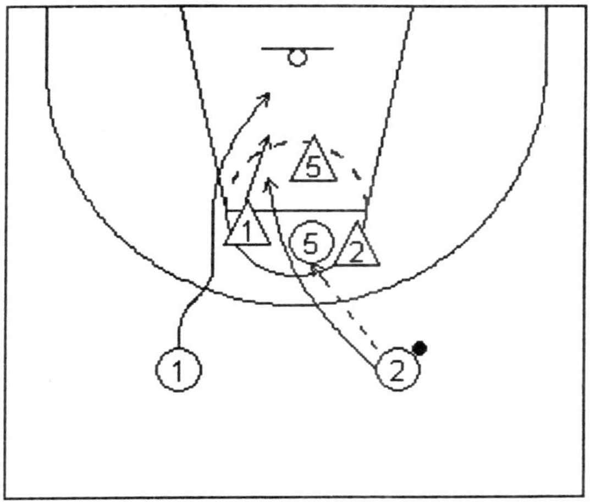

Player 2 passes to 5 and cuts outside his pass. Teammate 1 starts his cut behind 2 and sees that 2's defender has stopped following 2 and that his own defender will pick up teammate 2. Player 1 immediately changes direction and cuts on the same side as the pivot as did his teammate.

The scissors movement can also be used by a medium pivot, the forward and a guard on the ball side of the floor. Usually, the forward makes the pass into the pivot and cuts first with the guard timing his cut behind the forward. This action opens up many good shooting opportunities. If the forward receives the handoff pass as the first cutter he is in excellent range for a short fake and jump shot. The guard cutting behind the forward, is also in good short jump shooting range if the defense drops back, and the guard could also continue in to the basket for a lay-up.

The pivot should step to the basket opening up toward the ball. He will have inside position if his defender switches. Many shooting opportunities for step-away one-handers, hook shots, or turn-around jumpers may be available to the pivot player.

Rule: It is important that the two players not involved in these maneuvers, lure their defenders away from the point of attack and retreat so that good defensive balance is maintained should the ball be intercepted or possession is lost in the rebounding action.

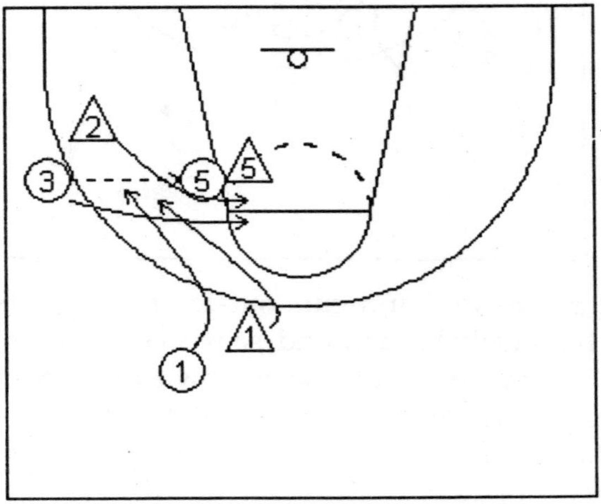

Scissor 5 - Movement (Using the center by a guard and forward)

First, forward 3 passes into the pivot, 5, and cuts to the outside of his pass. Next, teammate 1, the guard fakes and cuts off 3's movement.

PLAY #6 (CUT THROUGH)

Cutting a player through to the opposite side of the court is another play that has been around for ages. The cut through is almost a necessary part of every offense designed to attack zone defense. However, the good old cut through can be used against man-to-man just as effective. I've seen teams us it to get into a stacked offense after a reversal of the ball.

Remember, the usual two-step rule applies to all players when receiving a pass from a teammate, Also, stress that the cutter and screener should always pass to shoulder to shoulder on the screen and the screener should always open-up toward the ball. Spend some time, teaching your players how to read a screen.

Keep in mind that the cut through, as any other play, has many options. All these other options need to be practiced in order to attain complete success with this play. Your advantages often multiply when the defense either denies a pass or over-shift in their effort to stop the play.

The Basic Set

In the next page the diagrams show examples of the cut through from the Wing, Guard, Forward, and Point positions:

Options for Play 6

As mentioned earlier, there are many options. The options that follow must be practiced in order to take advantage of situations that develop during the running of this play. Your players must recognize and counter whenever the opponent attempts to deny a pass or over-shift in their attempt to defend the play.

Teach Players to read the Defense

Do what defender allows

This is a good drill for teaching the offensive fundamentals of reading your defender. The way the defender moves dictates three counter moves:

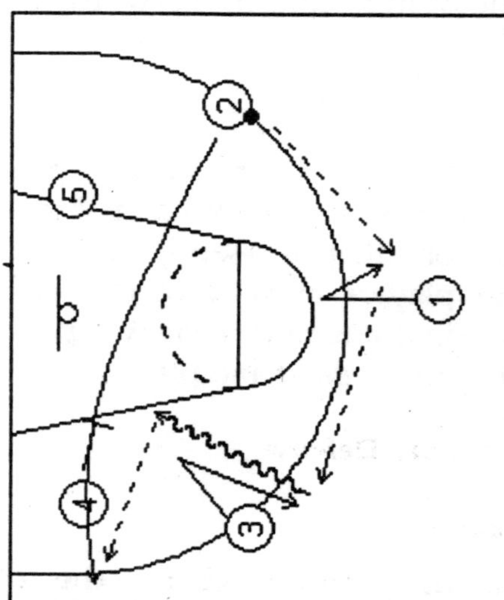

Play 6 from a 1-2-2 set

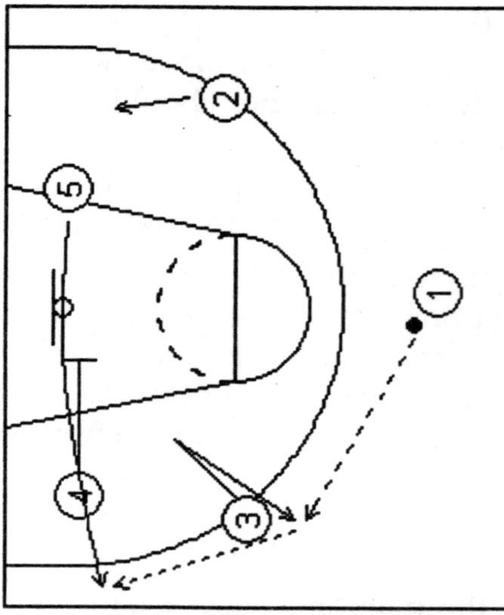

Play 6 from a 1-2-2 set - forward

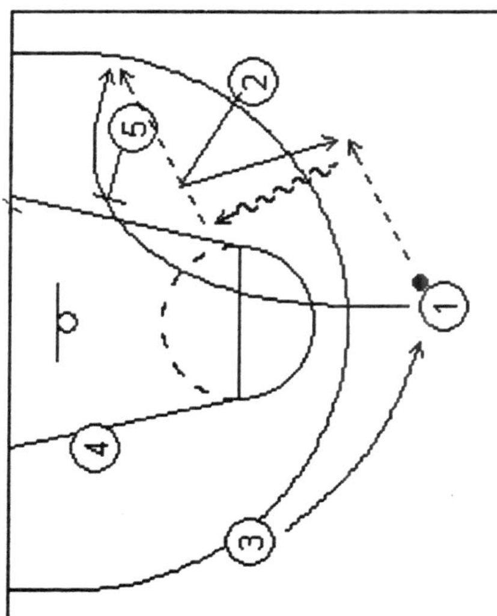

Play 6 from a 1-2-2 set - Point

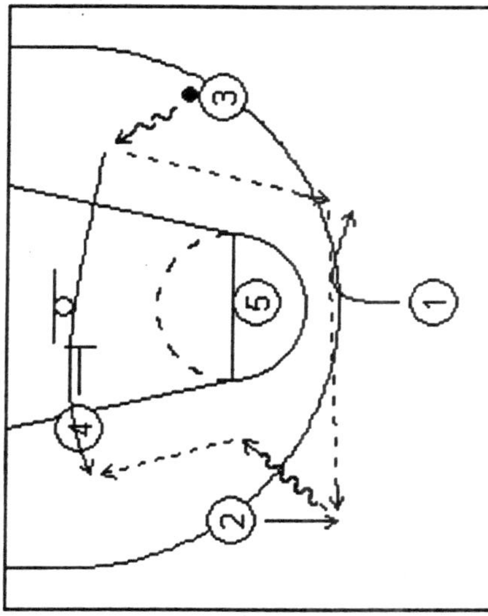

Play 6 from a 1-3-1 set - Wing

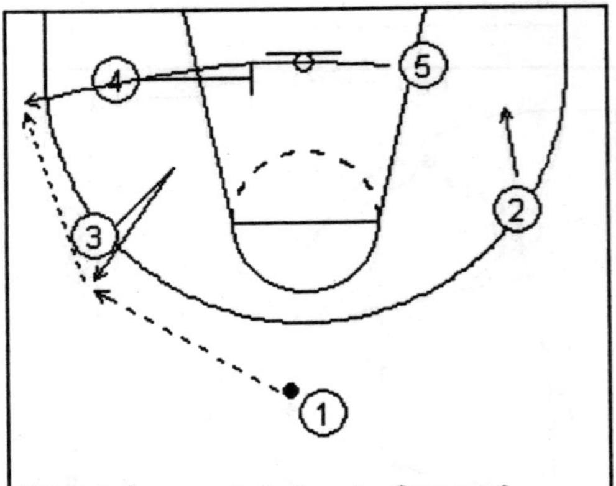

Play 6 from a 1-2-2 set - forward

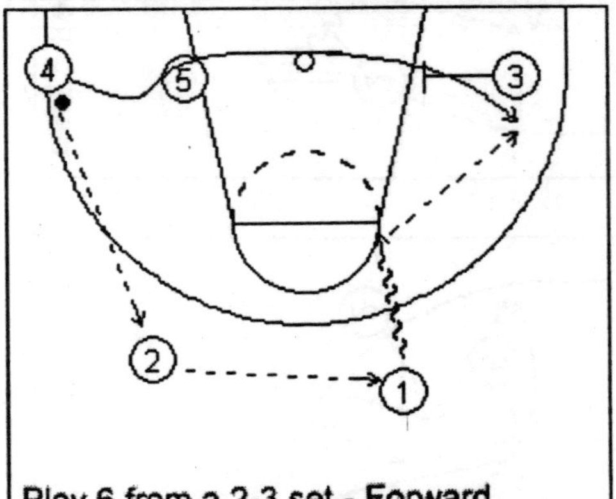

Play 6 from a 2-3 set - Forward

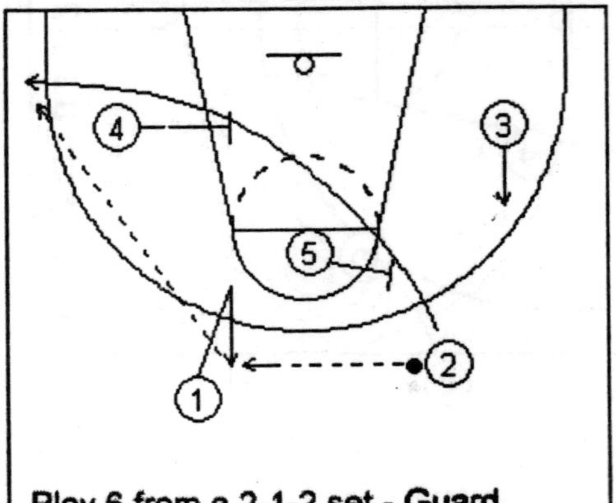

Play 6 from a 2-1-2 set - Guard

— The Curl
— The Flare
— The Pocket

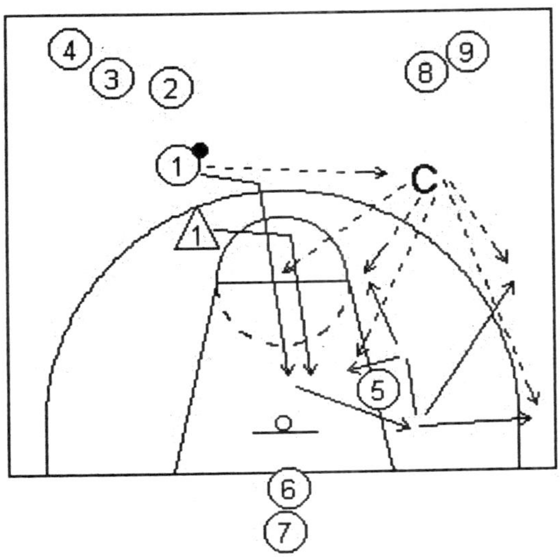

The drawing illustrates some of the passing options available during the exercise of this drill. In the beginning, the coach serves as the feeder and as he teaches ... always catches the ball in a triple threat position.

Once players become adept to this drill, the feeding position can be filled by #8 or players rotate clockwise, whichever if preferable. The purpose of this drill is to teach players the proper way to use screens by teammates. Use these options with any play using screens.

The Give and Go

Drill starts with #1 being closely guarded, making a crisp two-handed chest pass to the coach, and cutting to the basket. If open, he/she receives a return pass, jump stops, and lays it in the basket. *(The coach must insist that all these are executed properly by every player.)*

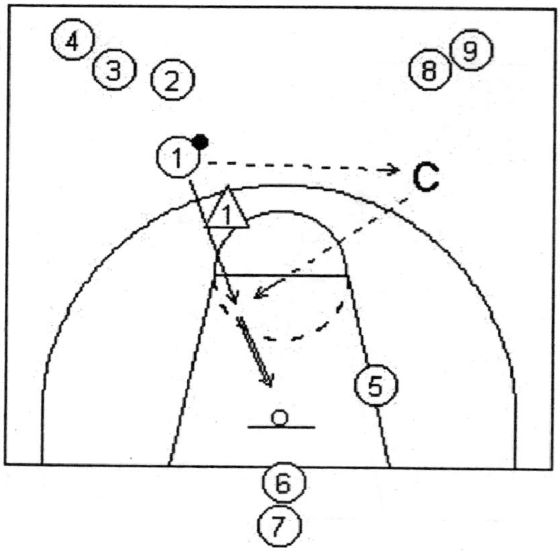

The coach is the feeder in the beginning; however, players are introduced once the players understand the proper execution of this drill. *(This also becomes a good drill for teaching young players to properly execute the jump stop and prevent charging calls.)*

All players must take their time using screens. Keep in mind the player receiving the pass can hold the ball 5 seconds, dribble it for 5 seconds, then hold it another 5 seconds. This is a long time! *(Use this to illustrate the importance of taking your time. At least, in most cases, it is desirable for every ball handler to hold the ball long enough for a scoring opportunity to present itself.)*

Flare Cuts

All players must take their time using screens. Keep in mind the player receiving the pass can hold the ball 5 seconds, dribble it for 5 seconds, then hold it another 5 seconds. This is a long time! Take time for a scoring opportunity to present itself.

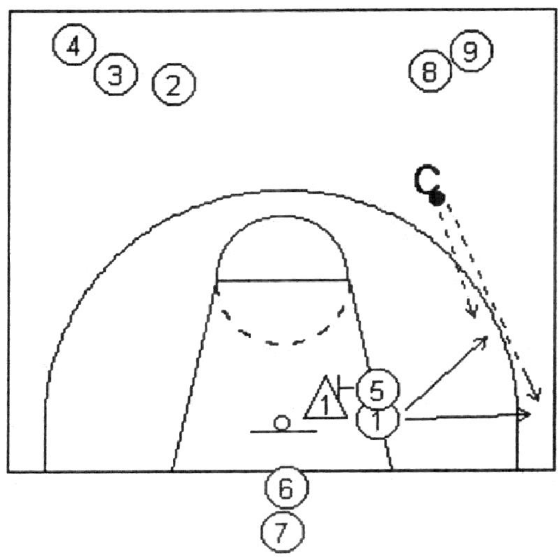

As the player comes off his/her screen, he/her, in this case calls, "Flare!" The player catches and shoots. For variety, the coach can have player, shot-fake then shoot, or shot-fake and drive.

Curl Cut

If the defender tries to follow around the screen, the curl cut give the cutter an open path to an easy basket. As the cutter recognizes this, he/she shouts, "Curl!", as he/she executes the cut.

You need to use a number of perimeter and post drills in teaching your players to read the defense and learn spacing and floor balance that is much required in today's motion defense. Break your offense down into two and three-man plays.

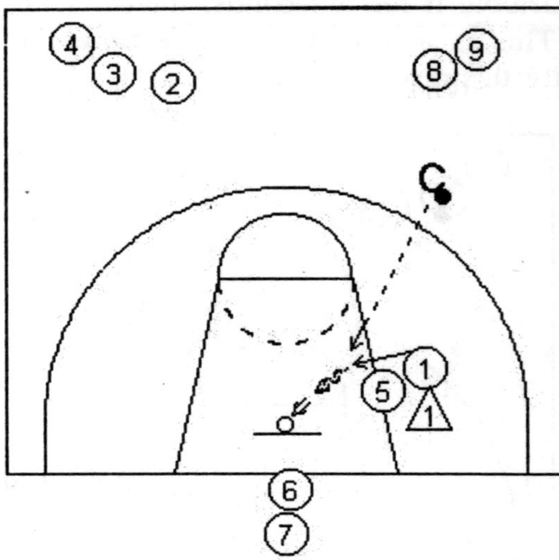

In motion offenses, some coaches only involve perimeter players in three-man plays and post players in two-man plays.

Pocket Cut

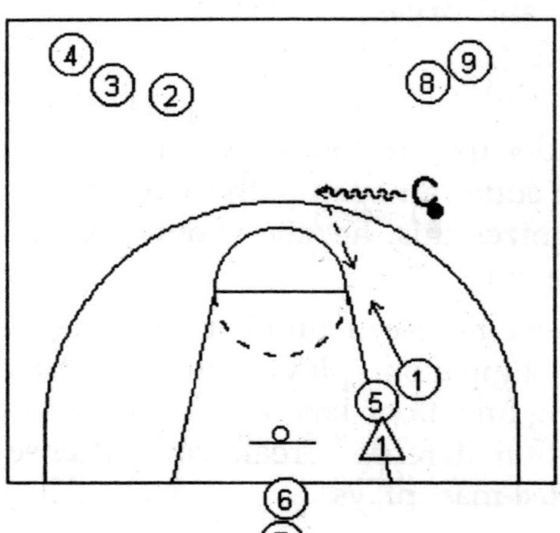

In this diagram, the coach has dribbled in order to allow more time for a scoring opportunity for #1 to develop. Player #5 helps obstruct the defender's route to the elbow. Teammate #1 catches the ball at the elbow and shoots.

— Run drill on both sides of the floor

— How to coach and teach the basketball shallow-cut play

PLAY #7 (SHALLOW CUT)

The shallow cut is used considerably in motion offenses; however, you can use it in many patterned offenses just as well. For instance, getting the ball to the wing is the key to starting most offenses.

Shallow Cut

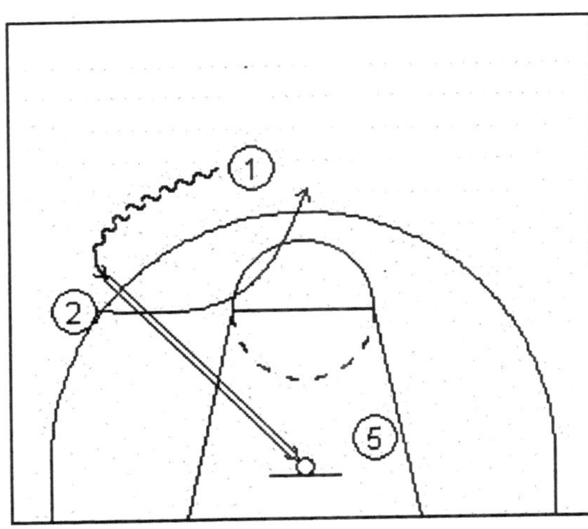

Player 1 dribbles over and shallows 2 off the right wing. Player 2 relocates to the top of the key using the 3-point arc as reference point to help with balance and spacing. Player 1 shoots the jumper from the wing. 5 rebounds and puts back all missed shots.

Shallow Cut - Return Pass

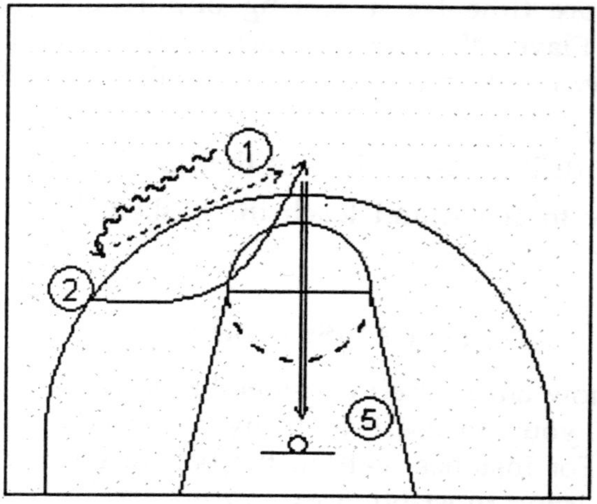

Player 1 dribbles over to the right wing and 2 relocates at the top and steps up for the return pass from 1. He shoots the jumper. (You also need to mix this drill a bit and have player 2 use a shot fake and move with a one-bounce dribble, then shoot or he could drive and dish off to 5 who lays it in.)

Shallow Cut - Drive and Dish

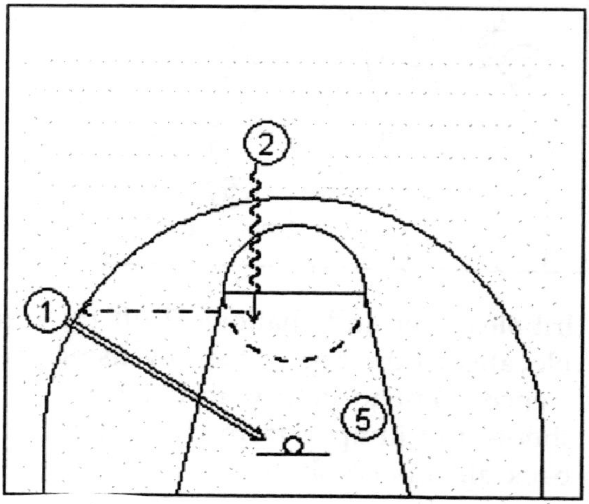

Player 1 dribbles over to the right wing and 2 relocates to the top for a pass from 1. Player 2 comes to meet the pass, catches the ball, squares up, fakes a shot, drives to the elbow, drawing 1's defender and dishes to 1. Player 1 steps up for the shot.

Shallow Cut - From the Wing

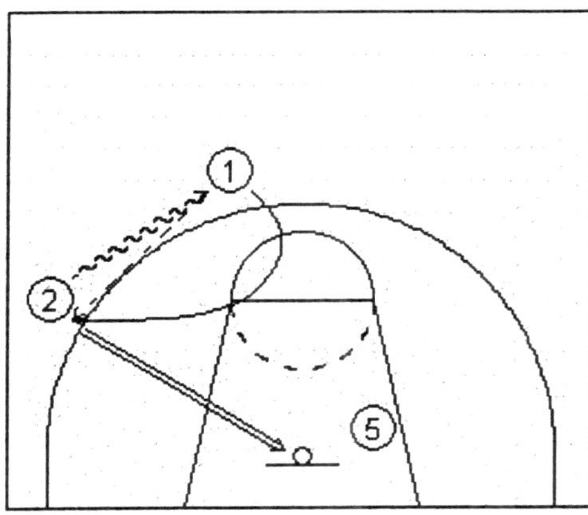

Player 2 dribbles to the top and 1 relocates to the wing. Player 1 receives a return pass from 2 and takes the shot.

Shallow Cut - Fake Relocate & V-Cut

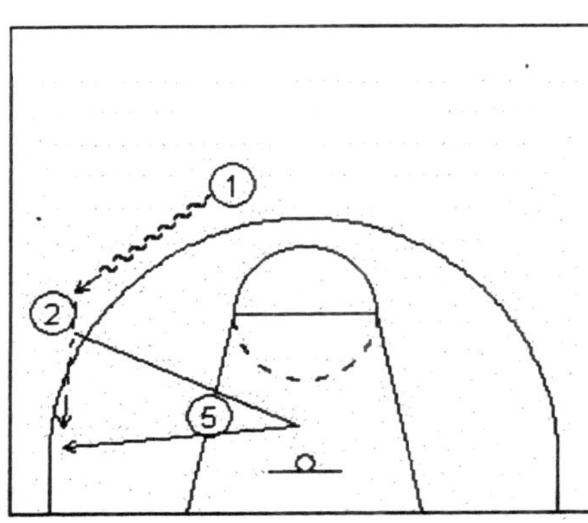

Player 1 dribbles at 2, as if to shallow him out to the top. Player 2 begins to relocate, but instead v-cuts, using 5's screen and fades to the corner for a pass from 1 and a shot.

For example, players 2 and 5 should pass shoulder to shoulder. If the defender follows 2, then 2 should curl. Don't try to hurry, but play it smart, like playing tag around a tree.)

Shallow Cut - Circle and Skip Pass

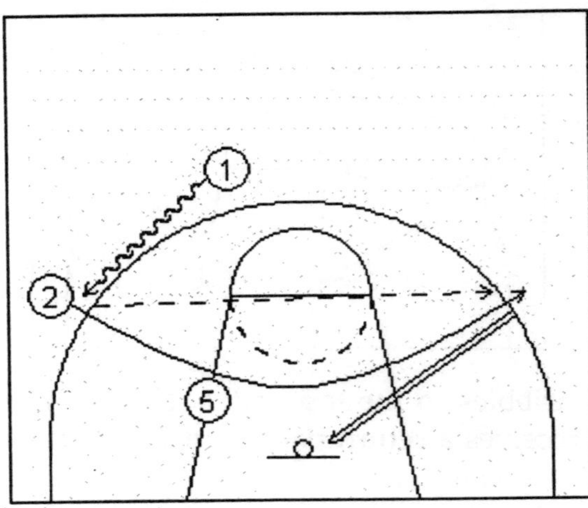

Player 1 dribbles at 2 who instead of shallowing to the top, continues through the lane to the opposite wing. Player 1 skip passes over the defense to 2 who squares-up for the shot.

Cut Through - V-Cut for Layup or Jumper

Player 1 v-cuts away. He can read the defense and either cut to the basket for a layup or replace himself for a shot.

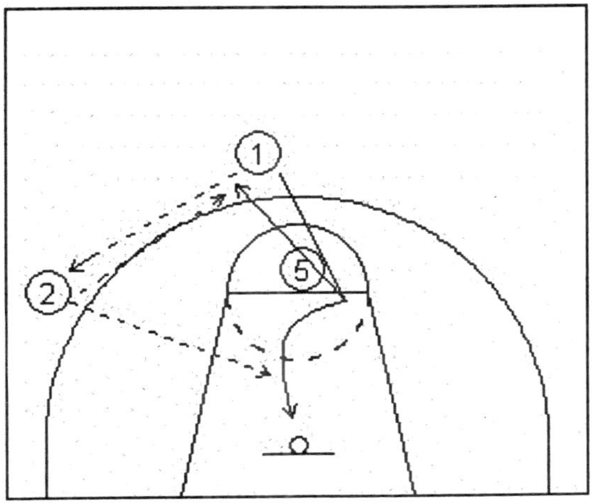

PLAY #8 (GUARD AROUND)

Here is another play as old as the hills. Kentucky's pride, coach Adolph Rupp used it very effectively to compile his impressive record. With the arrival of the three-point play and if coach Rupp were alive and coaching, today, he would be running the old guard-around until the "cows come home."

The guard-around play, as Coach Rupp called it is still effective, today. Coach Rupp considered the following play options to be the best fundamental ball handling drills the he ever found. The old coach set his up in the same way as is illustrated in the first five diagrams that follow on the next few pages; however, you can fit it into most any offensive set known, today. The next four diagrams following Coach Rupp's drills are a couple of typical examples of how to use the guard-around with other sets.

Offensive Guard-around Plays

As can be seen from the next five diagrams, the setup is the same in every case with five options for the guard to exercise as he sees fit. Here are a few pointers to help coaches in developing this play:

— A guard must be an excellent ball handler.

— A guard must be quick.

— All guard-around plays must be run with maximum speed in ball handling and footwork.

— A guard must always be in a triple threat position when he catches the ball.

— The guard-around play works best when the guard is near a sideline.

— The guard should cut right off the tail of the forward in a straight line at the basket, not a circular route.

The following four diagrams with explanations will show how each option is executed. These series of guard plays will work with any type defense. Regardless of how a defender maneuvers, one of these plays will fit the situation.

It was from these options that Coach Rupp developed the famous Kentucky offense. It can easily be seen that Rupp depended a great deal on his guards being scoring threats as his forwards and centers. He felt with clever ball handling, two of his smaller players could set up a well defined five player offense that fit well in his Kentucky patterned offense. When they exhausted the possibilities of two-man plays, they included the third (pivot) man into the play and many other high-percentage scoring opportunities than shown here were used by Coach Rupp. These plays can be used on either side of the floor. They are excellent ball handling drills in teaching basic fundamentals of basketball. Coach Rupp sent his players through these drills most every practice Not only did the develop ball-handling ability, change of direction, goal shooting, rebounding, and other necessary fundamentals, but, at the same time, built his complete offense.

Guard Around - First Option:

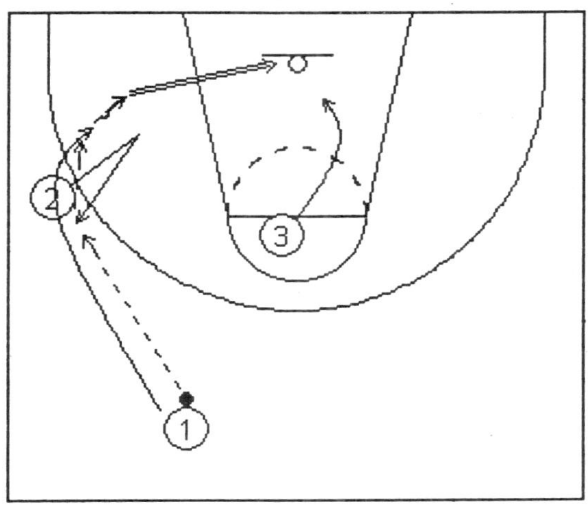

Guard #1 passes to Forward #2 who steps out to meet the pass in every case and turns his body as if to pass to #3 at the high post; however, he flips the ball to #1 who is cutting outside. If #1 is a good 3-point shooter, he can usually get an open shot here, take one dribble and shoot, or dribble all the way in for a lay-up, whichever best presents itself.

Guard Around - Second Option

Guard #1 passes to #2 who turns toward the free-throw lane, takes one dribble, jumps in the air, and hooks a pass to #1 who cut by him.

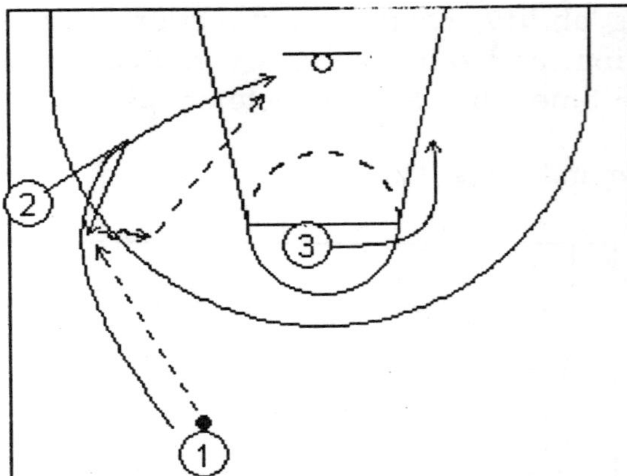

Play #8 Guard-Around (Option 2)

Guard Around - Third Option:

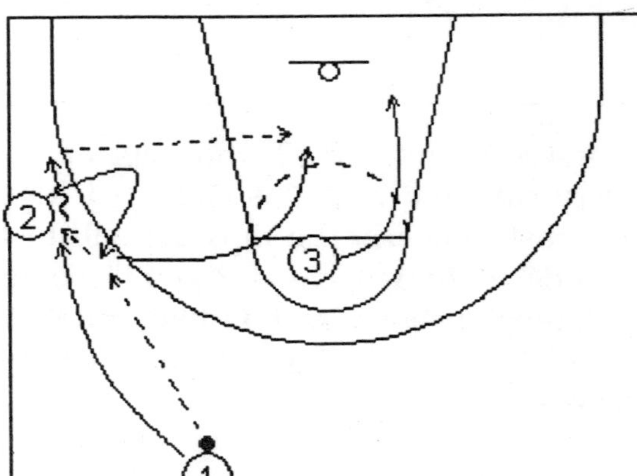

Play #8 Guard-Around (Option 3)

Guard #1 passes to Forward #2 who flips the ball back to #1 as in Option 1, but this time #2 rolls to the basket expecting a return pass from Guard #1.

Guard Around - Fourth Option:

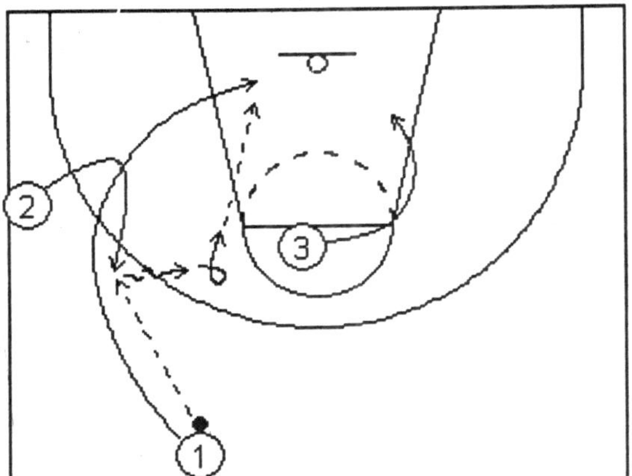

Play #8 Guard-Around (Option 4)

Guard #1 passes to #2 who takes one dribble, pivots, and passes back to #1 who cut around him to the basket.

In the guard-around play, the player with the ball may hand off to a teammate crossing behind him and set a lateral screen, or a player can set a lateral screen for the dribbler as the dribbler crosses behind him. In either case, the screener can stop close to the defender, because the defender can see the screen coming.

When the man with the ball hands off or passes to the dribbler and sets a lateral screen, he should stop and use an offensive roll immediately after the teammate move by him. Stepping imperceptibly toward the second opponent, in the direction of the end line, with the foot nearest the end line he pivots on that foot, away from the opponent he has screened. With this move he avoids causing any contact and obtains and holds an inside advantage on the opponent if there is a defensive switch, His pivot foot steps directly toward the basket. He should continue toward the basket quickly with his inside hand up as a target for a pass if the defensive switch occurs, the best passing lane opens immediately after the defensive exchange is made.

In the guard-around play, the player with the ball may hand off to a teammate crossing behind him and set a lateral screen, or a player can set a lateral screen for the dribbler as the dribbler crosses behind him. In either case, the screener can stop close to the defender, because the defender can see the screen coming.

When the man with the ball hands off or passes to the dribbler and sets a lateral screen, he should stop and use an offensive roll immediately after the teammate move by him. Stepping imperceptibly toward the second opponent, in the direction of the end line, with the foot nearest the end line he pivots on that foot, away from the opponent he has screened. With this move he avoids causing any contact and obtains and holds an inside advantage on the opponent if there is a defensive switch, His pivot foot steps directly toward the basket. He should continue toward the basket quickly with his inside hand up as a target for a pass if the defensive switch occurs, the best passing lane opens immediately after the defensive exchange is made.

Guard Around - Fifth Option:

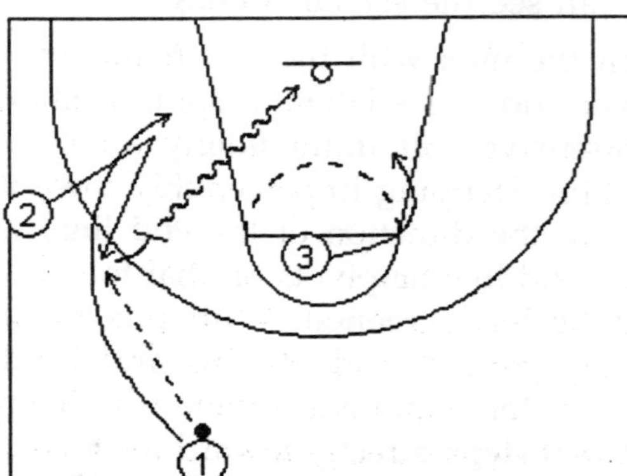

Play #8 Guard-Around (Option 5)

Guard #1 passes to #2 and cuts outside. #2 catches the ball with a jump stop, pivots, fakes a pass to #1, and dribbles inside to shoot.

Guard Around - Lateral Screen Guard for Guard:

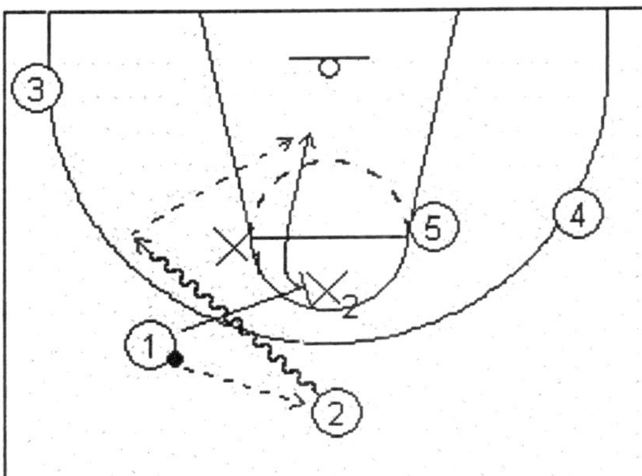

Play #8 Guard-around Option 6

1 passes to 2, then set a lateral screen on X2, 2's defender. 2 on moving to meet the pass, dribbles hard to his left off the screen. As 2 begins his drive, 1 slides his left foot imperceptibly toward the left corner. It is a very slight adjustment. As he makes this slide, X2, moving to stay with 1, bumps into 2, causing him to pivot on his left foot. 1 then takes a long 180-degree-arc swing with his right foot so that he steps directly toward the basket. He is now in front of X2. 2 makes a return pass to 1 if X1 switches. The lateral screen is set with 1's body perpendicular to the direction of X2's body.

Guard Around - Lateral Screen Forward for Guard:

Forward 3 has passed to guard 1 and set a lateral screen on X1. As 1 starts his dribble to the left, shoulder to shoulder off the screen so that X1 can not slide through,

3 slides his left foot slightly forward toward the free-throw lane.

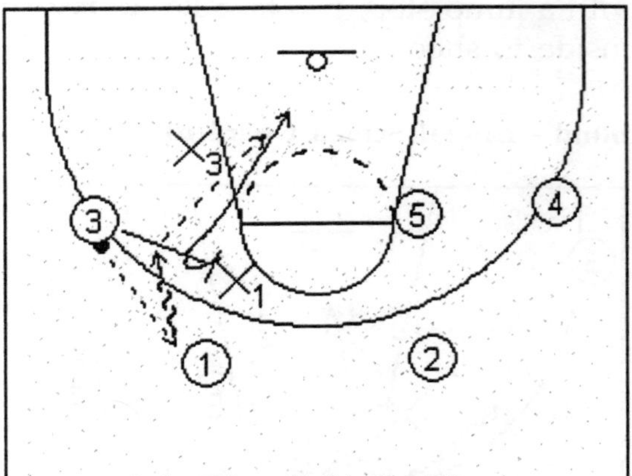

Play 8 Option 7

As X1 moves moves to stay with 1, he bumps 3. 3 makes a 180-degree-arc swing, pivoting on the left foot and swinging the right leg, stepping toward the basket with this foot. As 1 comes off the screen, X3 switches onto 1 leaving 3 in front of X1 and wide open for a return pass from 1.

Guard Around - Inside or Outside

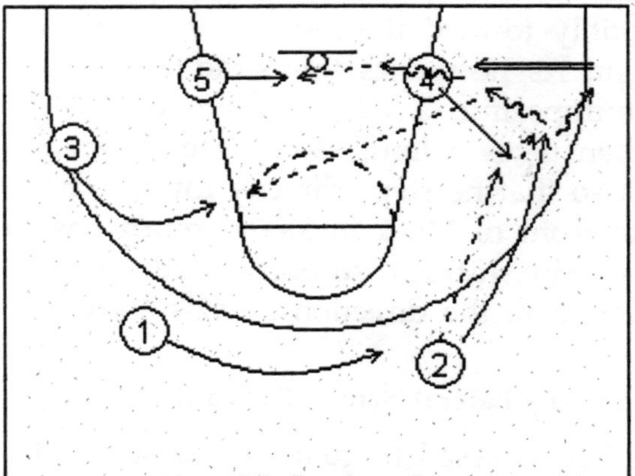

Play #8 Option 8

Guard 2 has the ball and passes to 4. Player 2 has two options. After the pass to 4, he may cut to 4's inside between 4 and 4's defender to receive an inside hand-off or cut to 4's outside and receive an outside hand-off. Player 2 can either shoot, dribble into the basket for a lay-up or dish-off.

Guard Around - High Post with a Screen

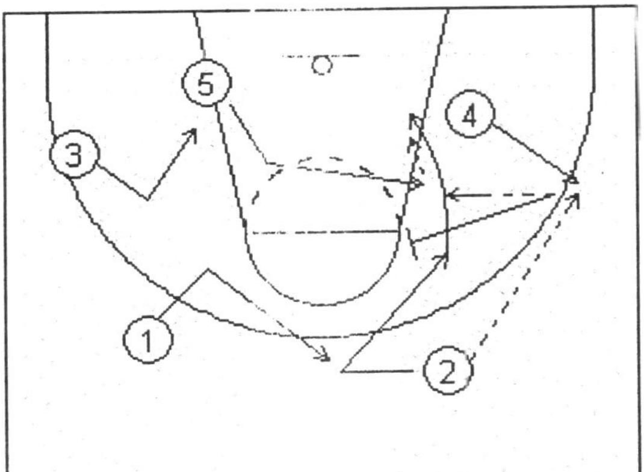

Play #8 Option 9

Player 2 passes to 4 and fakes away. Teammate 5 starts up from the low post opposite the ball and reverses direction to a medium pivot. Player 4 passes to 5 and follows his pass and sets a screen above the circle. Player 2 reverses and cuts off the screens set by 4 and 5 receiving a pass from 5. Player 2 can take a short jump shot, drive to the basket or kick it back outside.

7

Basketball Shots

FUNDAMENTALS OF SHOOTING

The objective of the offense in Basketball is accuracy of each attempted shot. Most players recognize this; but, only the better shooters learn how to practice correctly and work at improvement year round.

Since most of this practice sessions are alone, every player must be his own critic. This means he\she must understand the proper mechanics that affect the success, or failure, of every shot.

Every player must know his range and know what is a good shot. Therefore, before examining the techniques associated with the various shots, a good basketball player is expected to have in his arsenal, here are the principles at work in every scoring shot from anywhere on a basketball court. These are divided into two parts, the mental aspect and the physical aspect:

Mental. At no time is psychological conditioning more critical than when shooting the basketball in a game. Knowing when to shoot and being able to do it effectively under pressure distinguishes the great shooter from the ordinary.

Regardless of how much he practices, or how well he conditions himself, only a modest amount of improvement is possible in speed, reflexes, or strength. History gives many examples of players able to achieve greatness despite mediocre physical talent. Usually, however, such successes are due to determination.

Concentration: is the fixing of attention on the job at hand and is characteristic of every great athlete. Through continuous practice, good shooters develop their concentration to the extent that they are oblivious to every distraction.

Ability to relax: is closely related to concentration. You often hear great shooters have "ice water in their veins".

Watch a good foul shooter as he approaches the foul line. They usually begin the ritual of adjusting the feet and bouncing the ball (nearly always a set number of times). As his/her eyes open wide in sighting the basket, the concentration is so intense, there is little wonder that he/she is undisturbed by the crowd or game pressures.

Confidence: That is a "gut certainty" the ball will drop through the basket without touching metal.

Although, a good shooter never takes a shot that he/she is not confident he/she will make, they often miss. Therefore, the probability of making any given shot is somewhat less than 100% that his/her confidence leads one to expect. Clearly, then, when we say, "Don't shoot when in doubt," we have something different in mind than we do when we say, "Don't take a low-percentage shot except in desperate circumstances."

There are reasons why a player might lack confidence when confronted with a shooting opportunity having a good statistical probability of success. He/she may be off balance. He/she may have had his/her confidence shaken by a string of misses; or he/she may be overly tense, or tired, or may have a lapse in concentration. As Coach David Hayden says, "one often contributes to the other."

Every player experiences off nights when nothing works. An equally familiar phenomenon is that a player's returning to peak form in the second half after a miserable first half. This ability to make a mental recovery is like the ability some players have of recovering in mid-air after an off-balance take-off.

Physical: Shooting a ball and connecting with the target involves the following factors:

Sighting or locating the target: The difference between sighting and aiming is that in aiming, a device (for example, a gun) is visually aligned with a target; thus, visual attention is equally divided between the pointer and the target. In sighting, however, the eyes are used merely to locate, or fix, the target in space, and the computing of an intercept trajectory is left for the brain.

Some coach once said, "To demonstrate the brain's ability to determine a trajectory to a known location, close your eyes and touch either your nose or your ear lobe with a forefinger. To convince yourself of this ability in relation to a visually fixed target, focus your eyes on a nearby object and, without aiming, point your finger at the object. Notice that there is a strong tendency for your attention to shift from the object to your finger and that considerable concentration is required in order to remain focused on the object."

Notice, too, that when concentrating on the object your eyes open quite wide. The reason it is so important for the eyes to remain focused on the target is that they, too, are a kind of computer, continuously updating a three-dimensional fix on whatever is being held in focus. Naturally, the smaller the area focused upon, the smaller the fix, and the greater the potential accuracy.

This brings us to the problem facing a basketball player of not having as his real target not a concrete object, but an open area just over the lip of the basket. Since his eyes can not focus on an empty space, the best he can do is to select a sighting point as nearly on line with the intended trajectory and as near the real target as possible.

When making a bank shot, the shooter solves the problem on a spot related to the painted rectangle above the basket. For all other shots, however, he must decide upon a sighting point somewhere on the rim.

Personal preference determines whether the point selected is on the front or the back rim, but he/she should decide on one or the other and stick with that sighting point for all similar shots. Then, for every shot, he/she should fix upon the same number of cords, while conscious that he/she wants to drop the ball either just beyond front of the rim, or just before the back of the rim, whichever point he chose to sight. The sighting point must be held in constant and clear focus from the moment the shot is begun to the completion of the follow-through.

Body Balance: When properly balanced, a shooter can coördinate the efforts of each muscle to produce a force in the direction of the basket. Although the degree of balance may vary from the near perfect stance of a two-hand set shot to the last effort recovery of an aggressive drive-in.

The shooter's ability to control the trajectory of the ball is directly dependent upon his/her ability to control the acceleration forces generated by his/her own body. However, it is doubtful whether a shot ever succeeds unless, at the moment of release, the shooter has enough control to complete a smooth, continuous follow-through.

Some players have such body control they can hit baskets from positions impossible for any other player. Each player must learn whether or not he/she is in a position to take a shot and complete a follow-through that will leave him/her in the position to rebound a missed shot.

Generating the force: In their book, *Basketball Concepts and Techniques,* Bob Cousy and Frank G. Power, Jr., tell us, "From physics, we know that when several forces act upon an object, the effect is the same as that of a single force equal to the vectorial sum of the force components..." In simpler terms this means, the more horses pulling in the same direction, the greater the horsepower.

They go on to explain, "To a weightlifter, this means that it is possible to synchronize the efforts of leg, back, shoulder, and arm muscles to lift a heavier weight above the head (as in a jerk) than is possible with the arms alone (as in press). To a basketball player, it means that the force he can impart to the ball ranges from that required for a long *two-handed set shot* to that required for a *tip-in* a few inches from the basket."

Therefore, beginning at the ball, each of the following add to the total transmitted force:

— A forward action of the wrists and fingers.

— A sudden extension of the arm, snapping the shoulder and elbow.

— Rising to the balls of the feet.

"Since the force imparted by a muscle under strain is difficult to control, best results are obtained when all muscles can be brought into a smooth, coordinated effort that is within individual limitations."

Obviously, with a *jump shot,* much of the energy generated is converted to altitude. The remaining force required must be provided by arms, wrist, and fingers.

Timing or rhythm: The timing of a shot begins with getting the correct foot down for takeoff (jump shot) and ends with the follow-through and recovery. In a *set-shot.* Perfect timing results in a smooth, continuous thrust from the floor upward, developing a peak force at the fingertips, the instant before, and sustained through, fingertip release.

In a *jump-shot,* body momentum decreases rapidly to zero and the shot must be timed so that fingertip release occurs just prior to the highest point of the jump. Any non-synchronized acceleration of the body, or its members (for example, jerking the head) will directly affect the path after launching of the ball.

Hand-eye coordination and fingertip control: All forces imparted to the ball by the shooter should pass through the fingertips. This technique allows the fingers to make fine trajectory adjustments at release and provides a soft natural backspin.

By stating that the optimum trajectory is that which results in the ball's entering the basket at the highest possible angle commensurate with the lowest possible velocity, we shall have said all that can be said about trajectory.

Combined with a soft natural backspin, a medium trajectory results in the "soft touch" kind of shot that even if slightly off target, will either drop in or hang on the rim for an easy tip-in.

In adjusting his/her hands preparatory to shooting, the shooter should space the fingers comfortably to hold the ball firmly in his/her fingertips and on the heels of both hands. The palms are held slightly clear and the three middle fingers aligned perpendicular to the seams. Players should practice their feel of this until this adjustment becomes instinctive as soon as they catch a ball.

Follow-through: Throughout the act of shooting, the brain continues to compute the precise amount and direction of the force needed to reach the target. Although these computations continue automatically in what computer people call, "real time," there is sufficient lag time to make compensations impossible for any abrupt accelerations at, or before, the instant of release.

Therefore, success depends upon the constant sighting and a smooth, continuous build-up of propelling force that reaches its peak at the instant the ball leaves the fingertips. This means that a follow-through period in which the forces generated are allowed to diminish is an essential part of the shooting sequence.

Techniques for Specific Shots

Before describing the techniques associated with the various shots a player might have in his offensive repertory, we again emphasize the importance of improvisation to the particular style of each player.

Basketball has changed in recent decades, largely due to innovations of individual players whose experimenting with accepted techniques led to development and recognition of revolutionary new techniques. For example, dunks, behind-the-back passes, jump shots, shot blocking, and one-handed set shots were once considered showboating.

Virtually every shot required can be adapted from a mastery of six basic techniques:

Lay-up

Approaching from the right (technique reverses from the left), the shooter grasps the ball in both hands as his/her right foot hits the floor, keeping the body between the ball and defender.

Come down hard on the left foot, and thrust sharply upward with the right knee, carrying the ball in both hands as high as possible with the right hand behind the ball, wrist cocked and facing the basket, and the left hand in front, wrist away from the basket.

This last step is a shorter step that enables the shooter to convert his forward motion into vertical jumping thrust. At the top of the high jump, with both arms above your head erect, eyes fixed on a spot high above and to the right of the basket, allow the left hand to fall away. Your right arm, wrist, and fingers extend to place the ball against the sighted point in a motion similar to that of trying to grasp the rim from a running start without the ball.

The backboard should be used for lay-ups approached from the side. After completing his follow-through, the shooter lands with hips down, knees bent, and body weight low, ready to rebound. or go on defense. A lay-up is used in the following situations:

— A player receives a pass, close in, while cutting for the basket.

— A player dribbles past defenders and under the basket.

One-handed underhand

Except in theory, this shot is never used from a set position; however, the usefulness of this technique for such special purposes as underhand lay-ups and pivots will reward the player who spends time mastering them. From the initial position with both hands holding the ball, reach toward the basket with one hand under the ball, allowing the helper hand fall away.

With your shooting arm fully extended and eyes focused on the sighting spot, lift the ball toward either the basket or a spot on the backboard by raising the arm and adding a soft flick of the wrist and fingers. Follow-through with the palm upward and the arm bent slightly at the elbow.

Executed as described, the ball will carry with a minimum forward rotation. Any side rotation of the hand position at release, however, culminating in a follow-through with the hand edgewise and wrist cocked upward, will impart a side-spin that must be compensated for when sighting.

Two-handed set

This shot is hardly used by modern-day players; however, Bob McDermott, the best shooter used it with great success. During his era, five-foot-eleven guard Bobby McDermott owned basketball's best two-handed set shot. The dazzling McDermott, who was voted the "Greatest Player of All-Time" in 1946 by NBL coaches, players and sports editors, had the raw athletic ability to score from anywhere inside half court.

At a time when teams played deliberate, slowdown basketball, McDermott often scored more than 20 points in a game. Known as "Mr. Basketball Man," McDermott turned professional after just one year of high school, and starred in the ABL and NBL for 17 years. After leading the Brooklyn Visitations to the ABL title in 1935, McDermott played for the Original Celtics from 1936 to 1939 and 1940 to 1941, and quickly became the player fans wanted to watch perform. In five seasons with the Fort Wayne Zollner Pistons, McDermott landed two straight NBL titles (1944 and 1945) and three straight World Professional Tournament titles.

As player/coach of the Chicago Gears in 1947, "Mr. Inside and Mr. Outside" teamed with George Mikan to bring the Gears an NBL championship. McDermott, the only basketball player to lead three leagues (ABL, NYSL, NBL) in scoring and the only pro basketball player/coach to guide two teams to championships, was annually among the NBL's leading scorers. McDermott was considered by many to be the dominant player in basketball from the mid-1930s to the late 1940s. He concluded his career in 1950, the year Collier's named him to the All-World Team.

In the set position, the feet are spaced and aligned for balance and comfort. Each player should determine the position of the feet that gives him/her the most confidence. He/she should forever-after use that position for all similar shots. The weight is on the balls of the feet, with the heels resting lightly on the floor. Both knees are flexed. The upper body is bent slightly forward at the waist with the back straight. The ball is held comfortably in the fingertips of both hands about a foot in front of the body slightly below chin level. The fingers are spread wide, the thumbs and little fingers on the same line with the thumbs close together in the rear. The elbows are held fairly close to the body. The head is stationary and erect while the eyes remain fixed on the sighting target.

Execution is a simultaneous thrust with arms and legs, rising from the heels, locking the knees and elbows, with a flick of the wrists and fingers in the direction of the sighted target. This imparts a soft backspin to the ball. The follow-through is a continuation of the inward and downward rotation of the thumbs, leaving the hands declining slightly at the wrists, the palms turned outward. Eye concentration is essential.

One-handed set

This shot retains much of the balance, range, and accuracy of the *two-handed set* while realizing an increase in speed of getting off the shot. Because the technique is essentially the same as all other non-hooking, one-hand overhead shots, including the jump shot, it should be the basic shot for every player.

For the one-handed set shot, position the foot under the shooting hand slightly forward of the other. The level the ball is carried may be a matter of choice.

Some players prefer to shoot from the chest, while others prefer to come from shoulder; however, the higher the ball is carried in the set position, the closer the shooter can be to the defender and still get his shot away.

The starting point also affects the range. The higher the ball, the shorter the range. The shooting hand is positioned on the low-back side of the ball, fingers spread comfortably wide, with palm facing the basket and held clear of the ball by the fingertips and heel of the hand. The off hand is on the low-forward side, palm away from the basket. The function of the off-hand is to provide balance and control.

The off-hand falls away the instant before release and the driving force to the ball is transmitted solely by the shooting hand. Otherwise, shot execution is the same as a two-handed set. The shooter rises to his toes and thrusts with his legs. Simultaneously, he thrusts his shooting arm to full extension, his hand and fingers flexing downward at the wrist in order to impart a gentle backspin as the ball is released.

Jump Shot

This shot is the most used, today. When preceded by a fake, a quick accurate jump shot is virtually impossible to block. In fact, the fake is essential to its effectiveness. Unless he/she is considerably taller, to defend the jump shooter, the defender must be able to synchronize his/her own jump perfectly with that of the shooter. This is a difficult task by even the simplest of fakes.

From shoulders-up, if movement is toward the basket, the shot execution is the same as for a one-handed set shot. Therefore, once the technique of set shooting has been perfected, it becomes easy to expand one's arsenal of shots to include the many varied jump shots.

Takeoff can either be from a stationary position, facing any direction, or from a position on the move after dribbling, pivoting, or receiving a pass.

Takeoff from the stationary position is generally with both feet, but, when moving, it is usually from the foot opposite the shooting hand. The position of the legs once in the air is a matter of preference. It all depends on what is comfortable for the individual. Some great shooters tuck their legs, others leave them extended and spread and some extend them, but keep them together. All this depends upon balance, distance from basket, and the defensive pressure. Regardless of individual style, the following technique is essentially the same for all jump shots. As he/she begins the crouch, the jump shooter carries the ball in both hands to a preliminary position near the shoulder of the shooting side.

If the player is moving, the crouch occurs on count two of a two-count stop and is initiated by the foot opposite the shooting hand. If he is stationary, the crouch is with both legs and weight evenly distributed on balls of both feet. The elbows are held slightly forward and not necessarily under the ball. The hands are positioned with the off-hand leading and the shooting hand trailing. Spread the fingers comfortably wide as for a one-handed set shot. While sighting the target and as the legs unflex at the start of the jump, the shooter raises the ball with both hands to a shooting position slightly forward and either straight above, or above and to the shooting side of the head.

Taller players tend to prefer a more overhead position than short players. Just prior to reaching the apex of the jump, the shooter with palm of the shooting hand facing the basket, the shooter cocks the wrist so that the palm faces up and forward and his off-hand rides high and in front. Considerable concentration is necessary to ensure continuous sighting as the shooter's hands and forearms cross his line of sight.

As mentioned above, when nearing the apex of his jump, the shooter uncocks the forearm and wrist in a quick supple motion, allowing the off-hand to fall away. The forward motion of the hand and fingertips impart a gentle backspin to the ball. The follow-through is completed with the shooting arm fully extended and hand and fingers declining as if taking a cookie from a jar.

Hooks

The hook shot is an extremely versatile and effective shot from close-in to medium range. Both centers and forwards should, early in their careers, master its technique with both hands. This type shot can be executed after dribbling to either side, receiving a pass and pivoting, or after rebounding and a pivot.

In each instance, the shot is taken off the foot opposite the shooting hand. For a right handed hook, the shooter pivots to the left, pushing off his right foot, turning his/her body and head to pick up the sighting point, while his/her right hand, palm up, extends out parallel to the floor.

Taking off on the left foot, he/she completes a continuous, sweeping overhead arc toward the basket. As in every other shot, success depends upon effective sighting, a soft wrist, fingertip control, and a smooth continuous follow-through.

Other check points include high knee lift, two hand raising of the ball for added control before extending the ball away from the body, and extension of the weak-hand elbow to a position parallel to the floor to keep his defender at a distance. A correctly executed follow-through will leave the shooter facing the basket and in good rebounding position.

Adaptations and Variations

After a player masters the fundamental techniques of hook shooting from various distances within his own optimum-percentage area, he/she should begin to elaborate upon the technique by incorporating the specialized fakes, pivots, turns, etc., that apply to the play situations most often developing from his team position. Informal practice to perfect close-in shots with either hand will add greatly to a player's value as an offensive threat.

Special Purpose Lay-ups: Although one of the two variations described previously, should be used in most lay-up situations, the exceptionally talented player may find that two additional lay-up shots will increase his scoring opportunities.

The floating two-handed underhand lay-up: Can be used by a hard driving guard coming down the lane in front of a closely defended basket. Instead of the high jump of the conventional lay-up, a broad jump is begun toward the basket, from six to nine feet out, with a takeoff from either foot. After takeoff, the player tucks the feet under the thighs and floats toward the basket, the ball held between both hands. The release is timed for the apex of the jump and is effected by extending both arms forward and flipping the ball up with wrists and fingers.

The driving one-handed underhanded lay-up: This is useful either for a miscalculated takeoff too far from the basket or as a calculated tactic to counter pressure from a defender in position to block a conventional overhead shot. Again, this shot is made from a broad jump, but in this case the takeoff foot is the same as that of a conventional lay-up. That is left-foot for a right-hand shot and right-foot for a left-hand shot.

The ball is initially held in both hands, the body between the ball and the defender; however, after takeoff the hand nearest the defender falls away, and the shot is accomplished by a reaching motion. The arm extends forward at shoulder level, the shooting hand under the ball, and the wrist and fingers flick the ball toward a sighting spot on the backboard, slightly above and to the shooter's side of the basket. Some rotation of the wrist may be required in order to impart a slight carrying spin to get it into the basket.

Under-the-basket shots: Frequently, a player cutting under the basket finds himself/herself with the ball too close in for a lay-up of any type. In this case, he has two alternatives for a high percentage shot:

A semi-hook or short-hook: Takeoff for both these shots is from the foot opposite the shooting hand, with the ball held high and in both hands. In the semi-hook, however, as the shooter rises from the floor, he turns to face the basket, allowing his off-hand to fall away, and hooking overhead and toward the basket with his shooting arm, the elbow and wrist inclined in a shallow arc. For a short-hook the shooter does not turn toward the basket. Instead, he gets the ball away by a full overhead hook, with the arm relaxed, extended, and a soft flick of the wrist and fingers.

A layback or reverse lay-up: Initiated from the side opposite the side from you approach the basket. The side can be approached from the side or from the rear, utilizing the four-foot area between the backboard and end line. You takeoff from the foot opposite the strong hand. Tilt the head back to see the sighting point, carrying the ball upward with both hands. At fullest extension, let the helping hand fall away with the shooting hand rotating inward toward the little finger. Release the ball with a flick of the wrist and fingers. If you are ambidextrous, try to master this shot with either hand.

Drive-in hook: An important weapon in the repertory of smaller back-court players is used when a taller defender switches to block a drive to the basket. While still in motion, the shooter begins with the same takeoff as for a conventional lay-up; however, when the ball is level with the shoulders, it is extended out, held in the shooting hand, away from the defender. A high trajectory shot is then effected with an overhead hook with the arm fully extended.

Close-in jump shot: Following a quick stop and fake, this shot can often be executed before the defender can react. The attacker moves from his weak to his/her strong side, stops, fakes, and takes off on his strong-side foot. Turning toward the basket in mid-air, he/she shoots quickly, with one hand slightly before reaching the top of his jump. The attacker uses the same technique when moving from the strong side, except that a slight fall-away may be necessary in turning toward the basket.

Close-in pivot shots: Most of these shot opportunities come to low or medium post players or a forward when his back is to the basket. Therefore, players at these positions must master the following:

Right and left-handed hooks: A close-in back-to-the-basket hook shot is almost impossible to block. Because of the three-second rule, however, speed in getting the shot away is essential.

Ideally, the pass-in should be shoulder high, with the ball caught with both feet off the ground, landing in a position where both feet in position for a pivot in either direction. However, should pass reception require establishing one foot as the pivot by taking a step in the direction of the pass, then the step should be taken with the foot nearest the basket.

Upon receiving the ball, the shooter should execute a head-and-shoulder fake while bringing the ball shoulder level and elbows extended. Obviously, the shooter must be capable of shooting with either hand if a fake is to be convincing. Depending upon opportunity and ability, the shooter follows his fake with a quick pivot obliquely toward, parallel to, or away from, the end line.

Turn-arounds: This is simple to master. A successful execution requires that a step, pivot, take-off, and shot be effected in one continuous motion. The ball is received in both hands, with the weight evenly distributed on both feet so that a turn may be made in either direction.

For a right hand shot, a head-and-shoulder fake to the right is quickly followed by a step to the left with the left, or non-pivot, foot. In the same motion, pivot to face the basket, thrust upward with the right knee, and a left foot takeoff. During execution of the turn, bring the ball up to a shooting position, above the head, with both hands.

Step-in pivots: From a close-in pivot position, it is sometimes possible to take advantage of a defensive lapse by following a fake with a pivot directly toward the basket. If the player sees that his defender is moving in the direction of the fake, the pivot player, synchronizing his movements with the defender's lapse, can drop his/her non-pivot foot quickly toward the basket, pinning the defender behind. The shot can either be a hook, a turn-around, and underhand pivot, or a simple lay-up.

Underhand pivots: Whenever a pivot player is close-in, back-to-the-basket situation and feels pressure of the defender on his back, he/she can fake to the side of the pressure, execute a step-in pivot in the opposite direction, and shoot under the defender's arm with an underhand upward motion. The ball is released toward the basket with a lifting rotation of the forearm and wrist of the shooting hand, imparting a soft carrying spin. Sighting must take into account both the spin and lower arc. Rhythm and follow-through are essential.

Step-aways: This is useful when the back-to-the-basket pivot player has the ball but not closely guarded because of a mental lapse by his defender. For example, when the defender reacts to a fake by moving away from the shooter and toward the basket, the shot can be executed by stepping away from the basket with the non-pivot foot, pivoting on this foot to face the basket, simultaneously thrusting upward with the other knee for a rear-foot takeoff, executing a one-handed shot. Since this shot is easily blocked by a close defender, the fake, pivot, and shot must be perfectly timed.

Jump-turns: Most pivot players consider the turn-around jumper to be their best back-to-the-basket offensive weapons. Its success is largely due to its simplicity and to the effectiveness of an easily executed fake. In making the shot, the back-to-the-basket pivot brings the ball up to the shooting position while simultaneously executing a straight-up jump-turn to face the basket, timing the one-handed release prior to the apex of the jump. The fake is accomplished by a quick straightening of the knees and upward motion that simulates the beginning of a takeoff, making it impossible for the defender to synchronize his jump with the shooter.

Tip-ins are not lucky slaps at the ball. They are practiced as any other shot in the shot repertory of any tall basketball player. An offensive rebounder should be ready to make a *tip-in shot* of any rebound in his area and within six feet of the basket.

Facing the basket, with knees flexed, hands up, and elbows wide at the shoulders, the tip-in shooter times his takeoff to make fingertip contact just prior to reaching the top of his/her jump. The shooting hand first controls the ball with fingers spread and flexible wrist, flicking the ball upward in a soft trajectory toward the basket. Even if control is not possible, some type of contact, such as a slap, should be made with the ball.

Sighting, fingertip control, and follow-through are the same for any other one-handed shot. Although some players, and coaches, prefer to go up for the ball with both hands in order to rebound, most players can jump quicker and higher with only one hand up. To me, the recommended method is the one hand-up around the offensive board.

The free throw shot should be a regular part of every practice session and should take place under as near game-conditions as possible. Every player must determine his/her best-percentage medium, or long-range, shot and use that shot for *all* free throws. To be proficient, a shooter should make at least 80% of his free throws in practice; however, should a player not be particularly proficient in any one medium or long-range shot, he should be taught to master the one-handed set shot with particular attention in getting him to use the legs to propel the ball in a high soft arc toward the basket. The following fundamentals should be practiced until they become second nature for any free throw, regardless of style:

Dry hands and fingers: Before entering the free-throw circle, dry hands on trunks and shake the arms, wrists, and fingers to relieve tension.

Look to both sides and behind: Before accepting the ball from the official, look all around to check the opponent's offensive alignment and teammate's positions.

Receive ball from official: Always accept the ball before taking position at the free-throw line.

Take exact position: Move up to the line and set feet in the exact position you aways use for free-throws. Most all basketball courts have a nail indentation in the center of the free-throw circle. Use this as your marker to position your feet.

Spin ball in hands: Do this to acquire proper feel of the ball; then, bounce the ball a certain number of times to relax the arms and body to accentuate the feel.

Inhale and exhale softly: After, assuming final hand placement, inhale and exhale, slowly.

Shoot the ball high and soft with gentle backspin: Rising to the toes with a thrust of the legs and simultaneous extension of the shooting arm, hand and fingers flexing downward smoothly at the wrist in order to impart a soft backspin to the ball. Hold the follow-through and keep the eye on the target until the ball strikes iron. Do not watch the flight of the ball.

The objective of the offense in Basketball is accuracy of each attempted shot. Most players recognize this; but, only the better shooters learn how to practice correctly and work at improvement year round.

8

Importance of Offensive Basketball

In his book, *Winning Basketball,* Nat Holman writes, "mastery of detail in fundamentals is the first principle of winning basketball."Before bigger things can be attempted, successful coaches must stress and practice the fundamentals of basketball. This groundwork lays the foundation for success. It is essential that the coach synchronize his fundamental teachings with his chosen system of play. Unless there is a progression of the fundamentals and a carrying out, much of his efforts result in wasted time.

Teams well drilled in the fundamentals usually possess a stronger degree of confidence in their ability. However, only proper preparation and presentation of these fundamentals will produce that confidence. If you can instill this among your players, they will be hard to beat.

Fundamentals of Offensive Basketball

This could also be called the psychology of groundwork. In the interest of the laws of learning, here are a few points for the *inexperienced coach* in the teaching of a specific fundamental.

Demand Strict Attention

The first fundamental drill should be simple and non-competitive. Only after the mechanics are learned, revert to game condition drill to gain efficiency in developing the whole. Never allow carelessness.

The coach and more experienced players should demonstrate the fundamental first at half-speed and later at normal speed. A good demonstration of a skill tends to give a group a more uniform mental picture of that particular fundamental. Most sport authorities generally agree that a coach should not scrimmage with his players; however, if the coach is competent enough, I think it wise that he demonstrate the fundamentals.

Use the whole method in explaining the fundamental and its place in your chosen offense. Such explanation gives a better understanding of the fundamental, its purpose, and your particular offense.

In the beginning, constantly stress correct form and habits. Speed can be emphasized, later.

If your squad is average to large, divide players into small units with an experienced player, acting as player-coach. Using a player in this manner develops responsibility and leadership. The coach can make the rounds, lending hand to players who need help.

Use the part method by stressing one, or two, main points at a time. As progress continues, go on to other points in the execution. Repeat the next day or two and the next week until well mastered. Players learn best when reviewed at regular intervals.

Do not practice too long and one particular fundamental. This tends to dampen enthusiasm of players.

How to Play Basketball Offense

Team Positions

Over the years, as shooting, passing, and dribbling have become more sophisticated, offensive alignments have changed. They probably will continue changing in the future. Rule changes often dictate this. For example, take the three-point shot. This is changing the philosophy of a lot of coaches. Previous to the three-point shot, big men were dominating the game. Teams constantly looked for only a close-in shot. As a result, most defenses packed back in tight.

The three-point shot is changing all this. This new rule has opened up the game. Defenses must come out. It is quite common to see coaches using 3 and 4 guard offenses. Some of them even have their offensive teams and defensive teams, substituting freely to suit the particular need. Fundamentals, however, remain much as they were 40 years ago. Things that worked then, still work today.

The terminology used to describe offensive alignments are different than they were 40 years ago. Some team offenses have evolved so that every player must be able to play at any and all positions. The flex offense is an example. Yet, this type offense is over 30 years old. Us old timers called it "the shuffle." In either offense, the center often finds himself out at a guard position. This type offense is well suited for today's rules; however, adjustments are made to fit the abilities of available players.

High school coaches always have to adapt. College coaches simply recruit the players to fill a void. Regardless, the level of play, specialized players still perform specific roles within the context of the total team. Then, show you how to prepare yourself mentally, so you can get the best out of your position. After that, we will learn the importance of playing offense as a team, not as a collection of individuals.

The Point Guard

The point guard runs the offense and watches the backcourt. His role is so important to the team that he is really an extension of the coach on the floor. He must have these qualities:

— He must have an instinctive knowledge of the game.

— He must be a good ball handler.

— He must be a good passer.

— He must possess speed and quickness of foot.

— He must be a good dribbler with either hand.

— He must be able to play good hard-nosed defense.

— He must be able to hit the outside shot when left open.

— He must be able to penetrate and dish off.

— He must be able to read defenses.

Above all, his ego must not be so inflated that it interferes with his basketball judgment. Normally, the point guard receives little publicity for his fine play; but, his coach and teammates know his value to the team.

The Off-Guard

The off-guard is also referred to as the guard or shooting guard. He is generally the better shooter of the two guards. The qualities that he needs to possess are:

— He must have an instinctive knowledge of the game.

— He must be a good ball handler.

— He must be a good passer.

— He must possess speed and quickness of foot.

— He must be a good dribbler with either hand.

— He must be able to play good hard-nosed defense.

— He must be able to hit the 15 to 20 foot shot with consistency.

— He must be able to penetrate and dish off.

— He must be able to read defenses.

— He must know how to move without the ball.

— He must be a student of the offense so that he can step in and run the offense if the point guard is being overplayed, or must leave the game.

— His ego must not be so inflated that it interferes with his basketball judgment. Normally, the off-guard's job is to put points on the board and help his teammates to score.

The Center

The center, along with the point guard, is easily the most important player on the team. Normally, he is the tallest player on the floor. The qualities he must possess are:

— He must have quickness.

— He must be an aggressive rebounder and lead the way in blocked shots. He needs to be a little arrogant with a streak of meanness. He is king of the paint. He must prove by his manner and actions that this territory is his.

— He must be a dependable scorer at short and mid range. He must be adept at the power lay-ups, with and without shot fakes, from both sides of the basket. He needs to develop a short hook and jump shot.

— He must have defensive leadership, always talking to his teammates.

— He must be a good passer and be able to see the floor and hit the open man if his shot is not there.

— He must be able to read how he is being defended and to take advantage of this when he is posting-up.

— He must have strong hands, good upper body strength, and good jumping ability.

The Small Forward

The small forward is the most gifted player on the team. He should possess the following characteristics:

— He must be quick and fast.

— He must be an adequate rebounder.

— He must be a good passer.

— He must be able to play defense anywhere on the floor.

— Most of all he must be a good scorer, capable of shooting from anywhere from the wings, around the key, and under the boards. The best of these, can score at will, and simply take control of the game with their exceptional athletic abilities.

— He must run the length of the floor on fast breaks.

The Power Forward

Like the point guard, the power, or strong forward, does not receive much recognition. Usually, if he's doing his job well, his role as the player doing the "dirty work" is taken for granted. He must possess the following:

— He must be a solid rebounder, both offensively and defensively. Along with the center, the power forward controls the area inside the key. Many of their characteristics should be similar.

— He must be an adequate passer.

— He must be an adequate scorer.
— He must be a "gutsy" dribbler and a hard driver.
— He must be a good runner and able to go the entire length of the floor on a fast break.
— He must stand up to the opposition at both ends of the court. In basketball parlance, he is known as the "enforcer."

The Sixth Man, or Role Player

At all levels of basketball, the sixth man has become something of an elite figure. He is the guy who has set aside his ego so that he can come off the bench at a moment's notice and fall right into the flow. He's able to do whatever is necessary to help his team win.

Sometimes his role calls for him to score, play exceptional defense, or a combination of the two. Sometimes, he is meant to add rebounding strength.

Whatever he's capable of doing, the sixth man is an important component to the game. He satisfies his coach's quest for an advantage, particularly when the game is close. He's a spark plug, capable of picking up the tempo when play gets sluggish.

Since he doesn't start the game, the sixth man must study the game tempo and prepare himself mentally so he is able to adjust to flow of the game the moment he steps on the floor. More than anything else, he gives his team quality minutes when he plays. His coach, then, must know the sixth man's capabilities and limitations. Furthermore, he must know how long the sixth man can deliver these quality minutes before losing his effectiveness to the team.

Mental Preparation

Give or take a few percentage points, basketball is 80

percent mental preparation and 20 percent physical. Sure, God packs more ability into some player's 20 percent than others. But, from the mental preparation aspect of the game, the percentage is equal.

There are as many ways to prepare mentally for a basketball game as there are players. A few of these follow:

— Some players go into a deep silence before a game, preferring to focus on the upcoming game.

— Some enjoy jabbering to everyone in sight, listening to music, and staying loose.

— Others choose somewhere between the first two.

— As long as it helps you to play well is all that counts. Your mental preparation should be to your own taste. Use one that works for you.

After preparing yourself mentally for a game, the concentration needed for actual play is another matter. Basketball is such a fast paced, emotional game. Decisions are made in split seconds. A player can lose his concentration at anytime. To play the game effectively, you must block out everything around you, except the following:

— The action on the court.

— Your coach's plan for that particular game.

— Once you have your game face, be all business on the floor. Never let an official or an opponent upset you. This breaks your concentration. This is often called, "Playing under control."

— Stay cool and be a "team player." We have all seen teams with one dominant player who goes for the bucket every time he gets his hands on the ball. Oh, he may get his points in the game; but, his teammates won't. More likely, than not, the team, scorer included, loses.

— The point is you can maintain a respectable scoring average. At the same time, you can help your teammates maintain theirs and win the game. Remember to play as part of the team. Stay cool! Stay calm and concentrate. You will get your points in the course of a game.

How to Play Basketball Defense

Nobody knows why; but, efforts to strengthen defensive skills seem to go into hibernation every summer. Players think it a necessary evil ... you pass through ...on your way to a score. Use some of the summer league or playground pick-up games to work on these skills.

There are about six or seven major points that you should be aware of when playing ball defense. These major points concern your position in the private area of a player with the ball. This is the area in which a defender must be in to worry the player with the ball.

The defender must make dribbles, passes, or shots difficult. This area is often referred to as "his bubble." These major points are: body weight, position of the hands, faking, forcing, slapping (or stealing), and a self commitment.

The last is more important. If you aren't committed to stopping your man, none of the other points matter. Begin, with a sincere desire to be known as a good defensive player. If you have this, then the six points that follow, will help.

Body Position and Weight

Most coaches seem to want players to get in a lower crouch than players want to do. Most players, it seems, want to stand erect. So, how low should you be? A good rule to follow is this:

— Make sure your head is always lower than the head of the guy you are guarding.

— If you stay lower than him, you will be more ready to move than him. If he lowers his head to drive, you need to lower your head even more to stay in front of him.

— Players get blocking fouls when their knees are out. If you will examine a little further, you will see that their heads were up, too! At the moment of the block, the defender's head is likely higher than the dribbler's.

— Besides being lower than your man, you should have your weight back. Be ready to move when he moves. Get in your man's bubble and have your weight back.

— Players often stay away from their man. When the man fakes or looks to shoot or pass, it's only then, they move forward So, what happens? You get to the bubble (to the man); but, your weight is forward so that you can not possibly beat him to where he is going.

— Imagine trying to win a hundred yard dash. One guy is in the starting blocks ready to burst forward. You start several feet in front of him; but, you have to touch the starting line when the gun goes off. Obviously, you would be several steps behind after ten yards. Apparently, this isn't as obvious to some basketball players. In games at all levels, players stay too far from their men. At times, they lunge forward, and the guy with the ball blows right by them.

— Why do players allow this to happen? If you want to win a race, you have to lean in the direction of the finish line. In basketball you have to lean in the direction of the basket.

Get in His Bubble

"Bubble" is not a term used by all coaches; however, the term is useful to remind YOU to play in a GOOD defensive position. Unless your coach gives you some other rule, Good Defensive Position means not so close that the player, with the ball, can step by you with ONE step. Yet, you want to be close enough that you could slap the ball if he should hold it in front. In other words, be close enough to bother him. Make him worry. Make him think you will touch his next pass, block his next shot, or steal his next dribble.

To play good defense you must consistently be in that bubble. Even along with playing good helping defense, you should be able to get in your man's bubble EVERY TIME he gets the BALL. Strive to get there the moment he gets it. If you can do this, YOU will be a constant irritation. This is exactly what you want to be.

You can not expect to be a good defensive player if: one day, you try stealing the ball ALL THE TIME because that player IS NOT TALENTED; then, the next day, you stay far away because he is MORE TALENTED.

Why should you be in his bubble if he is forty feet from the basket? Well, that's so You can bother his ball handling. Make it difficult for him to take the ball exactly where he wants it, or to make the exact pass at the exact time he wants to make it.

If YOUR COACH tells you NOT to pick him up UNTIL he's within shooting range, DO WHAT HE SAYS! But, if he DOESN'T GIVE YOU a rule, OR it's a SUMMER LEAGUE or PICK-UP GAME, ... GET IN HIS BUBBLE ... AND ... STAY THERE!!!

Now, use common sense! I don't mean for you to be beside your man ALL THE TIME. DO NOT BE THERE when the BALL is on the OTHER SIDE OF THE COURT. When things are this way, YOU need to be in a position to HELP

A TEAMMATE. REMEMBER: The CLOSER the BALL to YOUR MAN, the CLOSER YOU MUST BE TO HIM. This is because the moment he gets the ball, YOU WANT TO be IN his bubble, ... NOT ON YOUR WAY, there. Be where you can WORRY him. Make him think to himself, "Oh, no! Here you are again!"

To be effective you don't have to block a shot or deflect a single pass. If you are merely in position all night long where you CAN, ... AND he can't GET AWAY from YOU, ... YOU will be a great defensive player.

Dictating the Way the Ball Goes

A player with the ball can do three things:

— He can SHOOT.

— He can PASS.

— He can DRIBBLE to the RIGHT or LEFT.

Your bubble defense and hand position makes the first two difficult. YOU will be showing your smarts by taking two of these three options away from him. Then, YOU can battle him for the third.

He still might shoot or pass; but, either will be difficult. This is what DEFENSE is ALL ABOUT! Thus, making those first two difficult, this leaves only the dribble to the RIGHT or LEFT. So, if YOU OVERPLAY to one side, forcing him to his LEFT or RIGHT, you take away HALF of HIS THIRD OPTION. He can only try to beat you the direction YOU DICTATED.

During the regular season, the type of defense YOUR COACH uses, will determine which option you leave open. LISTEN to him! In the meantime, during SUMMER LEAGUE play or Pick-Up Games, PRACTICE MAKING HIM KEEP THE DRIBBLE IN HIS WEAK HAND. In other words, if he's LEFT HANDED, slant him on that SIDE, or, he's RIGHT HANDED, do the opposite.

The advantage of this type of defense is that you DO NOT have to be PREPARED for "EVERYTHING." You DON'T EVEN have to worry about FAKES. You know what the player is going to do.

Either he is going to take a bad shot or he must make a good pass by YOUR hand. If he does neither, he must force the ball in the direction he is being overplayed. Chances are, he will choose to try to beat you in the one thing YOU ARE PREPARED FOR! This will happen nine times out of ten.

By dictating the action, not only do you make your own job easier; but, it will be easier for your TEAMMATES. When they see in advance where the battle is to be fought ... where the ball is going to be taken ... they have a better chance of getting into effective HELPING position.

Position of the Hands

All coaches urge "HANDS UP!" They want you to do this because it distracts the offense. YOU are in a better position to guard against a shot or deflect a pass. Players, invariably, want to play with their hands at their sides.

This is understandable. It's easier to move with hands at your side. In guarding the ball, there are times you want your "Hands UP" and there is times, they are better "Down."

If you are guarding a dribbler, YOUR hands DO NOT have to be up. They should be DOWN, faking at the ball, or HELPING YOUR BODY to stay on BALANCE and in POSITION.

The difference regarding your hands comes when YOU are guarding a player who has the BALL, but has not yet dribbled. If that player is out of shooting range, YOUR HANDS can be down at WAIST or KNEE level. One of them to the side and the other stretched out to the ball handler's belt buckle. The out-stretched hand should be the same as whichever foot is forward. The out- stretched hand should be PALM-UP. This is so you are always prepared to SLAP-UP anytime the ball is held out front.

If the player with the ball is in SHOOTING RANGE, you should have ONE HAND UP, almost touching your shoulder. Keep it poised to JAB UPWARD. This lets the player known that YOU ARE PREPARED TO BLOCK HIS SHOT (although, really ALL YOU ARE TRYING TO DO is DISTRACT him by getting your hand up near the ball and your ARM in FRONT of HIS FACE.

NEVER RAISE YOUR BODY UP TO BLOCK THE PASS OR SHOT OF A PLAYER WHO HAS NOT YET DRIBBLED! Stay low. Keep your weight back. Stay in that bubble. SLAP UPWARD from the waist if he is OUT OF SHOOTING position, or SHAKE YOUR HAND over the shoulder if HE IS IN SHOOTING POSITION.

When a Dribbler Gets By You

There are two possible reactions to this. The most common, it seems, is to turn and watch his butt grow smaller as he gets further down court. The other is what you should be doing, once you realize he has you beaten.

React to this, immediately. Turn quickly! Get down low where you could bite his butt, if it were sticking out. If you get yourself into the habit of this second reaction, you will get a lot of steals. This is especially true if you have been slanting him on his strong side. Here is the reason. Once he thinks he has you beaten, the tendency is to put the ball back into his strong hand. This would be the side you would be on. It's very possible that the first dribble with his strong hand will be right in front of your face. You can pick his pocket here without fouling. You don't have to reach across his body.

There is a reason more steals, like this, are not made. Players, so lackadaisical on defense to let themselves be beaten, are usually too slow-thinking to recover. It don't even occur to them to "bite him in the butt." Instead of thinking about the next play, they are thinking about the last.

This maneuver is so good you can use it on purpose. It might get you a "game winning steal, some night." Because of the psychology of the moment, especially, if your team is behind and needs a steal, it has a better chance of working in the closing minutes of a game. This is because the opponents think more of protecting their lead than trying to extend it. Their chief concern is to run out the clock.

If you use this on purpose, early in the game, there is a good chance it won't work. If it doesn't, your coach will probably take you out of the game. So, with this in mind, save it for the end of a game. DEFENSE WHEN YOUR TEAM IS BEHIND LATE IN THE GAME ...

The rules are different when you're behind. Now, you DON'T get anything for staying between your man and the basket and playing "solid defense." The clock will soon run out ... and YOU lose. It is at this point that many players fail to adjust. The things you need to be doing, NOW, is to discourage PASSES more than SHOTS.

Often, at the closing moments of games, you can hear the coach shout, "Go get 'em! Go get 'em!" Yet, nobody really gets anyone.

The defenders let their men receive the ball; then, make a show of useless hustle. They crowd their man, huff and puff, and reach in to swat the ball. This type of show doesn't fool anybody.

IF YOU WANT TO PLAY GOOD DEFENSE, in these closing minutes, YOU MUST MAKE IT DIFFICULT, preferably ... IMPOSSIBLE ... for YOUR MAN to RECEIVE a pass.

There is a Time For Fouling

By this time, you have reached a point of desperation. Simply put, YOU are hoping for LUCK! This is the time to foul; however, make EVERY attempt look like you ARE GOING FOR THE BALL. You don't want any intentional fouls called.

This point in time will come less often if YOU REALIZE what adjustment on defense you need to make BEFOREHAND. If you KNOW that the OBJECTIVE is to deflect, intercept, or stop PASSES. If anything, give up the RISKY LOB or backdoor BOUNCE PASSES. If you do this, you will get your SHARE of COMEBACKS.

It's easy to find excuses when you are tired and discouraged. You should NEVER GET BEAT TO THE BALL. DIVE FOR IT! Please, do not use excuses. They never win games. Good players KNOW their job is to PREVENT PERIMETER PASSES, in spite of screens or other diversions. They know that HUSTLE, once their man gets the ball, IS TOO LATE.

When your team is behind, toward the end of a game, it takes GUTS! Stick to your man and DON'T let him TOUCH the ball. If anything, force him to get a lob going AWAY from the passer.

Sure, he may score. You have to take chances. If you stand back and LET your man break out and receive passes, you will surely lose. Realize that a team protecting the lead won't throw a backdoor lob, unless, there is a man WIDE OPEN. Thus, you have the advantage. You know what type of passes they would like to throw. Don't let them! Prevent your man from catching a pass while moving toward it.

Offensive Basketball Rebounding Wins Games

Height and good jumping ability have certain advantages in offensive rebounding. They are by no means the only factor in becoming a good rebounder. There are many instances, at all levels, that a seven foot center is out battled for a rebound, even out- rebounded for an entire game by a player as much as six inches shorter.

Rebounding is an important basketball skill that is developed and improved through these three ingredients:

— Aggressiveness

— Positioning

— Determination

Combine these factors, even though you are not 6'11" and don't have good jumping ability. You will be well on your way toward being a good rebounder.

How do you pick off all the loose balls that come from your teammate's, and your own, missed shots? You try to anticipate where you think the ball will come off the rim. Position yourself so that you have a better position to get the ball. The big problem is that you usually have a defensive man in front, blocking you to keep you away from the basket. It always takes extra effort to establish good rebounding position, especially on offense.

One of the biggest mistakes young players make is standing around watching the flight of the ball, maybe only for a moment. They should be going for the rebound. If your teammate misses a shot, and you watch it first, before going for the rebound, you give the defense plenty of time to effectively box you out. This will keep you from ever getting to the basket.

A good way to get out of the habit of watching shots before going in for the rebound is to always think that every shot will miss. This will force you to think where the shot will come off the rim.

Determination

Your rebounding motto should be, "The ball belongs to me and, come hell or high water, I'm going to have it!"

Take a lot of pride in your offensive rebounds. They are harder to come by. It takes a lot of work to be good at rebounding; however, there is nothing more satisfying than a rebound pulled down in a crowd under the glass, and then going back up with it, scoring, and getting a foul shot, too.

Mental outlook is one of the most important factors in rebounding. You need the proper frame of mind when going for the ball. You have to be determined that you will do your best to get the ball. Rebounding starts with determination. There are nine other players on the court; but, you have to want the rebound the most. This mental and physical toughness will pay off.

Many times the ball will come off the rim and not be grabbed right away. It may even bounce off your fingers. It might slip through outstretch hands. A lot of times you have to go up two, maybe three times on one play to get one rebound. Rebounding is hard work; but, never give up. By concentrating, going up that many times for the ball, and then finally coming back down with it, and putting it back in the hole for two points, you can take the energy and heart right out of the other team.

One important thing to remember, once you have the ball in your hands, is to bring it down to your chest with elbows out wide. This protects the ball. When you land on the floor, with the ball, be sure to come down with a wide and strong position. This will keep you from being knocked over when the defense bumps you. This, also, helps you to protect the ball.

If you are in a crowd, under your offensive board, the tip-in is a good thing to use. Even if you miss, you are keeping the ball alive. Even if you can't get it with your second and third effort, perhaps a teammate might.

Positioning

Positioning for offensive rebounds is important. A good strong position is the secret of both offensive and defensive rebounding. First of all, you have to reach that spot in the lane where you think the ball will come down. Don't get too far under the basket. You don't want to be too far away from the rim, either.

Once you are here, you must be able to hold your position for two or three seconds. Keep low with knees bent, and legs wide to provide a large and strong base. This will keep you from being pushed out of position by the defense. Your back should be slightly bent forward and your arms at a 45-degree angle over your shoulders. By holding your arms like this, the defense will not be able to hook you and pin your arms at your sides. Do all these things and you will be in a good position to rebound.

Another thing you should always remember, don't try to dribble the ball when you grab a rebound and come back down to the floor. Immediately go back up strong to the basket.

Aggressiveness

The painted area is one of the most physical places in the world of sports. When you are there, your job is too rebound. Be prepared to be elbowed, shoved, pushed, or even knocked to the floor. That's the nature of the game. If you are not willing to take the pain, you will never develop into a rebounder.

Even though it is so physical in the paint, even in high school, you must be extremely aggressive to get in there and rebound. Whenever you are blocked out by your defensive man, keep moving around and try for a better position.

Quickly note where your teammate has shot from. Tell yourself, "That ball is not going in!" Then, move in aggressively for rebounding position.

Remember that 75 percent of all missed shots go in a direction away from the shooter. Generally, the further away the shooter is from the basket, the higher and further out the ball will bounce. Shots taken from the side have a tendency to bounce to the opposite side. Shots taken straight on at the basket will generally bounce straight back to the shooter.

Study the way your teammates shoot. Note the type of arc the give their shots. This will tell you approximately where you can go for the rebound.

How to Go for the Offensive Rebound

There are many simple moves you can make that will help you to become a good rebounder. Make yourself aware of them and use them in practice and games.

When Not Blocked Out

If your defensive man is facing you, when a shot is taken, and hasn't begun to block you out, take a strong step in one direction. Make a head and shoulder fake at the same time. Follow this with a change of direction and a change of pace to go over him.

When Blocked Out

If your defensive man has effectively blocked you out, lean on the middle of his back with your shoulder. Using his back as the pivot point, make a reverse by actually rolling around his back, placing your lead foot in front of his feet. If you do this correctly, you will end up in front.

Over With the Arms

Another trick to use if you find your defensive man beside you on a rebound is the old "hook the arm" trick. When your defensive man has his arms raised, raise your arms and hook one of them over the crook of his arm and push it down. As you do this, step in front of him and take his position. If you can't get in front of him, at least try to get parallel with him. Tip with your other hand. It may surprise you, how high you can reach. At least, you will have a better shot at keeping the ball alive.

Rebounding Drills

On a strictly physical level, rebounding is an explosive act that involves the contracting and tensing of the leg muscles. Then, jumping upward by straightening out those muscles. The higher you can jump, the better your chance of getting the rebound. Not everyone has natural jumping ability; however, everyone can improve what jumping capabilities he possesses. The following drills will help you improve your jumping ability and lateral movement.

Leg Bounds

This drill will develop strong muscles in your upper legs. This gives you the explosive power needed to leap quickly and continuously. The drill goes like this:

— Stand at an end line with your legs together.

— With your arms at your sides, bend your knees until you are in a half-squat.

— Jump out as far and as high as you can, thrusting out your arms and straightening your body.
— When you land, end in the same crouched position and take off again with your next bound.
— Continue these bounds until you reach the far end line.
— Grab a ball and shoot 10 free throws, then bound back.
— Start by doing this once, then gradually increase the number until you can do it five times each session.

Squat Jumps

This drill will develop tremendous leg strength. Remember to jump as high as possible on each jump. Perform the drill as follows:

— Stand with your feet shoulder's width apart.
— Put your hands behind your head, lacing the fingers of your hands together.
— Drop to a half-squat position and then explode upward as high as possible. Keep your hands behind your head.
— When you land, begin the squat-and-jump process all over again. Continue until you have completed 25 jumps. This constitutes 1 set.
— Do 3 sets and shoot 10 free throws between sets.

String Jumping

This drill will help develop quickness, endurance, and power in your legs. Perform this exercise as follows:

— Place two chairs about four feet apart. Tie a string between them, about 12 to 18 inches off the floor.

— Stand sideways on one side of the string with your feet together.
— Hold your arms at your sides and flex the knees until you are in a half-squat.
— Explode up and over the string using your legs and arms for power.
— Land on the balls of your feet.
— Repeat the motion and jump back over to the other side.
— Do this continuously for one minute, keeping track of how many jumps you performed.
— Grab a ball and shoot free throws for one-minute, then repeat two more times.

Back to the Basket

This drill will help develop power and quickness. You will need a friend to help you with this drill. Do it this way:

— Have your friend to stand about 6 or 8 feet from the backboard.
— You stand with your back to the backboard about 2 feet closer than your friend.
— Have your friend throw the ball up underhanded.
— When you hear the ball hit, pivot and face the backboard. Spot the ball as quickly as possible.
— Jump up for the rebound. Bring the ball down to your chest, with your elbows out wide.
— Spring up with the ball and put it in the hoop.
— Repeat this over 10 times. This constitutes 1 set. Shoot free throws for one-minute between sets. Do 3 sets per session.

Continuous Tap-Ins

This is a good exercise to develop jumping ability, timing, and fingertip control of the ball. Two players are needed to perform this drill. The drill goes like this:

— Start by facing the backboard, one player on the right side, the other on the left of the rim.

— The first player begins by tossing the ball over the rim to the opposite side of the backboard and then runs to that side.

— The second player then jumps up and taps the ball over to the other side of the backboard and then quickly runs over to that side.

— Repeat this drill 20 times, which constitutes 1 set. Shoot free throws one minute between each set. Do 3 sets per session.

Lateral Movement Drill

This is an excellent drill to enhance lateral movement, an important, yet, often neglected aspect of rebounding. Do it like this:

— With a basketball in your hand, stand four feet away from the backboard. Face the direction of the baseline with one foot inside the lane and the other, outside.

— Toss the ball over your head to the opposite side of the backboard.

— Quickly move and catch the ball, with arms extended, before it hits the ground.

— Step back, once again keeping one foot in the lane and one foot out, and toss the ball back up again. Repeat this until you have done it 10 times. This constitutes a set.

— Shoot 10 free throws and repeat.

9

Basketball Fouls

Players who accumulate too many fouls during the course of a game are said to be in foul trouble. Teams need to avoid the total number of team fouls reaching more than six in each half. Once they reach this number, the other team is "in the one-and-one" and goes to the charity stripe for all subsequent fouls in that half.

The following is a break-down of some of the most common basketball fouls:

Away-From-the-Play Foul

In the last two minutes of the game, illegal contact by the defense which occurs either deliberately away from the ball, and/or before the ball is released on a throw-in.

Blocking

Physically impeding the progress of another player who is still moving.

Charging

When an offensive player runs into a defender who has established position.

Double Foul

When two opponents commit personal or technical fouls against each other at about the same time.

Elbowing

Throwing your elbows during play in order to hit another player or push him away; it's a basketball foul if contact is made.

Fighting Foul

When two or more players engage in fighting one another.

Flagrant Foul

Unnecessary or excessive contact against an opponent. Actions by players which break the rules but are not floor violations.

Hand-Checking

Using the hands to check the progress of an offensive player when that player is in front of the defender who is using the hands.

Holding

Restricting the movement of an opponent.

Illegal Blocking

Illegal contact which impedes the progress of an opponent.

Illegal Screen

A form of blocking in which the player setting the screen is still moving when the defender makes contact.

Loose Ball Foul

A basketball foul committed while neither team has possession of the ball (such as when going for a rebound).

Offensive Foul

Illegal contact, committed by an offensive player, after the ball is live.

Over-the-Back

Infringing on the vertical plane of, and making contact with, a player who is in position and attempting to rebound.

Personal Foul

Contact which occurs with an opponent after the ball has become live that may result in injury (including a push, hold, trip, hack, elbow, restrain or charge).

Punching

Personal foul where one player punches another.

Pushing

Impeding the progress or otherwise moving a player by pushing or shoving.

Reaching In

Extending an arm and making contact with a ball handler in an attempt to steal the ball.

Team Foul

Each personal foul committed by a player is also counted

against his team; when a team goes over the limit, its opponent is awarded free-throw opportunities.

Technical Foul

Misconduct that officials believe are detrimental to the game; can be assessed against team members on the floor or seated on the bench. penalized by a free-throw opportunity to the non-offending team; also called a "T".

Tripping

Extending a leg or foot and causing an opponent to lose balance or fall.

Tips For Players, Parents & Coaches

The game of basketball is a contact sport! There are ten players on the court that are in constant motion - running, jumping, shooting, and moving throughout the entire game.

Because of this constant movement by the players, basketball fouls are often committed. The rules of basketball discourage rough or overly-aggressive play.

The game is meant to be played in a competitive and fun nature -not in a violent way. Therefore, the rules are designed to penalize the players that are playing in an excessively rough manner.

Basketball fouls are called when the official feels there has been physical contact between two players and that one player has gained an advantage because of that contact.

Here are some basic guidelines used by the officials to determine which player has committed the basketball foul after contact has occurred:

— The first player to become set in a position on the court has the rights to that position.

— When a player moves into the path of an opposing player, obstructs their path, and contact is made - that player is responsible for the contact made.

— A player cannot extend an arm or leg in the pathway of an opponent. When this happens, that player is responsible for the contact made.

— Players have the right to the area extending from their feet, which are set on the floor, up. This is their floor space.

10

Basketball Injuries

Basketball injuries can be separated into two general categories: overuse injuries and traumatic injuries.

Overuse Injuries

Injuries caused by stressing an area over and over until it is damaged and begins to hurt are described as overuse injuries. One such injury is patellar tendinitis, or "jumper's knee," which is characterized by pain in the tendon just below the kneecap.

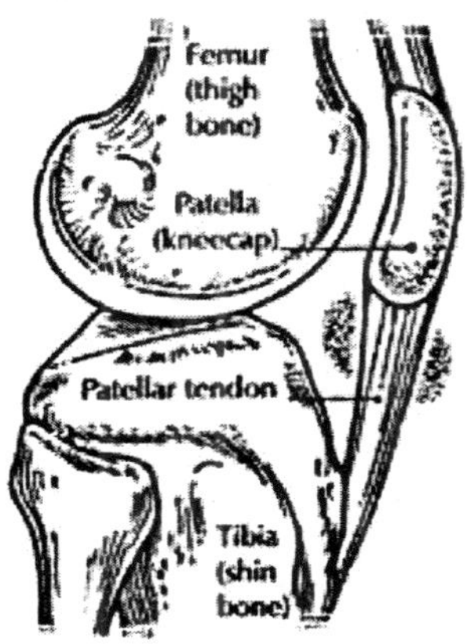

Achilles tendinitis is another common overuse injury in basketball players. This injury of the tendon connecting the muscles in the back of the calf to the heel bone causes pain in the back of the leg just above the heel. Occasionally, the Achilles tendon can tear. To treat a torn Achilles tendon, the doctor might tell you to keep the area immobilized for some time so the tendon can heal, or you might need surgery to repair the damage.

Some basketball players overuse the tendons in their shoulders. The rotator cuff of the shoulder is composed of four muscles. The tendons that attach these muscles to the shoulder bones can become inflamed and painful, particularly when you do repetitive overhead activities, such as shooting the basketball.

Traumatic Injuries

Traumatic injuries are those caused by a sudden forceful injury. Some of the more common traumatic injuries in basketball are jammed fingers. The severity of a jammed finger can range from a minor injury of the ligaments, which connect bones, to a broken finger. Splinting may be needed to allow the injured finger to heal. Another type of traumatic injury is a muscle pull or tear. In basketball players, these injuries occur primarily in the large muscles of the legs. To prevent them, stretch your thighs and calves well and do warm-up exercises before playing.

Ankle Sprains

The most common basketball injury is the ankle sprain. This injury often occurs when a player lands on another player's foot or the ankle rolls too far outward. When this happens, the ligaments connecting bones and supporting the ankle are stretched and torn. The ligaments can tear partially or completely. To treat your sprain, your doctor prescribes a short period of immobilization, keeping the joint still, so the ligaments can heal. After immobilization, you begin special exercises to strengthen the muscles that help hold your ankle in place.

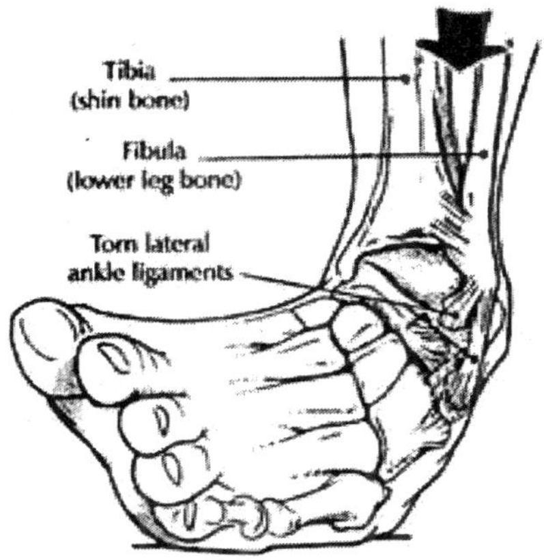

If your muscles and ligaments are not strong enough to prevent reinjury, you might need surgery to repair the damage and to help stabilize your ankle.

Knee Injuries

Knee injuries are some of the most serious basketball injuries. One type of knee injury is a sprain.

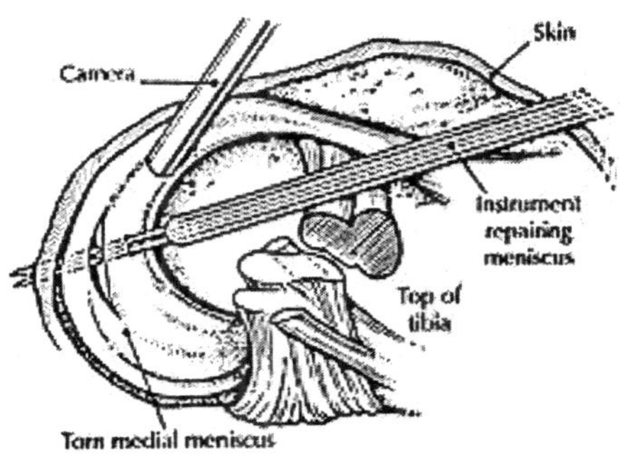

A knee sprain is a small tear in the ligaments or joint capsule that is not severe enough to cause your knee to give way. To help the tear heal, you must protect your knee for a short time by immobilizing it. After the tear heals, your doctor will prescribe stretching and strengthening exercises for the muscles that help hold the knee in place.

If you twist your knee, you can tear a meniscus, which is tissue that acts as a cushion between the bones of the upper and lower leg at the knee. To repair or remove a torn meniscus, you might need arthroscopic surgery. The surgeon inserts a camera and instruments into the knee joint through small skin incisions.

Running Injuries

When injury rates are expressed per hour of activity, risk of injury can be ranked by sport. Not surprisingly, such rankings show that sports like rugby and lacrosse produce the most mayhem, with about 30 injuries per 1000 hours of activity (rates above 5 per 1000 hours are considered high). Basketball and squash are also problem producers, with around 14 injuries per 1000 hours. Running and high-intensity aerobic dance follow fairly closely, with 11 injuries per 1000 hours (or about one per 100 hours).

Of course, injuries in sports such as rugby and lacrosse are often the result of impacts with other players - or with other players' equipment, as in squash. Such injuries are often very difficult to avoid. Your body may be strong, flexible, and injury-resistant, but if another player's racket catches you in the eye, you're going to be hurt, no matter how well prepared you are. However, in sports such as running, cycling, swimming, stair climbing, and walking, most injuries are not the result of sudden catastrophes but occur because of what is popularly called 'overuse'. This is one way of saying that a key part of an athlete's body simply can't stand up to the regular pressures of training and competition without breaking down.

To think about how such injuries can be prevented, it is instructional to consider the sport of running, which can certainly be classified as a high-injury sport. As mentioned, 65 percent of runners are injured in an average year, one running injury occurs for about every 100 hours of running, and runners miss about 5-10 per cent of their workouts due to injury. Those very high 65-per cent-injury and 10-per cent-absence rates could probably be significantly lower - if runners knew more about the actual causes of injuries, made a few simple adjustments in their training schedules, and routinely strengthened their muscles and joints. In fact, research suggests that running injuries could be cut by around 25 per cent.

To understand how to prevent injuries, it is first necessary to clear away some misconceptions. For example, coaches and runners often believe that males have higher injury rates than females, but male and female runners actually have about the same injury rate per hour of training. Large numbers of runners believe that training speed, racing speed, running surface, and body weight are closely related to the risk of injury, but research suggests otherwise. If you're heavier than average, you're not more likely than a lightweight runner to be injured during a typical year of training, for example.

Likewise, if you carry out most of your training on concrete roadways, you're probably not hurt more often than the runner who pads along softly on forest trails. In addition, your foot-strike pattern - whether you prefer to land on the heel or forefoot while running - doesn't have much impact on your injury risk. Such factors are just not very important in predicting injury.

Knee Joint Injuries

Instability of the knee joint - experienced as a sense of the knee 'giving way' - is an important symptom of knee injury and a predisposing factor for both acute knee injuries and osteoarthritis. Despite its importance, however, not much is known about the prevalence of knee instability among athletes and its association with particular sports and occupations.

Knee instability did not seem to be related to the type of sport preferred by the participants, whose chosen sports included football, handball, basketball, badminton, tennis, competitive gymnastics, swimming and jogging; neither was it related to weekly hours of participation in a specific type of sport or years of participation in that activity. However, it was strongly linked with female gender, years of predominantly standing occupational work and hours of predominantly sitting occupational work per day.

The researchers point out that the observed prevalence of knee instability was considerably lower than that of knee pain among athletes, while the reported 1% prevalence of absence of work could suggest it is not a serious problem. However, the fact that only 17% of the young participants were in occupational work raised the prevalence of absence to 6%, similar to that of absence from sport.

Neck Pain

Shoulders and arms do a lot of the work, but the neck also gets into the act. Throwing that ball up, pushing it through a basket, looking up, these actions curl the neck into uncomfortable, strenuous positions.

Eye Injuries

Many players are sidelined by eye injuries, unable to play because their eyes are swollen shut and bandaged, or because their sight is impaired.

Preventing Injuries

Some acute injuries occur following mid-air collisions, erratic lunges for a rebound, or scrambles after a loose ball, and can't be helped. But chronic injuries can be averted with proper conditioning, equipment, and good sense on the court.

Podiatric physicians recommend stretching exercises and gradual warm-up before beginning vigorous play. A separate weight-lifting regimen of both upper and lower body muscles helps minimize the impact of chronic injuries before they happen.

Another means of preventing injuries while playing basketball is a proper shoe. Shoes should be basketball-specific, with lots of ankle support and shock absorption.

Some high-topped shoes offer more ankle support than others and are preferred by many doctors of podiatric medicine. Shoes should fit well and be replaced before the soles become smooth, or before the uppers begin to tear or come apart. A typical basketball shoe should be replaced every two to three months for five days a week worth of play. Acrylic socks should be worn to avoid blistering.

Vollyeball-specific shoes should also be worn by devotees to that sport. They are similar to the basketball shoe, but typically are lighter, have less midsole support, and a "tighter" sole more responsive to quick starts and stops.

Acute injuries require immediate medical attention. After a bad fall or painful twist, the game's over. When an injury occurs, podiatrists advise, get off the court immediately and apply first aid. The best initial treatment for acute injury is ice, rest, compression, and elevation of the injured extremity. See your podiatric or family physician as soon as possible.

When bothered by a chronic injury, reduce activity level in accordance with the severity of the pain. If nagging pain gets worse in the course of a game, get off the court and apply ice and a compression bandage, and elevate the foot. Over-the-counter anti-inflammatory medications such as aspirin or ibuprofen can be taken at proper dosage for temporary pain relief.

If pain does not subside within three to five days, see a podiatrist, who will explore possible causes of the injury. Chronic pain can often be traced to a biomechanical abnormality that is placing undue stress on a particular part of the foot or ankle. Biomechanical imbalances can be corrected by prescription orthotic devices—specially constructed shoe inserts that redistribute the body's weight evenly on the foot and ankle.

Selective stretching and strengthening programs, shoe modifications, or strapping of the foot and ankle can also correct biomechanical problems. Lower extremity structural problems that often lead to injury include high arches, flat feet, bow legs, and tight calf muscles.

11

Diet and Nutrition

Young basketball players tend to be tall with large energy needs for growth. A single game of basketball does not provide a great threat to the fuel capabilities of trained athletes. However, in many situations players struggle with their recovery, due to a combination of regular training and matches, and an unorganised meal plan. Games tend to be at night, which impinges on meal times. Many young players are offered contracts to teams in the major basketball competitions, which require them to move out of home before they have learned all the tricks to domestic life. The following ideas can help to get organised to eat well.

At the beginning of each week, take a look at the schedule ahead and plan your meals around this. If you are living in a group house, use teamwork to share out the shopping and cooking tasks. Make the most of quiet days or rest days to get these tasks done. It makes sense to cook ahead in batches on these days, so that meals are ready in the freezer or fridge for the busy days. You will appreciate coming home after a tiring game or practice and being able to zap up a meal in minutes.

A household of young players without cooking skills is a high-risk situation for nutritional problems. When energy needs are high, increase the frequency of your meals and snacks, rather than trying to over-eat at a few meals. This means being organised to have snacks available throughout the day. Things that can be carried around and eaten 'on the go' include cereal bars, fruit, dried fruit and nut mixes, and muffins or slices. If refrigeration is available, the options can expand to include yoghurts, flavoured milks, liquid meal supplements, pre-packed sandwiches, or a bowl of breakfast cereal and milk.

Action-packed drinks such as fruit smoothies, liquid meal supplements, and flavoured milks provide a low-bulk carbohydrate and energy boost. If games or practices are scheduled for late at night, make sure your meal plan for the day is ready to cope with this. If you want to stick with the tradition of having your main meal at night, have it prepared before the game or practice so that it can be ready within minutes of arriving home. Although it is important to refuel and recover after the workout, many people feel uncomfortable going to sleep on a very full stomach. An alternative is to restructure the day to make lunch the main meal, and then refuel after the session with a lighter meal or snack before going to bed.

Iron Status

Iron is an important nutrient for growth. Impact against other players or the floor may increase iron losses through increased red blood cell destruction. Some players may have problems with low iron status especially females with low iron intakes. Iron levels should be checked regularly when in heavy training. Iron-rich foods such as lean red meat and breakfast cereals fortified with iron should be included regularly in the diet. Iron-rich plant foods such as wholegrain cereals, spinach and legumes should be combined with animal iron sources (e.g. wholemeal pasta and bolognese sauce) or vitamin C sources (a glass of juice consumed with breakfast cereal) to improve iron absorption. A sports dietitian will be able to provide specific dietary help.

Pre-Game Meal

The pre-game meal should fuel and hydrate players, but leave them feeling comfortable for the game. Ideally, the menu calls for a high-carbohydrate choice eaten at least 2-3 hours before a game. Pasta with low-fat sauces, rolls or sandwiches, baked potatoes with low-fat fillings, creamed rice, and fruit salad with yoghurt, are all examples of suitable choices. Each player or team should experiment to find the routines that work best for their situation. Eating together as a team can be a great way to raise team morale and get focused for the game. It also ensures that all players have their pre-game nutrition needs looked after.

Drinking Strategies

High-intensity exercise in a controlled atmosphere stadium can lead to large sweat losses - especially in large players. The good news is that basketball offers plenty of opportunities to hydrate during the game - time outs, quarter or half time breaks, and time spent on the bench. Hopefully, the coach will organise frequent drink breaks during practice. Each player should have their own drink bottle courtside, so that they can keep track of how much they are drinking. In professional teams, the job of refilling bottles is often left to the team manager or other support staff member.

Water is a suitable fluid, but a sports drink may promote better performance by topping up fuel stores for both the muscle and brain. Remember that basketball is not only a game of high-intensity running, but of skill, concentration and decision-making. These last factors are impaired both by dehydration and lowering of blood glucose levels. Sports drinks top up carbohydrate needs during the game, but may also encourage you to drink more fluid.

It is an interesting exercise to monitor weight changes of players and their drink bottles during practice and games, and estimate their sweat losses and fluid intakes. The fluid losses are still high during winter sessions when it is chilly outside and many players don't think they need to bring a drink. Remember that the stadium is kept warmer than the outside conditions, and the players are working hard and producing their own heat.

The performance-depleting effects of dehydration on sports performance have long been known. But what's the best kind of drink to take to prevent dehydration during exercise and thereby maintain sports performance? That's the question US scientists set out to investigate in a double-blind, randomised study on basketball players at Pennsylvania State University.

Fifteen basketballers (aged 12 to 15 years) underwent three separate two-hour exercise sessions in hot conditions with different drinking strategies:

— No drinks consumed leading to 2% dehydration (loss of fluid equivalent to 2% of body mass);

— Consumption of a 6% carbohydrate/electrolyte drink to maintain hydration levels (ie 0% dehydration);

— Consumption of a flavoured water placebo drink to maintain hydration levels, but with no added carbohydrate/electrolyte.

After each exercise session, there followed a recovery period after which the subjects performed an orchestrated sequence of continuous basketball drills designed to simulate a game (12-minute quarters with a 10-minute half-time). The researchers looked at a number of performance measures and component drills required during basketball; these included various individual and combined shooting percentages (3-point, 15-foot, free-throw shots), sprints (suicides, court widths), lateral movements (zigzags, lane slides), and defensive drills (combining lateral and front-to-back movement) times.

The results showed that, compared with the flavoured water drinking strategy, dehydration significantly impaired shooting ability (as expected), but that consuming the carbohydrate/electrolyte drink improved shooting compared with flavoured water. The same results were found with sprinting performance – ie drinking carbohydrate/electrolyte produced the quickest sprint times, plain water slightly slower times and dehydration markedly lower times (76 vs. 78 vs. 83 seconds, respectively). Moreover, the carbohydrate/electrolyte drinking strategy significantly improved total defensive drill times compared to no drinking.

This study provides persuasive evidence that using carbohydrate/electrolyte drinks to maintain hydration or rehydrate at half-time yields superior physical and skills performance to using just plain or flavoured water.

Half-time Nutrition

The days of sliced oranges and a cup tea at half-time are long gone. As Tim Lawson explains, optimum half-time nutrition is a complex science in which a number of factors need to be considered.

The half-time nutritional strategies employed by many sports teams often rely as much on tradition, fashion and even sponsorship deals as they do on sound science. But with sports like football becoming so high profile, nutritional strategies are becoming increasingly sophisticated, with many teams employing full-time nutritionists and sport scientists. Increasingly, top teams are using specialist sports drinks and other products with an emphasis on different priorities for different positions and individuals.

The traditional approach to half-time nutrition usually involves a cup of tea and a slice of orange, and like many nutritional practices that have stood the test of time, this almost certainly has some merit. Similarly, other foods such as high-carbohydrate cakes, confectionery and even jelly babies have been advocated because they contain useful energy. Some scientific papers have even recommended snacks like pretzels because they contain high levels of sodium.

However, these kinds of products may also contain other ingredients that are not entirely beneficial for sports performance. For instance, it may not be possible to measure the performance detriments of hydrogenated vegetable oils or trans-fats in a single game but their negative effects on health are well documented, which is why they're banned in several countries. Similarly, colourings and other additives are often contained in these kinds of products, which have at least been associated with disruptive behaviour and poor concentration in school children, if not some of the crazy on- and off-ball fouls often seen on TV.

Since the first World Congress on the Science of Football was held at Liverpool in 1987, there has been much published research on the physical demands of football and other team sports, and the nutritional status of participants. Fluid, electrolyte and carbohydrate needs have been studied during training and in match simulations, as well as the effects of dietary manipulations on sport-specific skills. Fatigue has been observed as a transient phenomenon during matches and general performance declines towards the end of matches. However, the underlying factors responsible for fatigue during football are still not fully understood.

Physical Demands

There are significant differences in the physical demands of team sports like soccer, American football and rugby, with soccer being more physically demanding in terms of distance covered per minute than rugby, for instance. However, most team sports show activity patterns that would be expected to have a considerable energy cost, with typical values for distance covered per match at around 8-11km.

The energy cost of competing in a match is much higher than an even-paced run of the same distance, as there are numerous changes of pace with many periods of intense activity, which is typically associated with heavy demands on carbohydrate energy supply. Within the same sport, different league standards are often associated with different activity levels, with top-class sport clearly differentiated from lower levels by the increased volume of high-intensity play.

Outcomes in team sports are highly influenced by skill, so it is also important to consider factors that may influence skill and concentration when considering strategies to optimise performance. Often these factors go hand in hand with carbohydrate depletion, associated with reduced exercise capacity and poor concentration – effects that may be compounded by dehydration. Both dehydration and muscle glycogen depletion have been associated with injury and accidents, so efforts to prevent these affecting performances could have repercussions well beyond the immediate match.

In the early 1990s, scientific publications commenting on nutrition for football tended to suggest that even when players were consuming sufficient calories to meet their energy needs, they should consume more carbohydrate in order to recover between training sessions and to maximise muscle glycogen stores prior to a match. However, studies using dietary analysis continue to suggest that many soccer players are failing to consume sufficient carbohydrate to optimise carbohydrate stores and two Spanish studies published in 2005 suggested that the eating habits of young players were so poor that nutritional intervention and education was necessary in order to improve general healthy dietary practices.

The impact of carbohydrate supplementation during the half-time interval could well depend upon the prior eating habits of the player. Similarly, the rehydration needs, and therefore the efficacy of half-time rehydration strategies, will depend on the pre-game hydration status as much as the playing conditions and player work rates. Researchers from Pennsylvania State University recently investigated the effect of dehydration and rehydration on basketball skill. Urine tests showed that some subjects taking part in the experiment were already dehydrated when they arrived at the experiment venue, even though they had been encouraged to stay well hydrated the day before each trial.

This situation is probably reflected in real game situations, especially where squads are not monitored closely in their build-up to games. Sport nutritionists working with Premier League football clubs have noted that players often turn up to training less optimally hydrated during cold weather than in the hotter months. This may be because players give hydration less priority when the sun is not shining and are unaware of the increased water vapour losses in cold conditions.

The growing use of under-pitch heating also means that more games can be played in very cold air temperatures, where water vapour losses are significant. If well-monitored players at high levels of sport are often sub-optimally hydrated, there's a good chance that players in other leagues are starting matches in a sub-optimal state and will therefore be in a worse state at half-time than necessary.

Just enough and no more

Scientific studies of sub-elite sportsmen and women show there is much to be gained by replacing fatty, energy-dense foods with more carbohydrate. However, at the very elite end of sport, nutritionists are fine-tuning energy and hydration provision to provide just enough.

This is to maximise power-to-weight ratio; each gram of carbohydrate stored as muscle glycogen is bound to 3g of water, so if a player starts with 500g of muscle glycogen and this is used during the game it will release 1.5kg of water. This released water is important when considering the fluid and energy requirements at half-time.

While dehydration resulting in a loss of body mass of 2% or greater can result in reduced endurance exercise capacity, and sprinting and sport-specific skills can be adversely affected by losses of 3% or more, players are able to tolerate a level of dehydration. There's no merit in encouraging players to consume more fluid than required to maintain performance, because this would be the equivalent of sending players out with a weight vest! However, any change in body mass should not be calculated by the difference between that immediately prior to the match and half-time, but instead baseline body mass should be established by early morning measurements taken before any carbohydrate loading has taken place.

Although there are some reports of soccer players losing up to four or five litres per hour of sweat in very hot and humid environments and up to three litres in temperate climates, sweat losses closer to two litres per hour are probably more typical. In such cases, a half-time fluid consumption of between 500 and 800mls should be sufficient to prevent a decrease in body mass greater than 1% during the second half.

Individual Differences

In an ideal world each individual would have a specific fine-tuned nutritional strategy, but this can be almost impossible in the squad culture that tends to exist in everyday training situations. Nutrients, especially electrolytes, may prevent fatigue and reduce muscle cramps in the second half. The most important electrolyte lost in sweat is sodium and research has shown a wide individual variation in sodium losses – as low as the equivalent of 1g of salt to over 6g in 90 minutes. Assuming that players start a match with reasonable sodium stores, most players are unlikely to become performance limited due to sodium depletion during one match; the main role of sodium in a half-time situation is to encourage fluid uptake in situations where large fluid volumes need to be consumed at half-time (because sodium stimulates thirst).

However, 6g is the suggested total maximum daily salt allowance recommended by the UK Food Standards Agency and there has been considerable pressure from the government for food producers to reduce the amount of sodium in food. It is not clear if 'high sodium sweaters' are so because they consume a high-sodium diet or for other reasons. It is clear, however, that sweat losses of 6g in 90 minutes cannot be sustained unless consumption is increased beyond the current recommended daily maximum. Unseasonably hot weather and reduced sodium foods may combine to leave players potentially short of this important electrolyte.

Research on many games players suggests that the status of other nutrients is often poor, and minerals such as zinc, magnesium and calcium (found as electrolytes in sweat) and other minerals such as iron may be sub-optimal prior to matches. Whilst a player suffering from fatigue or cramps due to poor nutrition prior to the match may benefit from carbohydrate/electrolyte supplementation at half-time, it's probably better to improve diet between matches rather than try to patch up poor general nutrition with a half-time fix.

CARBOHYDRATE

In players starting with an adequate nutritional status, fluid or electrolyte losses are not usually a limiting factor in performance towards the end of games. However, carbohydrate shortfalls are almost certainly responsible for fatigue in games, irrespective of player position or standard. Low carbohydrate levels can compromise mental skills as well as physical performance, and there is consensus that carbohydrate supplementation can improve performance. Muscle glycogen stores are generally quite low at the end of games, and even when overall stores are not depleted, carbohydrate may be depleted in specific limiting muscle fibres.

Carbohydrate supplementation to replace lost muscle glycogen makes sense and has been shown to help prevent deterioration in the performance of soccer players in simulated matches and to improve performance in soccer- and basketball-specific tests. However, gastric-emptying studies have shown that the activity levels in competitive games are such that they are likely to delay gastric emptying and possibly reduce the effectiveness of carbohydrate drinks given immediately prior to or during matches.

To counteract slow gastric emptying, glucose polymers (maltodextrins) have been recommended for many years; they have a lower osmolality than simple sugars, can improve gastric emptying and are relatively light on the stomach. Recent research from Birmingham University suggests that energy drinks using multiple energy substrates may result in improved energy delivery to the muscles. Combinations of maltodextrin and fructose would therefore seem to be a sensible combination to form the basis of a half-time nutritional strategy, combining good gastric emptying with the benefits of multiple energy substrate transport across the small intestine.

Half-time is, however, relatively short and care should be taken to maximise the opportunity to refuel when gastric emptying is not limited by intense match activity. Isotonic energy gels can be a practical solution, providing players with a bolus dose of carbohydrate as they leave the field, gaining valuable recovery time over a team waiting until they reach the changing rooms to get drinks. Although this article is about half-time nutritional strategies, it also makes sense to use any natural breaks in the game to take on carbohydrate, and fluid/electrolytes in hot conditions.

It's worth cautioning against a 'one size fits all' policy with regard to player nutrition. A strategy of ensuring that each player consumes at least 400-500mls of 10-12% glucose polymer/fructose solution is a good baseline for half-time refuelling. In hot conditions, and for players with very high sweat rates, more fluid may be needed to prevent dehydration reaching detrimental levels. Fluid requirements can be checked by comparing half-time weights to baseline measures in training matches, and players should be encouraged to fine-tune their thirst perception using this feedback. When 800mls or more of fluid needs to be drunk at half-time, it is possibly useful to consume solutions containing at least some electrolyte, especially sodium.

CAFFEINE

Caffeine proves less of a help to team sports sprinters. Team sport athletes should not expect caffeine to enhance their sprint performance: that's the conclusion of a New Zealand study comparing the effects of caffeine and placebo on performance in a test designed to simulate the repeated brief sprints of team sports.

While numerous studies have established that caffeine improves endurance performance, there have been few studies of its effects on short-term performance. Those which have been done suggest that caffeine produces an enhanced performance of a single 30secs sprint that would be worthwhile for a track-and-field athlete.

However, when fatigue develops during repeated sprints, caffeine appears to make it worse. Repeated sprints are the norm in team and court sports, but each sprint generally lasts only a few seconds and the effect of caffeine on such sprints is therefore unclear.

In this double-blind study, 16 male sport-science students, all competitive team-sport athletes in basketball, hockey or rugby, were tested in a temperature-controlled gym on two occasions 2-3 days apart. Sixty minutes before each test each subject ingested a capsule containing either caffeine or a glucose placebo in a dose of 6mg/kg of body mass. The test consisted of 10 20m sprints, each completed within 10 seconds, followed by a rest for the remainder of the 10 seconds.

The results were as follows:

1. In comparison with placebo, ingestion of caffeine resulted in a 0.1% increase in mean time to complete

the 10 sprints, although individual variation ranged from a 2.7% decrease to a 2.9% increase.

2. Fatigue was apparent as an increase in time for each sprint. But while the increase in time over the 10 sprints was 14% with placebo, it was 0.7% higher with caffeine.

Neither of these effects was large enough to be of any practical significance for a team-sport player,' comment the authors, 'but the confidence limits allow for the possibility that the true effect on mean performance could be small and beneficial or small and harmful. The true effect on fatigue could also be small and beneficial, but there is more likelihood of a larger harmful effect. Further research with a larger sample, more trials or a more reliable performance measure would give more precise estimates of these effects.'

In conclusion, the observed effects of caffeine on mean sprint performance and on fatigue over 10 sprints were negligible for the average team-sport athlete and the true effects are unlikely to be anything more than small.'

Magnesium

Ask most athletes to name some key minerals for human performance nutrition and you'll probably find calcium, iron, zinc and even chromium popping up in their lists. But they are unlikely to mention magnesium. Despite magnesium's pivotal role in energy production, many coaches and athletes remain unaware of its critical importance in maintaining health and performance. Indeed, dietary intakes of magnesium in the West have declined to less than half of those recorded 100 years ago, and are still falling. Yet many scientists believe that the amount of magnesium required for optimum health has been underestimated in the past, and now new research suggests that even small shortfalls in magnesium intake can seriously impair athletic performance. Clearly, magnesium nutrition is an area that no serious athlete can afford to overlook!

Pure magnesium is a silvery-white metal, which burns with a dazzling brilliance – something you've probably seen demonstrated by your science teacher at school! It is the second most abundant mineral in cells after potassium, but the two ounces or so found in the typical human body is present not as metal but as magnesium ions (positively-charged magnesium atoms found either in solution or complexed with other tissues, such as bone). Roughly one quarter of this magnesium is found in muscle tissue and three-fifths in bone; but less than 1% of it is found in blood serum, although that is used as the commonest indicator of magnesium status. This blood serum magnesium can be further subdivided into free ionic, complex-bound and protein-bound portions, but it's the ionic portion that's considered most important in measuring magnesium status, because it is physiologically active.

Magnesium is well supplied in unrefined whole grain cereals, such as wholemeal bread, and also in green leafy vegetables, nuts and seeds, peas, beans and lentils *(table below)*. Fruit, meat and fish supply poor levels, as do refined foods. Contrary to common belief, milk and dairy products are not particularly rich sources of magnesium The magnesium content of plant foods tends to reflect soil magnesium concentrations and growing conditions, especially as magnesium is not routinely added to soils by farmers during intensive fertilisation.

Table 1: the magnesium content of common foods

Food	MAGNESIUM Content (milligrams per 100g)
Pumpkin seeds (roasted)	532

Almonds	300
Brazil nuts	225
Sesame seeds	200
Peanuts (roasted, salted)	183
Walnuts	158
Rice (whole grain brown)	110
Wholemeal bread	85
Spinach	80
Cooked beans	40
Broccoli	30
Banana	29
Potato (baked)	25
White bread	20
Yoghurt (plain, low fat)	17
Milk	10
Rice (white)	6
Cornflakes	6 ('Frosties' or 'Honeynut')
Apple	4
Honey	0.6

Magnesium is a fairly soluble mineral, which is why boiling vegetables can result in significant losses; in cereals and grains, it tends to be concentrated in the germ and bran, which explains why white refined grains contain relatively little magnesium by comparison with their unrefined counterparts.

Magnesium plays a number of roles in the body, being required for more than 325 enzymatic reactions, including those involved in the synthesis of fat, protein and nucleic acids, neurological activity, muscular contraction and relaxation, cardiac activity and bone metabolism. Even more important is magnesium's pivotal role in both anaerobic and aerobic energy production, particularly in the metabolism of adenosine triphosphate (ATP), the 'energy currency' of the body. The synthesis of ATP requires magnesium-dependent enzymes called 'ATPases'. These enzymes have to work extremely hard:

the average human can store no more than about 3oz of ATP, yet during strenuous exercise the rate of turnover of ATP is phenomenal, with as much as 15kgs of ATP per hour being broken down and reformed (from adenosine diphosphate and phosphate).

In normal adults, a magnesium deficiency results in altered cardiovascular function, including electrocardiographic abnormalities, impaired carbohydrate metabolism, with insulin resistance and decreased insulin secretion, and high blood pressure. Disease states that have been associated with magnesium imbalances and deficiencies include coronary heart disease, neuromuscular disorders, kidney diseases, asthma, migraines, premenstrual syndrome, pre-eclampsia and eclampsia (both potentially serious complications of pregnancy), menopausal bone problems and even obesity.

The UK recommended intake for magnesium (the daily amount deemed adequate to prevent deficiencies in 97.5% of the UK population) is set at 300mgs for men and 270mgs for women. The US has recently revised its figures upwards and now recommends an intake of 400mgs per day for men aged 19-30 and 420 for those over 30; the figures for women under and over 30 are 300 and 310mgs per day respectively. However, some investigators believe these should be set even higher at 450-500mg/day.

Dietary intakes of magnesium in the United States have been declining over the last 100 years from about 500mg/day to 175–225mg/day and a recent national survey suggested that the average magnesium intake for women is as low as 228mgs per day. But since this figure is derived using a one-day diet recall method, it may actually be an overestimate of actual magnesium intakes. Meanwhile, the UK's Food Standards Agency estimates that the average daily intake of magnesium in Britain for both men and women is just 227mgs – only two thirds of the US recommended daily amount (RDA).

The figures above suggest that many people fall short of optimum magnesium intakes, and this has been confirmed in a number of studies. For example, American researchers found that more than 60% of US adults were failing to meet even the previous (lower) RDA for magnesium. Even athletes, who might be expected to take greater care with their diets, are not immune from magnesium deficiency; for example, studies carried out in 1986/87 revealed that gymnasts, footballers and basketball players were consuming only around 70% of the RDA, while female runners fared even worse, with reported intakes as low as 59% of the RDA.

Given magnesium's vital role in energy production, two key questions emerge:

— Can these all-too-common sub-optimum dietary magnesium intakes impair athletic performance?

— Could extra magnesium intake, over and above RDA levels, enhance performance?

While there is plenty of evidence that oral magnesium therapy improves cardiac function and exercise tolerance in coronary heart disease patients, until recently, there has been little hard evidence about the effects of sub-optimum magnesium intakes in healthy exercising adults.

However, in a very tightly controlled three-month US study carried out last year, the effects of magnesium depletion on exercise performance in 10 women were observed – and the results make fascinating reading. In the first month, the women received a magnesium-deficient diet (112mgs per day), which was supplemented with 200mgs per day of magnesium to bring the total magnesium content up to the RDA of 310mgs per day. In the second month, the supplement was withdrawn to make the diet magnesium-deficient, but in the third month it was reintroduced to replenish magnesium levels.

At the end of each month, the women were asked to cycle at increasing intensities until they reached 80% of their maximum heart rate, at which time a large number of measurements were taken, including blood tests, ECG and respiratory gas analysis. The researchers found that, for a given workload, peak oxygen uptake, total and cumulative net oxygen utilisation and heart rate all increased significantly during the period of magnesium restriction, with the amount of the increase directly related to the extent of magnesium depletion.

While many studies on magnesium supplementation and exercise have been carried out, the results have been inconsistent and may indicate that there is nothing to be gained by supplementing an already magnesium-sufficient diet. One study of male athletes supplemented with 390mgs of magnesium per day for 25 days resulted in an increased peak oxygen uptake and total work output during work capacity tests; in another, on sub-maximal work, supplemental magnesium elicited reductions in heart rate, ventilation, oxygen uptake and carbon dioxide production; in a third, physically active students, supplemented with 8mgs of magnesium per kilo of body weight per day, experienced significant increases in endurance performance and decreased oxygen consumption during standardised, sub-maximal exercise.

However, other studies carried out on physically active people with 'normal' serum magnesium and muscle magnesium concentrations have found no functional or performance improvements associated with supplementation. On the evidence available so far, the scientific consensus is that extra magnesium can enhance performance when (as is all too often the case) magnesium intakes fall below optimum levels. But in subjects already consuming magnesium at or above this optimum level, there is little hard evidence to suggest that taking more confers extra benefits.

Given the growing body of evidence pointing to the need for optimum magnesium nutrition in athletes, what tests are available to coaches for determining magnesium status? Muscle magnesium (obtained through a needle biopsy) is one of the most accurate methods of assessment, but it is time-consuming, very invasive and can cause discomfort. Magnesium status can also be measured by means of a 'magnesium load' test, followed up with measurement of urinary excretion. However research suggests that urinary magnesium is too variable to accurately evaluate magnesium status.

Total blood magnesium (TMg) is the most widely used assay, but this has the disadvantage of including complex and protein-bound magnesium, whereas it's the ionic portion that's physiologically active. This test is also insensitive to the movements of magnesium that occur within the body as a result of exercise.

However, the recent introduction of ion-selective electrode (ISE) technology now enables scientists to measure ionic magnesium directly, and this is considered one of the best methods. But even then it's not all plain-sailing, since ionic magnesium levels tend to fluctuate significantly according to the time of day, with higher values recorded in the morning and lower values in the evening. This 'circadian magnesium rhythm' is believed to be linked to changes in physical activity levels through the day, but the whole subject of 'intra-body' magnesium fluctuations remains poorly understood. Nevertheless, the best results seem to be obtained when ionic magnesium is sampled from fasting, non-exercised subjects first thing in the morning.

So what's the take-home message for athletes? First, it's all too easy to go short of magnesium, especially if your diet is light on foods like whole grains and cereals, green leafy vegetables, pulses (peas/beans/lentils), nuts and seeds. To make matters worse, excessive sugar intake, alcohol consumption and diets high in fats, protein and calcium have all been shown to impair magnesium absorption and/or increase excretion. And even when the quality of food is good and the diet carefully balanced, diets containing fewer than 2,000 calories per day often struggle to meet magnesium needs, placing those on weight loss or maintenance régimes at added risk.

Magnesium intakes above the RDA are unlikely to boost performance further, but supplements are cheap and non-toxic, so can safely be used as an insurance policy. Most forms of supplemental magnesium are well-tolerated but it is inadvisable to supplement more than 400mgs per day. Some forms, such as magnesium oxide, are quite alkaline forming and can have the side effect of neutralising stomach acid and interfering with digestion. These should not be taken with meals. Finally, magnesium is best absorbed in small, frequent doses; so, for example, it is better to take 100mgs three times a day than 300mgs in one go!

Use of Drugs

The use of performance enhancing drugs in the modern Olympics is on record as early as the games of the third Olympiad, when Thomas Hicks won the marathon after receiving an injection of strychnine in the middle of the race. The first official ban on 'stimulating substances' by a sporting organisation was introduced by the International Amateur Athletic Federation in 1928.

Using drugs to cheat in sport is not new, but it is becoming more effective. In 1976, the East German swimming team won 11 out of 13 Olympic events, and later sued the government for giving them anabolic steroids. Yet despite the health risks, and despite the regulating bodies' attempts to eliminate drugs from sport, the use of illegal substances is widely known to be rife. It hardly raises an eyebrow now when some famous athlete fails a dope test.

In 1992, Vicky Rabinowicz interviewed small groups of athletes. She found that Olympic athletes, in general, believed that most successful athletes were using banned substances. Much of the writing on the use of drugs in sport is focused on this kind of anecdotal evidence. There is very little rigorous, objective evidence because the athletes are doing something that is taboo, illegal and sometimes highly dangerous. The anecdotal picture tells us that our attempts to eliminate drugs from sport have failed.

Drugs are much more effective today than they were in the days of strychnine and sheep's testicles. Studies involving the anabolic steroid androgen showed that, even in doses much lower than those used by athletes, muscular strength could be improved by 5-20%. Most athletes are also relatively unlikely to ever undergo testing. The International Amateur Athletic Federation estimates that only 10-15% of participating athletes are tested in each major competition.

The enormous rewards for the winner, the effectiveness of the drugs, and the low rate of testing all combine to create a cheating 'game' that is irresistible to athletes. Drugs such as erythropoietin (EPO) and growth hormone are natural chemicals in the body. As technology advances, drugs have become harder to detect because they mimic natural processes. In a few years, there will be many undetectable drugs.

The recent Olympic Games in Athens were the first to follow the introduction of a global anti-doping code. From the lead-up to the games to the end of competition, 3,000 drug tests were carried out: 2,600 urine tests and 400 blood tests for the endurance enhancing drug EPO. From these, 23 athletes were found to have taken a banned substance – the most ever in an Olympic Games.

Human sport is different from sports involving other animals, such as horse or dog racing. The goal of a horse race is to find the fastest horse. Horses are lined up and flogged. The winner is the one with the best combination of biology, training and rider. Basicallv this is a test of biological potential. This was the old naturalistic Athenian vision of sport: find the strongest, fastest or most skilled man.

Drugs that improve our natural potential are against the spirit of this model of sport. But this is not the only view of sport. Humans are not horses or dogs. We make choices and exercise our own judgement. We choose what kind of training to use and how to run our race. We can display courage, determination and wisdom. We are not flogged by a jockey on our back but drive ourselves. It is this judgement that competitors exercise when they choose diet, training and whether to take drugs... Far from being against the spirit of sport, biological manipulation embodies the human spirit – the capacity to improve ourselves on the basis of reason and judgement.

Should we limit drug use in sport? There is one limit: safety. We do not want an Olympics in which people die before, during or after competition... Rather than testing for drugs, we should focus more on health and fitness to compete. Forget testing for EPO, monitor the PCV...What matters is what is a safe concentration of growth hormone – not whether it is natural or artificial.

We should permit drugs that are safe and continue to ban and monitor drugs that are unsafe...there are of course some drugs that are harmful in themselves – for example anabolic steroids. We should focus on detecting these because they are harmful not because they enhance performance.

Far from harming athletes, paradoxically, such a proposal may protect our athletes...the current incentive is to develop undetectable drugs, with little concern for safety. If safe performance enhancement drugs were permitted, there would be greater pressure to develop safe drugs.

It should also be noted that the prohibition of a substance that is already in demand carries its own intrinsic harms.

The prohibition of alcohol in America during the 1920s led to a change in drinking habits that actually increased consumption. Driven from public bars, people began to drink at home, where the alcohol was more readily available, and the incidence of deaths due to alcoholism rose or remained stable, while they dropped widely around the world in countries without prohibition. Furthermore, as the quality of the alcohol was unregulated, the incidence of death from poisoned alcohol rose four-fold in five years.

The direct risks from prohibiting performance enhancing drugs in sport are similar, but probably much more pronounced. Athletes currently administer performance enhancing substances in doses that are commensurate with the amount of performance gain they wish to attain, rather than the dose that can be considered 'safe'. The athletic elite have near unlimited funds and the goal of near unlimited performance, a framework that results in the use of extremely unsafe doses. If athletes were excluded when their bodies are unsafe for competition, this kind of direct consequence from prohibition would be reduced.

Bibliography

Ambler, V. *Basketball: Scoring Skills and Strategies.* Barrie and Jenkins, 1976.

Anderson, F. *Basketball Techniques Illustrated.* New York: The Ronald Press Company, 1952.

Auerbach, A. *Basketball for the Player, the Fan and the Coach.* New York: Simon and Schuster, 1975.

Barnes, M.J. *Women's Basketball.* London: Allyn and Bacon, 1980.

Bonsor, Kevin, *How Basketball Works: Who's Who. HowStuffWorks,* Retrieved on January 11, 2006.

Eric Sacharski, *Blackboard Strategies: Over 200 Favorite Plays From Successful Coaches For Nearly Every Possible Situation,* Lessiter Pubns, August 30, 1999.

Frank Lloyd Wright , *Ultimate Basketball Book: A Complete Shooting Guide,* Sierra Vista Publications, December 31, 2003.

Gail Gibbons, *My Basketball Book,* HarperCollins, September 5, 2000.

Hal Wissel, Basketball: *Steps to Success (Steps to Success Series),* Human Kinetics; 2 edition (2004).

Howard Garfinkle, Will Klein, *Five-Star Basketball Drills,* McGraw-Hill; January 11, 1998.

International Basketball Federation, June 2004, *Official Basketball Rules.*

Jay Mikes, *Basketball Fundamentals: A Complete Mental Training Guide,* Human Kinetics Publishers, January 1991.

Sachare, Alex, *100 Greatest Basketball Players of All Time,* New York: Pocket Books, 1997.

Reimer, Anthony, "FIBA vs North American Rules Comparison". *FIBA Assist* (14): 40–44, June 2005.

Robert G. Price, Barb Greenberg, *The Ultimate Guide to Weight Training for Basketball,* Sportsworkout.com; 4 edition (September 1, 2006).

Sharman, B. *Sharman on Basketball Shooting.* Englewood Cliffs, N.J.: Prentice-Hall, 1965.

Shibukawa, K. "Velocity conditions of basketball shooting". *Bulletin of the Institute of Sport Science*, The Faculty of P.E., Tokyo University, 59-64, 1975.

Stimpson, P. *Basketball. The Skills of the Game*. London: The Crowood Press, 1986.

Stone, W.J. and Steingard, P.M. "Year-round conditioning for basketball". *Clinics in Sports Medicine*, 12, 173-191, 1993.

Strack, D.H. *Basketball*. Englewood Cliffs, N.J.: Prentice-Hall, 1968.

Tan, A. and Miller, G. "Kinematics of the free throw in basketball". *American Journal of Physics*, 49, 542-544, 1981.

Ted St. Martin , *The Art of Shooting Baskets*, McGraw-Hill; 2 edition, September 19, 2005.

Veenker, G.F. *Basketball for Coaches and Players*. New York: A.S. Barnes and Co, 1937.

Withers, Tom, *How to play the All-star Way*, Austin, Texas: Steck - Vaughn Co.,1994.

Index